WORD WARRIORS

rs in the
Revolution

EDITED BY Alix Olson

FOREWORD BY Eve Ensler

SEAL PRESS

WORD WARRIORS
35 Women Leaders in the Spoken Word Revolution

Copyright © 2007 Alix Olson

Published by
Seal Press
A Member of the Perseus Books Group
1400 65th Street, Suite 250
Emeryville, CA 94608

Library of Congress Cataloging-in-Publication Data

Word warriors : 25 women leaders in the spoken word revolution / edited
by Alix Olson.
p. cm.
Includes bibliographical references and index.
ISBN-13: 978-1-58005-221-4 (alk. paper)
ISBN-10: 1-58005-221-5 (alk. paper)
1. American poetry—Women authors. 2. American poetry—20th centruy.
3. American poetry—21st century. 4. Women—United States—Poetry. 5.
Oral interpretation of poetry—History—20th century. 6. Oral interpretation
of poetry—History—21st century. 7. Oral interpretation of poetry—
Competitions. 8. Poetry slams. 9. Poetry—Authorship. I. Olson, Alix.

PS589.W77 2007
811'.540809287—dc22
2007032584

9 8 7 6 5 4 3 2 1

Cover design by Rowan Moore-Seifred, doublemranch.com
Interior design by McGuire Barber Design
Composition by Steve Connell
Printed in the United States of America

This book is dedicated to my mom, Laura Katz Olson,
for dressing me in blue overalls
and for gifting me with the bright side.

Contents

Eve Ensler

The Way Girls
Word

I WANT TO TALK ABOUT THESE WOMEN, THESE words, these fierce flying no scheming, no vetted, no trying to land in the white house or sell me a toaster words. These words that grow in the jungles of the bellies of these women who stand on land they never owned or felt at home but the words grow and make a place a space for the others to live. Words in the mouths of these women slam, shoot like alphabet guns, fire fast digit letters and sounds into silence, into the invisible that lives forever visible right in front of us, the invisible that can't be spoken until it's spoken and so these brave chicks speak and speak, "breathless red faced and pissed off." Speak the heretical, speak the blood body, speak not as representatives of their dark skinned selves or dyke diving selves or Gaza stripped selves. Not representing but presenting, not claiming we, but an unapologetic escalating have to say it see it be it me, me that is jammed slammed stuck in the dead center of invisible wastelands; malls, the too beautiful suburban roads, mean anonymous streets, soap opera reality TV symphonies. Me, me that has been so fucking programmed, conditioned to be skinny white ass, not taking up too much space, not round, not black, not female, not ethnic, not loud. Girl words the way girls word, the way pussies poem, not all proper theoretical proving a point. Pussies don't need to prove points they need to create magic and sound alarms and wipe the blood off the wall. Not just clever words so you marvel at their abilities and memorization skills, you never really *really* hear those words. It's pussy, not personality, pussy not all sexual on your lap, on her back. No—pussy words that have to say it see it have to chomp down wrap their mouth, their verbal staccato hips coming straight from the adjective quick wet—get off me. Get back. Come stand by me. Not yet. Go deep. Now slow.

Words, better than bullets cause they don't lodge and kill, they lodge and spin, lodge and free, lodge and learn, lodge and spread like possibility through the whole fucking system. The story can be told. It lives in these word warriors, in their outrageous spells and tells. It lives in their bus rides and bar fights. It lives in their pierces and tears. It lives in the trans planes and trains traveling them through gender and Georgia, napalm and bras, traveling through this concept this memory this made up dreamed up mad desire still desiring America.

Count on these girls, these pussy pointing spraying their wet word poems, these poetry midwives with their pushing and breathing anarchic rhyming and dominatrix thing, rapping, rapping slamming releasing, bringing us, birthing us, wording us home.

Alix Olson

Introduction

ORAL TRADITION HAS BEEN INTEGRAL TO women's experience since the beginning of recorded time. Women, often denied access to writing and reading skills and materials throughout (his)story, have *verbally* passed down individual stories, documented poetry, preserved recipes for physical and emotional healing, and ensured survival of what might otherwise be lost or suppressed in a male-dominated world. I consider this past collective amalgamation of voices to be the true backdrop for the current women's spoken word movement.

However, the popular phenomenon and relatively new cultural art form, known as "slam poetry," is probably most specifically responsible for the recent upsurge in spoken word poetry overall. Slam poetry began in the United States in the 1980s, when Marc Smith, a blue-collar Chicago worker with an affinity for verse, decided to prompt the resurgence of poetry in the "average" person's life. He implemented a format wherein each person would have three minutes to perform and, in an effort to keep poetry palatable, engaging, and in keeping with a U.S. competitive sports mentality, audience members were randomly tapped as "judges." This design not only allowed for poetry to be redemocratized, but also provided it with an anticapitalist and antiestablishment flair. Anyone could do it, anyone could be good at it, and the "winner" was not in the hands of an "expert," but rather at the mercy of the crowd.

As a result of Smith's concept, poetry began to enjoy a rapid reentry into the national consciousness. Regional slam poetry venues popped up all over the country and, soon, all across the globe. A national slam was implemented, with teams composed of the winners from cities nationwide. Shortly thereafter, a world slam was created. Poetry was no longer owned by the publishers, academia, or the literary elite.

I first heard about "slam poetry" from Kate Rushin, my African American Women's Poetry professor at Wesleyan University. Not only had Kate written the inimitable poem "This Bridge Poem" (which was part of *This Bridge Called My Back: Writings by Radical Women of Color*, edited by Cherríe L. Moraga and Gloria E. Anzaldúa), she also gave spoken word performances around campus—reading in an ardent but mellifluous voice. I was spellbound (and a little in love).

One day in class, Kate mentioned the Nuyorican Poets Café in New York City, a venue that might be fitting for some of her students' particular brand of rather "unruly" poetry. It was also, she implied, a radical forum for continuing postcollege education. Petrified, but thrilled about life outside of my prepackaged and stamped learning center, I had the address of the Nuyorican memorized by graduation day.

On one of my first evenings in New York City, I left my new roommate and close friend to unpack our small box of dusty kitchen appliances, and position our scuffed futon. I tucked some poems into my windbreaker pocket and anxiously orange-line-subwayed to the Lower East Side.

That early September evening altered my correlative personal, artistic, and professional worlds forever. In fact, becoming a part of slam poetry's planet was quite likely the most influential episode of my life. The words on that open mic stage exploded before me like a personal pyrotechnics display: electric, sparkly, in bold bursts of fierce authenticity and shining life testimonies. The shoulder-to-shoulder crowd was exuberant—the applause a mix of stomps, shrieks, and howls, heads casually tossed back in laughter. It was unlike any response to poetry I had ever envisaged. My poetry had finally sited her audacious ancestral sanctuary.

In addition to my poetry, I had also subconsciously brought along another significant item: a sharply attuned queer-feminist nose, one that had been buried in women's and gender studies books for the past four years, and so one that quickly sniffed out the slam scene sexism like a newly radicalized crime dog. I noted not only the misogyny in too many of the poems, but also the heavy male domination onstage, even within that progressive poetic lexicon, the "artistic democracy" known as slam.

I flipped through my papers, nervously. Was this urban underbelly, for a white dyke with newly cropped hair from a decidedly small Pennsylvania town, really the right spot to showcase her potentially immature "angry feminism"? Bolstered by the synergy of the space, however, and by a righteous stubborn demeanor, I stomped toward the sign-up list for the open mic. The response was enthusiastic. I was awarded a spot in that Friday's slam competition, and I went on to become a member of the 1998 Nuyorican Slam Team. My teammates were a Puerto Rican revolutionary man, a Trinidadian feminist woman, and a socialist-informed white guy with two lesbian mothers; our mentor, and ringleader of the Nuyorican at the time, was Keith Roach, a former Black Panther. I jokingly referred to our team as the Rainbow Poet-lition. We won first place at the National Poetry Slam competition in Austin, Texas, toured nationally as a group for the next year, and signed a book deal with Soft Skull Press (*Burning Down the House*). I believe that the reason we were so fundamentally successful as a group is that we each approached our art from a different identity-based vantage point, but with a common pathos and political ideology. We individually drew different types of audiences and, together, it was a beautifully sundry crowd. Shortly thereafter, we each went on to develop independent spoken word careers.

I booked my first tour by contacting slam venues across the country, begging to be featured at their open mic events, and slowly these nights connected dot by dot into a two-month tour. I distributed my first handmade spoken word tape, the covers individually cut and folded by my group of friends, hunched over pizza in my living room for a week. Tracks from the collection began to circulate on mix tapes, and I began to be invited to college campuses, primarily by the women's and LGBT centers.

It was really only then, once I began to plunge into the life of a full-time touring artist—and to look for women spoken word mentors and allies, whose lives I might imitate, or at the very least borrow from—that I began to notice once again the underrepresentation of feminist and/or queer voices within the movement. Certainly, I was aware of the formidable troupe of touring artists known as Sister Spit, as well as of women like Patricia Smith, Jessica Care Moore, and Lisa King, poets who were well known on a national level. However, women's voices, on a professional level, still seemed sparse. The few spoken word anthologies that I gobbled up were mainly edited and foreworded by men, the movies made about slam poetry were produced by men and revolved around male characters, the majority of the regional venues where I performed were run by men, and many of the acknowledged originators of the movement were tagged "fore*fathers*"—the creator of "the slam," the founders of the Nuyorican, the beatniks credited for the style, the rappers who were considered artistic cousins, and so on and so on.

And yet, as the spoken word movement began to gain momentum over the following decade, it also began to acquire an increasing number of women's voices. Women, quite familiar with the tenet that "the personal is political," caught on quickly to slam poetry's populist notion, and were more than ready to add their truth(s) to the tapestry, contributing invigorating voices of protest, reflection, and resistance. The combination of the eminent slam movement and the upsurge of our bold underground feminism(s) began to create a unique pool of women verbally challenging society on all fronts. Since my first foray into the movement, I have witnessed spoken word develop as one of the most undiluted expressions of art available to women, particularly as a vehicle for social change.

Indeed, this demanding oral poetry of the early twenty-first century began to define a vanguard of lithely muscled voices— women who think and act decisively to create their distinctive and desperately earned realities. These female spoken word artists have become spokeswomen for a new generation.

When I was asked to edit the first U.S. collection of women spoken word leaders, I felt a salmagundi of emotions: excited about the opportunity, relieved that the documentation of these women's voices would finally come to fruition, but mostly, anxious. How could I possibly begin to amass these voices; how would I know who to include, or what it meant to be "a leader in this movement"?

I started from scratch, first pinpointing other touring artists I had shared stages with at festivals, conferences, and rallies. Because I tour for a living, I also had ample access to the artists people were talking about: what spoken word CDs the college students had blaring in their cars when they picked me up at the airport; which artists' poems were tacked up in women's and LGBT centers; whose work was discussed when I forced myself into the world of the Internet. Little by little, I composed a list of both recently emerged and long-renowned women spoken word leaders.

The women contained within these pages are the new keynote speakers at feminist organizations' annual conferences and inspire the masses at national marches on Washington. They kick off college Take Back the Night events and LGBT rallies and serve as the feature speakers for university awareness months of all kinds. Collectively, these women have been on the covers of dozens of magazines, had full-length features in *The New York Times*, appeared on HBO and CNN, and won Tony Awards for more than one spoken word Broadway show. They have toured countless countries with their art, garnered innumerable awards, fellowships, and book prizes, and topped best-seller lists. These contributors draw hundreds of expectant faces in the tiniest of communities, and thousands at national and international festivals. With origins in spoken word and/or slam poetry, these women are also now successful bandleaders, hip-hop artists, playwrights, actors, and novelists.

Word Warriors is a collection of some of the most influential female spoken word artists in the movement, the writer–rock stars of our time. And even though all of these female spoken word artists have become well known and have had a profound influence on the movement, the idea for a collection that honors their contributions has somehow slipped under the mainstream publishing radar. *Word Warriors* is not only the first U.S. all-women spoken word anthology, but also, unimaginably, the first time that women make up more than 50 percent of a spoken word anthology's contributors.

The contributors offer original essays about pivotal moments and significant experiences within their spoken word careers, accompanied by two spoken word pieces, one well-known work and one new and/or unpublished poem. Each essay offers an illuminating peek into the artist's thought process, a rare chance for the reader to become intimate with the poet.

I am honored to include work by Tony Award–winner Sarah Jones, who discusses her incredible transformation from spoken word artist to Broadway dramatist/actress, as well as by remarkable spoken word foremother Patricia Smith, who encourages us to listen to the Baptist preacher, the pump jockey, kids, our lovers, or drivers cursing in traffic as inspiration for our art. Multiple-award-winning author Michelle Tea contributes her always resoundingly original stream-of-consciousness reflections upon her Sister Spit touring years, while my discussion with Palestinian-born Suheir Hammad includes an honest reflection upon writing her first poem about a young uncle killed as a resistance fighter during the Palestinian liberation movement. We learn how being watched onstage "out of openness, not abnormality" shifted Natalie E. Illum's understanding of her physical disability, and how fat activist Nomy Lamm performed for years, balancing her growing strength with a prosthetic leg that once broke in the middle of a tour. Southern gentleman and self-identified "cowboy-loving Jewish transsexual" Katz exposes how words have served as "a personal brand of revival" and survival, while openly intersex artist Thea Hillman explains how this performance genre has given her the tools to empower herself more fully. And so on, and so on, these voices laugh, argue, retaliate, shudder, and dance through the pages.

Poetry should, Adrienne Rich argues, break the silence, forcing us to ask, "what kind of voice is breaking silence, and what kind of silence is being broken?" It is inarguable that this anthology shatters sound barriers across the board. These poets build upon our political and feminist/womanist vertebrae, contributing unabashed and flawed, precise and untethered voices to the spine of persistence.

It is a kind of hokey-pokey we spoken word artists are forced to play, one foot in and one foot out of mainstream existence. Together, we form this essential community, a hip-hop ballet—coming together, twirling, lifting, dizzyingly determined to be en pointe.

I invite you to join this crazy dance: to write, speak out, and challenge these thoughts and your own, to plug into the movement that uses language to claim, reclaim, and rediscover this tattered but glorious world.

Sarah Jones

Cast of Characters

SARAH JONES IS A TONY AWARD-WINNING POET, playwright, and performer whose latest Broadway production, *Bridge and Tunnel,* was produced by Meryl Streep. Jones's career has taken her from a sold-out run at the Kennedy Center to tours in India, Europe, and South Africa, and to performances for such audiences as the United Nations, members of the U.S. Congress, and the Supreme Court of Nepal. Jones sat down for a chat with anthology editor Alix Olson to reflect upon their old Nuyorican days, her successful lawsuit against the FCC, and her creative process.

You embrace the power of language so organically. Was your family one that promoted a culture of words and strong political beliefs?
My parents were both undergraduate students when they got married, so I was born into a house full of textbooks, volumes of poetry, spoken word albums, folk song lyrics, and the kinds of verbose discussions you might expect from a mixed-race, mixed-gender group of college students circa the 1970s civil rights, women's, and antiwar movements. I think my first words were "Power to the people!"

What year(s) did you consider yourself a part of the Nuyorican Poets Café and what were your impressions of the Café at the time?

I became a regular member of the audience at the Café in 1996. I remember listening to Samantha Coerbell, Cheryl Boyce Taylor, Tracie Morris, Sekou Sundiata, Tish Benson, Carmen Renee, Edwin Torres, Evert Eden, Everton Sylvester... there were so many voices, too many to list. And honestly I can't remember everyone I saw, or exactly when or where, because there was just so much going on. It seemed like almost every night of the week there was a reading somewhere. There was the Brooklyn Moon Café, sort of an Afrocentric hotbed of spoken word and hip-hop flavored poetry, and there were probably two dozen other popular spots ranging from tiny dives to regular readings at clubs like SOB's, the Fez, and at St. Mark's Church. There were even spoken word opportunities at Lincoln Center; I gave one of my first performances there as part of a live jazz and dance piece. But that was before I had the nerve to try slamming. Imagine that, I wasn't afraid to read my poetry at Lincoln Center, but a slam at the Nuyorican? Now that was a challenge I was not sure my pen or ego could handle just yet. But by 1997, after reading around a lot and developing a name for myself alongside my '97–'98 "classmates" Jamaal St. John, Roger Bonair Agard, Lynne Procope, you [Alix Olson], Steve Colman, Dot [Antoniades], Felice Belle, and others, I won the Grand Slam. That was pretty exciting—ranks right up there with my Tony Award—I only wish I had a Nuyorican statuette.

Were you writing poems in college, or did you begin writing them for the slam?

Right after college I had been writing all the bad, angst-ridden stuff you might imagine, laments about ex-boyfriends, one rant against the marriage industrial complex, lots of stuff about racism, sexism, the awful state of the world. Little did I know how much worse it would get so quickly. I had heart, but I wasn't writing anything that was ready for public consumption. Listening to other poets in the performance and slam environment enhanced my understanding of, and relationship to, both the poetry I had studied in college courses and the scribbling I had been doing in my notebooks. I began to see the two as connected, and in a way I guess I began trying deliberately to write in the spaces between them for the slam.

What was it like leaving the formal university system and entering the underground world of the Nuyorican Poets Café?
I learned quite a bit about myself and the world during my truncated career as a Bryn Mawr student (I believe I am still technically a junior!), including feminist values which complemented the multiculturalism I embraced during my junior high and high school years at the United Nations school. The Nuyorican added to these layers by exposing me to its unique mixture of organic class consciousness and validation of traditionally marginalized voices. I listened to poets whose cadences or accented English or lack of formal education or radical subject matter might have excluded them from the rarefied ranks of New York's elite poets and their readings in hushed, wood-paneled rooms. There was nothing hushed about the Nuyorican, especially during a slam, and while many poets followed a rigorous course of writing, workshopping, editing, and self-critiquing their work, there were no standardized entrance exams or ivory towers. In fact, the only "canon" around was the writer and professor Steve Cannon, who, along with other Café elders, such as founder Miguel Algarin, Lois Griffith, Keith Roach, and Bob Holman, helped nurture and manage the rich, sometimes chaotic, often sublime, always edifying experience that was the Nuyorican.

What is your theater background like, and how did you transition from poet to playwright and actor?
I can't say I have any theater background unless you count a

Shakespeare competition in the fifth grade in Washington, D.C. My
public school was great, with highly paid teachers and a robust music
and arts curricula. I guess I'm just lucky I got my early, free, democ-
ratizing education before the Reagan/Bush defunding revolution
could really take hold. And of course my eighth grade turn in *The
Importance of Being Earnest*. But my experience at the Nuyorican,
developing my voice as a performance/slam poet, emboldened me to
transition from poems to monologues in character, and then from indi-
vidual monologues to cohesive theater pieces.

**What has this style mergence taught you about language, the fluidity
of style, and varying art forms?**
I think words are words are words, and if you develop a loving rela-
tionship with them, deep and committed, they will accompany you
along any path you choose. And as you move forward, whether inten-
tionally seeking out new disciplines or just meandering the way I
have, the words will keep propelling you around each bend, helping
you navigate the seemingly impossible intersections, and they'll get
you through all the ditches and forks in the road and even back you
out of the occasional dead ends. So however we travel, from poet to
playwright or songwriter to screenwriter or rapper to librettist to
blogger, what matters is how well we employ the words.

**You were the first artist in history to sue the Federal Communications
Commission for censorship, and the lawsuit resulted in the reversal of
the censorship ruling, which had originally targeted your hip-hop poem
recording, "Your Revolution." From where, and how, did the idea to sue
the FCC germinate and what took it from an idea to the next level?**
I sued the FCC because I could not let the indecency ruling go unan-
swered. While the radio station itself had some recourse in terms of
responding to the FCC directly and trying to defend itself, I as the
writer and performer of "Your Revolution" had no rights as far as the

Commission was concerned, since they technically weren't fining me, they were fining the radio station over my song. Of course it didn't occur to them that publicly labeling my work "obscene" and "sexually indecent" might have just a smidge of an effect on my career and reputation as an artist.

Were you surprised by how quickly word of your case spread? What and who served as your support network during the legal process?
It's unfortunate that many people first learned about me because of the indecency ruling, but many other people had heard "Your Revolution" on the radio before all the FCC madness, or they had seen my off-Broadway show, or seen me on TV or on the cover of *Ms.* magazine, or knew of my work with Equality Now for the human rights of women and girls, or my performance at the United Nations, et cetera. So I had the support of all the people who knew me already and were outraged at the absurdity of the ruling. Then, because the ruling itself was so public (the FCC had only done this "cracking down" in response to one other song, Eminem's "The Real Slim Shady," and as an incredibly profitable artist with a corporate conglomerate behind him, his indecency ruling was quickly reversed), I got a lot of response from people who were concerned with free speech issues. Among them were People For the American Way and Frankfurt Kurnit Klein & Selz, lawyers who worked on my case pro bono and filed the historic lawsuit.

Did you feel as though it were a personal, political, and/or community obligation for you to do so?
Looking back, I remember how much it hurt personally to have the government characterize my work as "obscene" and "intended to pander and titillate" knowing that my intention had been just the opposite. I worked with kids in schools, for crying out loud. I was trying to offer an empowering, culturally relevant alternative to the

dehumanizing, corporate-sanctioned version of the urban experience the FCC seemed to have no problem with. So yeah, it was very personal. But at a political and community level, I was also conscious of the hypocrisy of the "family values" espoused by the Bush administration and its allies (FCC included, though Michael Powell was a Clinton appointee). I was disgusted that the same people who claim to be the arbiters of decency are also proponents of a right-wing agenda that includes consistently censoring political dissent and attacking the basic rights of women, black people, and urban communities, among others. All it took to censor my poem/song was a phone call from a conservative who knew and/or cared nothing about my culture, my values, and the context of my parody of misogynist pop/hip-hop lyrics on the radio. This to me was yet another indicator of how much the power of Bush, his cabal, and their base could be brought to bear on every aspect of the lives of people in a nation that had never actually voted him into office in the first place. I wanted to do whatever I could to reject that power.

You do such a brilliant job of adding laughter within the context of serious global issues. What role does humor play in your life perspective and your work?

Growing up, I was drawn to humorists and comedians. I was fascinated by their ability to make observations, sometimes about the touchiest of issues or situations, and somehow leave audiences more relaxed and receptive to even controversial ideas than they would have been if someone had politely avoided the same subject matter. I think humor is one of the most precious resources we have as people, whether we are creative artists or philosophers or teachers or parents. We live in a world that won't continue to exist much longer unless we make sweeping changes. If we are going to raise peoples' awareness of issues like our rights as women or people of color or workers in a culture that is often hostile to the protection of those rights, we must reach people in a space in which they are open to ideas that may not seem to be in their interests at first. And that's gonna take everything we can throw at them: vice presidential documentaries, rock stars in favor of debt cancellation, and jokes. Lots and lots of jokes. I find wherever there's an open, laughing mouth, the open heart can't be too far behind.

The cast of characters in your head seems endless. How do you go about creating these "people"? Have you ever been concerned about depicting people accurately, and genuinely, without veering into a stereotype?

No, I can't say I have been concerned. My experience growing up surrounded by people from so many different backgrounds has attuned my ears to the specificity of the ways people sound and given me an underlying comfort level with the human experience in all its permutations. So I don't feel any more uncomfortable portraying a person of any particular background than I would listening to that actual person speak. The only problem arises if there are audience members who bring with them an inherent prejudice against a certain accent or portrayal of a certain kind of experience. For example, I've had people ask why a certain character is black and working-class instead of being a doctor. My response is there is nothing wrong with working-class black people, their values or accents. It's only images from mainstream media that consistently degrade poor people, or people of color, or women, or members of the LGBT community, based on the negative values the dominant culture attaches to some of our real-life characteristics, such as how we speak, or our income levels, or how we dress. In general, I just try to observe and listen to people carefully (sometimes even going so far as to record various people from a particular place), and in this way I can avoid creating a stock caricature that doesn't reflect a person's real human dimensions. The rest is up to the audience!

your revolution

inspired by Gil Scott-Heron's "The Revolution Will Not Be Televised"

your revolution will not happen between these thighs
your revolution will not happen between these thighs

the real revolution
ain't about booty size
the Versaces you buys
or the Lexus you drives

and though we've lost Biggie Smalls
your Notorious revolution
will never allow you to lace no lyrical douche in my bush
your revolution will not be you killing me softly with Fugees
your revolution won't knock me up and produce
    li'l future MCs
because that revolution will not happen between
    these thighs

your revolution
will not find me in the
backseat of a Jeep with LL
hard as hell
doin' it & doin' it & doin' it well

your revolution will not be you
smackin' it up, flippin' it, or rubbin' it down
nor will it take you downtown or humpin' around
because that revolution will not happen between
    these thighs

your revolution will not have me singing
ain't no nigger like the one I got
your revolution will not be you
sending me for no VD shot

your revolution will not involve me feeling your nature rise
or helping you fantasize
because that revolution will not happen between
    these thighs
and no, my Jamaican brother, your revolution
will not make me feel boombastic and really fantastic
have you groping in the dark for that rubber wrapped
    in plastic

you will not be touching your lips to my triple dip of
french vanilla butter pecan chocolate deluxe
or having Akinyele's dream
a six-foot blow job machine

you wanna subjugate your "queen"
think I should put it in my mouth
just 'cause you made a few bucks

your revolution will not be me tossing my weave
making believe I'm some caviar-eating, ghetto mafia clown
or me givin' up my behind just so I can get signed
have someone else write my rhymes?
I'm Sarah Jones, not Foxy Brown
your revolution makes me wonder, where could we go
if we could drop the empty pursuit of props and the ego
revolt back to our Roots, use a little Common sense
    on a Quest

to make love De La Soul, no pretense ... but

your revolution will not be you flexing your sex and status
to express what you "feel"
your revolution will not happen between these thighs
will not happen between these thighs
will not be you shaking and me faking between these thighs
because the revolution, when it finally comes, is gon' be real

wax poetic

a multicultural affair
this trim trimming party
she speaks mandarin and cantonese
I would speak english french or spanglish
were I not sworn to a vow of stoicism
(silent and dignified, even prostrate and naked
this an african american thing)
my breathing is prana from india
her technique, born brazilian, now a citizen of the world

from waist down I am a brown
brooklyn bagel with a schmear
a flick of the wax
a twist of her tongue depressor
(would that it were only my tongue being
spread thick then tugged clean)
she hovers, coats, yanks, with swiss precision
and soon I am smooth as a saharan dune

in hong kong she was educated to be a teacher
she speaks of the rising cost of a climbing class
how america grinds bones to make its bread
at bryn mawr I was educated to be a feminist
to be a torch and find my sexiness where it was buried, hidden
    in plain insight

we never speak of how we both got here
or pause to ponder the private, pubic filigree
the tiny pile upon the sterile floor

we do not interrogate the sticky strips
the traps for tortured tufts and tangles

it would be unseemly to tease
apart the reasons some women must touch
other women's pussies for
train fare and tips every day and
so instead we leave it to the wax
in the melting pot

On Sister Spit

THERE IS SOMETHING ABOUT THE SORT OF FEMINISM
I have always organically embodied, and that has been likewise
embodied by the majority of my closest and most admired lady writer
friends. You know how earlier eras of feminism sort of forgot that
there were poor women? Remember there was that whole lavender
menace wariness of queer women butting in with their own experi-
ences, messing up our heterosisters' stab at media acceptance? I think
that the people who made up Sister Spit, "the all-girl performance
tour that tore up the U.S. at the end of the last century," were the
living, breathing responses to those overlooked patches of feminist
experience. We were the lavender menace and the broke-ass menace;
we were the never been to college menace and the drunken menace;
we were the shove your dogma menace and the my poetry can beat
up your theory menace.

This was not a conscious thing, this acting out. We were grind-
ing our axes when we arrived, the combination of cynicism and ide-
alism pumping through our very nature, unnoticeable. We were all

feminists who knew exactly how and where feminism had failed us
with its assumptions, or its ignorance, about our lives. We knew the
best revenge would be to wrap our stinky, drug-addled, badly behaved
selves in feminism, which, we also knew, saved our lives. We would kick
out some space for others like ourselves: slightly feral, hungry to con-
nect with others, inappropriate, wild, reckless, and feminist.

This is not to say that everyone who ever toured with Sister Spit
was a poverty-stricken alcoholic with little formal education and a
penchant for starting bar fights. There were middle-class girls in the
van. Clean and sober recovering alcoholics and addicts somehow man-
aged, no doubt with some difficulty, to tour with us, and there were
others who, miraculously, just didn't have those issues. There were
college graduates. There were girls who, though they had tried really
hard, weren't even queer. Some had had relatively happy childhoods.
There were performers who had real problems with the bar fights
that others instigated. Also, there were people who would hook up on
tour and have sex with each other. Sometimes right in the van. Next
to you. Some people really didn't like that, and others really didn't like
the kind of sex their tour mates were having. The bruising and the
bite marks could be over the top. Somehow, we managed to get along
with each other, mostly. Somehow, everyone's candida diet or vegan
needs were met, mostly. Incredibly, the money we made, a single wad
of cash, never got lost, though it was found lying around unattended at
least three times during the tour: at a Nevada gas station parking lot,
in the van window in the French Quarter in New Orleans, and sitting
lonely at a table in New York City. That wad was not enough to pay
us, but it got us from city to city.

When our $1,500 van, bought from an indie rocker whose own
band had just had a vehicle upgrade from money raised from a full
year of benefit shows, pulled out from San Francisco, we had no reason
to believe that fate wouldn't have us turning around and driving back
home in no time. Why would anyone come to our shows? We were two

vanfuls of nobodies, with a couple of underground sensations we were hoping would pull in enough of a crowd to fill the gas tank. Why did we think we could pass through America unmolested? We all had friends who were fearful for us, going out into our hateful country, leaving the bosom of our cities. So many people had commented on how we were bound to all hate each other by the end of the tour that I made a plan in my head about how to handle anyone who got bitchy—drive their asses to the nearest Greyhound station, and leave them there.

Nobody's fears came true. We took right to the road, hanging our feet out the window, chain-smoking, buying real scorpion paper-weights at truck stops, watching the sun set to classic rock stations, scrawling new poems into our notebooks. No one got dumped any-where (except that time we inadvertently left one of us behind at a Mexican restaurant in Albuquerque). And, most amazingly, though none of us necessarily believed that the world cared about us or our poetry, people came to our shows. Sometimes quite a lot of people. We were astonished. Entering a coffeehouse in Athens, Georgia, I felt nervous at what would happen when the large coffee-drinking crowd was confronted with a bunch of "debaucherous" queer and feminist storytellers. I was shocked to realize they were actually there to lis-ten to us! A crowd that had gathered to hear us in the basement of a sushi restaurant in the South clapped wildly for us before we even said anything, they were that proud that we had just made it to their town. And they were correct, it was a huge accomplishment. With no money backing us, no cell phones, no credit cards in case of emergency, no laptops, no way to MapQuest our way into the next town and often no actual plan of where we would all sleep that night, we made it to our shows, rarely if ever late. And we always found a place to sleep.

Sometimes the shittiest, most oppressive thing about being a girl is how good you're supposed to be all the time. And sometimes that feeling of an enforced, expected integrity can come from feminism. The thing about being a poet, a writer, and an artist is that you can't be good. You shouldn't have to be good. You should, for the benefit of your art, your soul, and your life, go through significant periods of time where you are defying many notions of goodness. As female artists, the Sister Spit group wanted the same opportunities to fuck up and get fucked up as dudes have always been forgiven for pursuing; we needed access to the same hard road of trial and error our male peers and literary inspirations stumbled down. We needed the right to ruin our lives and crawl out from the wreckage, maybe wiser. We needed the right to start a stupid brawl and emerge victorious or with a black eye. We needed to cheat on our lovers and quit our jobs. We definitely needed to shoplift. We weren't everyone's role models, but if we were yours, you'd know it.

In a ton of ways, the tour itself was an act of defiance. We were, largely, a group of people who had heard the word *No* too much. *No* to being queer, to wanting to be artists, to thinking anyone would want to listen to our attitudinal manifestos. So it was more than a little gutsy to think we could do what rock stars did, tour the country, delighting audiences and racking up adventures. It was possibly delusional. It was amazing that we did not get seriously hurt, or arrested. It helped that there were thirteen of us, two vans full. If a creepy cop pulled one of us over, he inadvertently pulled both cars over. That was a lot of bother if he was just looking to fuck with some freaks. And we were freaks. Our hair was blue or it was pink. It was short to the scalp or looked like it had never been combed. We had tattoos, many of them not too well crafted. We had scars, many of them deliberate. Our clothes were mostly secondhand, if not third- or fourthhand. Many of us were butch, not passing as a girl or a boy, but as some new sort of human a lot of gas station denizens had never seen before. In the beginning of each tour—there were three major cross-country ones and a bunch of shorter, regional excursions—we would have to figure out who was the most normal looking. That person would be called upon to deal with authority, be they cops, auto mechanics, or hotel workers.

We lost our first van due to an oil leak that blew a rod in the engine. This happened on the Mississippi-Alabama border, at around midnight on a weekend night. The tow truck driver was drunk and scary. Some of the performers were towed away in the van. I can't remember why we thought that would be a good idea. We stayed overnight in a hotel room, one hotel room for all thirteen of us, I believe. We snuck in through a side door. In the morning everyone had to dump some of their luggage in order for us to keep going. Someone had brought a skateboard; someone else, a tennis racket. A health food store back in San Francisco had donated tons of healthy food to us; we still had a lot of it, and all of it was dumped in that hotel parking lot. One of our more financially stable performers had an honest-to-goddess credit card and was able to rent us a van. A cargo van. With no seats in the back. The one menopausal writer claimed the one actual seat in the air-conditioned cab; the rest of us tumbled around the back. It felt, perhaps, like going over the falls in a barrel. It was illegal to have passengers in the back of the cargo van. Of course, it was also illegal to drink in the van, or to do drugs. Or to buy drugs, though many times we were simply given the stuff. Once, a yellowed page torn from a paperback and soaked in LSD was donated to us by some guys selling tie-dyed thong underwear outside an adult bookstore in Reno, Nevada. A Cambridge police officer once let me go in spite of my belligerence, me screaming in the streets, drunk, in velvet hot pants and a rainbow-spangled tube top. There were many transgressions, and mercifully, amazingly, we never got arrested.

But we always had style. And smarts. When a southwestern cop wanted to search the van, because the devil stickers in our windows led him to believe there were drugs inside, performers knew their rights and didn't let him in. There may not have been drugs in the van that time, but that particular van, our second, was so shabby that if you shut it off it wouldn't necessarily turn back on. So allowing the cop to come on board could have cost us that night's show.

We encountered many expected foes, like the man at a sandwich shop in Mississippi who said if he had his gun he'd blow our heads off, or the gang of security guards who were called to wrestle one of our "men" out of the women's room at Niagara Falls. But for the most part our friends and supporters were not always who we expected them to be, nor were our foes. A Catholic townie from Boston took great offense to our antics at a bar there, prompting a brawl replete with flying glass jars of mustard. We had befriended a group of circus performers, straight dudes, and they fought alongside us, for the right to whip out your dildo in a public establishment. An East Coast dyke promoter was majorly offended by our onstage drinking and our public revelations of shoplifting snacks across America. Bar dykes in Buffalo, New York, tried to kick our asses, ostensibly for flicking cigarette ash onto the floor of their dive bar, but really I just think they thought we were freaky nerds, with our weird hair and our poetry. Other lesbians, at a bar in Ohio, tried to prevent us from performing, then heckled us throughout the show. They couldn't wait 'til we were done so they could turn the k. d. lang back on and slow-dance on the lit-up dance floor. Seriously. The tragedy is, these ladies should have been our comrades. A great many assumptions about who we were stoked a resentment toward our presence in their neighborhood bars, their second homes. But truly, I felt we had a lot in common (working-class backgrounds, scant college, alcoholism); that our differences (mullets, acid-washed jeans, dream catcher earrings) were largely cosmetic. A bunch of older dykes let us camp out at their lesbian separatist land and swim in their pond, which was awesome, and *L Word* prototypes, who we judged on sight, bought up all our merchandise in Los Angeles.

But for all the asshole guys and aggro dykes we encountered, the scary rednecks and the coppish cops were actually the folks who embraced us most. We charmed the Carhartts off a bar full of punka-billy and assorted fratlike dudes at a bar in Las Vegas; one performer even sucked a hickey onto the neck of a jock who had, inspired by our performance, penned his own poem, a sappy-sweet ode to everybody being friends with everybody else. We heard him on the pay phone after the show explaining to his girlfriend that a lesbian had given him a hickey. Some Christians stuck around for our performance in Atlanta, much more open to us than we were to them.

All across the U.S., we wrote and caused trouble, and wrote about the trouble we caused, and read it each night to audiences. It was stunning. To have our improbable ambitions validated. To have the chips on our shoulders polished and praised. To have our zines and chapbooks purchased by brand-new fans who wanted us to sign them, like we were real writers! Some of us had already had books published before Sister Spit, but the majority of us had not. To know that there would be strangers in North Carolina, Arizona, and upstate New York reading our writing was incredible. We were writers. People bought us drinks and took us home to stay in their beds. They cooked us food. Mostly we were grateful for this, but occasionally our generous hosts had ulterior motives: observing our bravado and braggadocious sluttery on stage, they thought they'd get lucky back at home. But what most of these folks ended up getting was a starring role in a Can You Believe It?! story, to be told and retold, often from the stage at our next show. Like the woman who whipped off her shirt when we got back to her house, all casual-like; or the woman who opened the shower door while someone was using it to recommend a bar of soap that smelled like "a sweet woman's pussy" (she didn't understand that after three weeks in the van, we were desperately trying to wash away the smell of any sort of pussy); or the girl who left baskets of sex toys around her house and unexpectedly shoved her tongue down my throat. Of course, people did get lucky; mostly in the van, with each other. Performers hooked up in ways both discreet and mind-blowingly indiscreet. Like, leaving lubey handprints on the back windows or getting it on in a room you're sharing with three other people. Like, steering the van with one hand while fisting someone with the other.

The fact that Sister Spit was a success is partly a miracle and partly a testament to how queer and feminist subcultures take care of their own. It is partly proof that some sort of god watches over the drunk and foolish, and definitely proof that if you want something bad you can make it happen through sheer will, ingenuity, and community support. It proved to all of us that our writing was important, at a time in our mostly young lives when, without such tangible evidence, we might have been discouraged from writing by the rigors of everyday living in a world that devalued art, especially the first-person narratives of such a band of ruffians. And it gave us a platform to misbehave spectacularly, to feel temporarily invincible, to feel safe in a world that had taught us to fear it.

Pigeon Manifesto

The revolution will not begin in your backyard because you do
not have a backyard. What you have is a back door that shits
you directly onto the streets of your city. What you have is a
back staircase of wood that resembles splintered matchsticks, it
trembles each time a bus rolls down Mission. What you have is a
patch of concrete, a splotch of weedy grass clumped with trash,
and this is not a backyard. What you have is a cement slab that
pools with rainwater, that catches the tumble of beer can and
sludgy condom that falls from the apartments above you. What
you have is empty of anything green but the slugs still find a
way to work it out, inkiest green like mold breathed to life, they
slide a wet trail across what is not a backyard. Maybe you have
never had, will never have a backyard, but you still could have
slugs, and always you will have the pigeons.

The revolution will begin at your curb, in the shallow pool of
shade that is your gutter. The revolution will begin with the
pigeon bobbing hungry in the street—it is now your job to love
her. It is now your job to not avert your eyes from her feet, your
job to seek out and find the one pigeon foot that is blobbed in
a chemical melt, a pink-orange glob, a wad of bubble gum. The
pigeon splashed in a pool of chemicals laid out to kill it because
so many of the people hate the pigeons. This is now why you
must love them. We must love the nature that does not make it
onto the Discovery Channel, onto Animal Planet. We must love
the nature that crawls up to our doorstep like sparechangers
and scares us with the thickness of their feathers, their mutant
feet and orange eyes. Someone could have made dinner with the
rice on the corner but instead they sprinkled it on the curb with
the hope that hungry pigeons ate it, and that the grain would

expand in their stomachs, tearing them open, felling them in the street, plump and feathered and dead in the gutter. I think perhaps this does not even work, because I watch the pigeons peck at the rice and fly off on grey wings. I hardly ever see them dead in spite of how many people try to kill them.

Pigeons are doves. They are rock doves, and I wonder if we began to call them that again if people would hesitate to hate them, as doves have that history as being mesengers of peace. It is true that in my neighborhood nobody hates the mourning doves, dusky and elegant with wings that squeak like they flap on rusty hinges. They roost on the wires like little Audrey Hepburns, while the pigeons troll the ground, tough and fat, they look like they should be smoking cigarettes, some of them. They look poor and banged-up, they look like they could kick the mourning doves' asses but they are wise to the divide and conquer tactics we use on one another, they coo wearily at the mourning doves and waddle forth in search of scavanged delights. What you might not know is when you call a pigeon a rat with wings you have given it a compliment. The only thing a rat lacks is a pair of wings to lift them, so you have named the pigeon perfect. When you say to me I hate pigeons I want to ask you who else you hate. It makes me suspicious. I once met a girl who was so proud to have hit such a bird on her bicycle, I swear, I thought that it was me she hit. I felt her handlebars in my stomach, and now it is your job to feel it also. The pigeons are birds, they are doves. They are the nature of the city and the ones who no one loves. When people say they hate pigeons I want to ask if they hate themselves, too. Does it prick the well of your loathing, do they make you feel dirty and ashamed, are you embarrassed about how little or how much you have, for how you have had to hustle? Being dirty is not a problem for the pigeon. You can ask it, How do you feel about having the city coating your feathers, having the streets gunked up in the crease of your eye, and the pigeon would say, Not a problem. You will now stop blaming the pigeon. It is not the pigeon's fault. The pigeon was once a dove, and then we built our filthy empire up around it, came to hate it for simply thriving in the midst of our decay, came to hate it for not dying. The pigeon is your ally. They are chameleons, grey as the concrete they troll for scraps, at night they huddle and sing like cats. Their necks are glistening, iridescent as an oil-slick rainbow, they mate for life, and they fly.

The Beautiful

a coke and a smoke
as we roam the gray prairie.
what sentiment do i want
to express at the end
of our world,
a terrific excitement
as we prepare
to exit
america.

its many eyes
america the
hydra
the milky stuffed
beast the roast beef
sandwich
of america.
i have no doubt we
created it.
the absent truckers
stitching the states
together, the moving
monuments
of this country.
we destroy
a little bit
of everything
we pass.
the bomb tucked
dearly

into farmland,
rest stops,
missing but
a simple bolt
of certain rage.
the wake of america
at our tail—oh
we could kill it,
couldn't we.

america
what shitty parents you were.
we have to run away
again and again
we keep
coming back
to see if you missed us
but you didn't
even know
we were gone.
we write tell-all books
about our rotten childhoods:
the bad food
you fed us,
the coat-hanger
beatings.
can i process
my bad relationship
with america,
can we go to
couples counseling,
can we sit down and talk about

all this
bad energy?

oh america i love you
i just want to
go on a date with you
and you won't even give me
the time of day
stuck up bitch
think you're too good for me,
america?
i could have anyone—
canada, london
amsterdam
is in love with me
but it's you i want,
america.
what could i do
to impress you?
i could write you
an anthem
but you have
so many.

fuck you
america.
you're just so
emotionally
unavailable
you act like
it's everyone else's
fault

you're a
really bad
communicator
and you have
serious
boundary issues.

i think you're
really fucked up
america.
i think you've got
a lot of
problems.
i keep getting all these
hang-up calls
i know
it's you
america.
you better cut the shit.
i'm getting a restraining
order: if america comes
within twenty-five feet of me
i'm throwing her ass
in jail.
how do you like that,
america?
you can dish it out
but you really can't
take it, america.
you're such a baby.
we've been together
all these years

and you still won't let me call you
girlfriend
you act like it doesn't mean
anything.

i'm over it america.
i think you're really
self-loathing.
you know,
i made you
what you are today.
i think you forget about that.
well, you can just forget
about everything,
america,
you can just forget
the whole thing.
i'm going home.

Lenelle Moïse

Protégée

IN 1985, MY UNCLE SERGO, FRESH FROM A MENTAL institution, moved into our small, government-owned apartment in Dorchester, Massachusetts. Sergo—as tall, vain, charming, and flamboyant as I imagine Oscar Wilde must have been—was my favorite eccentric relative and also a poet. One would never have guessed he was unemployed. He owned countless pairs of handmade Italian leather shoes. He wore silk-blend Spanish suits, exclusively. He generally scoffed at blue jeans but once bought a designer pair from a strung-out street vendor in Roxbury. When lined up in his closet, his expensive, imported clothes had the effect of an open box of crayons. My uncle was the color of ground coffee, cruelly handsome, a bit of a philanderer and slightly effeminate. He blended three different women's perfumes to create his potent, aura-outlining signature scent. His hair shone like a gel-induced halo. And when he smiled his saccharine, secretive smile, he flaunted a top right canine tooth encased in gold. Sergo was a Caribbean Adonis. His mildest flaw was an aggressive stutter, but when he stood behind pulpits to recite his epic poems, even the stutter disappeared.

My uncle was famous in our Haitian American Seventh-Day Adventist community. Church services usually went from 9 AM to 3 PM, but every Sabbath Sergo's performances broke the monotony of an excruciatingly long day. Since he wrote poems in Haitian Kreyol, we considered him to be a literary revolutionary. In old-school Haiti, French was the language of business, politics, and literature while Kreyol—the language of the people, the *langue-lakay* or "hometongue"—was dismissed as common patois. Despite the fact that over half of the Haitian population could not read or write in French, for too long French was the only official national language of the island. Our church in the U.S. was committed to this classist, colonized thinking. In an effort to sound more holy, most hymns, psalms, testimonials, and sermons were delivered in somber, formal French.

Sergo rebelled. He felt determined to craft and deliver Kreyol in a way that was unmistakably ceremonious. His poems always rhymed. They were didactic but clever and often funny. He was a gregarious, generous performer. Sweat poured from his forehead as he leapt off the pulpit into the congregation, punching his fists into the air to punctuate his words. Sergo was a sanctified slam poet. Whenever he finished reciting, the congregation erupted into one booming, collectively uttered *"Amen!"* His work appealed to the members of our church with multiple degrees and to the illiterate. My uncle was never published or awarded or even interviewed, but in our enclave, he was a brilliant star.

When I was five, Sergo took me on as a protégée. "Write me a poem," he demanded one afternoon when he was babysitting and I was bored. He pulled out a blank yellow legal pad and specified that I should fill at least one side of a page with rhymed couplets. I dutifully took on the assignment, laboring over a soulless rant about *fat cats wearing big hats and breaking bats.* When I returned with my completed, albeit amateur, assignment, Sergo slowly stroked his goatee in seemingly serious contemplation of my work. "Not bad," he said, marking my stanzas with his red pen, "but you can do better."

An hour later, I approached him with my second draft. "I'm done," I sung. I stuck the paper out for him to grab, eager for easy praise, but he only held my wide-eyed gaze, crossed his arms and shook his head no.

"This time you have to read it to me," he said, and after I did, he asked, "What do *you* think of it?" I had to admit that what I had written made very little sense. "Keep writing," he told me. "Practice every day until it is perfect." That day, I learned three lessons: (1) You should write about things you feel passionate about (I owned no fat cats, big hats, or bats), (2) Serious writing requires meticulous editing, and (3) A poem is not finished until you share it.

Sergo did not join us when my mother moved us to nicer projects in Cambridge, Massachusetts. He got his own small apartment and a day job as a cab driver but continued to serve as a sounding board for my earliest work.

A lot went down in the early 1990s: Bush Sr. declared war. Haiti's Jean-Bertrand Aristide was democratically elected and then violently forced into exile (for the first time). Old men started to stare at my budding breasts and catcall to me on the street. Dozens of friends and family members died of a white-cell-sucking disease they were too ashamed to name. Rodney King got his ass beat by racist cops and some of my female classmates were raped. I filled several seventy-page spiral notebooks with my outrage and grief about the increasingly harsh, confusing world around me. I then crafted these free-writes into hopeful poems. By the time I was twelve, I had written a song against the Gulf War, a rant about the L.A. riots, and an educational rap about AIDS, among many other pieces. I memorized my writing, swallowed my preadolescent self-consciousness, and performed in school talent shows in front of my teachers, parents, and peers. Since the competitions were actually popularity contests, the lip-synching cool kids garnered the top prizes. Nevertheless, even today, old classmates from the seventh grade can recite the lyrics to my rhymes, and that is more encouraging to me than any $50 gift certificate I could have won back then.

By the time I went off to college, Sergo had fled to Haiti to avoid jail time for a crime he claimed he could not remember committing. Missing him, I followed a colorful flyer to the Oak, a now defunct café-slash–used bookstore in Ithaca, New York. The Oak was hosting an open mic poetry night every Wednesday to attract customers. At first, the hip-hop-loving, Saul Williams–emulating Jewish boys and I were the only ones rocking the mic. But word spread quickly about our tight-knit community of reciting writers, and soon enough, every week, a racially diverse crowd consisting of student artists, neohippie professors, activists, the local schizophrenic, and other misfits filled the joint to fire hazard capacity. In the late 1990s poets became celebrities, featured on the covers of major magazines and in award-winning feature films. All over the world, poetry was the new cool. Ithacans flocked to the Oak to experience the phenomena of the spoken word, live. The atmosphere was always celebratory and unconditionally supportive. Anything went. An open mic poet could recite something abstract about the sun and stars, something intimate about her dying grandparent, a journal entry about her cheating lover, or a didactic political rant about reproductive rights; she could recite rhymed couplets, sonnets, haiku, free-form verse, or a freestyle rap. Unless a poem was racist or misogynist, almost every poet who had the courage to get up and read was met with rock star applause. We praised poets' bravery when we couldn't praise their craft.

I thrived at the Oak. Every week, Jordan the host reserved the seventh slot for me to practice performing my texts. Between the acting, writing, dance, and sociology courses I took at Ithaca College and my regular spot at the Oak, I developed my artistic voice and a highly physical performance style. I also made really good friends at the café: the bisexual sex major who organized an annual How to Make Your Vagina Sing conference; the long-haired, long-winded, goddess-worshipping, yoga-practicing massage therapist who would be my last boyfriend; the sexy chain-smoking photographer in chic vintage clothes who became the first girl I ever kissed.

When I went home for winter breaks, I desperately missed my "Oakies." Since I was a first-generation college student, my family members and I were ill-equipped for how much I would evolve at school. I lost interest in their strict Christianity, male-dominated conversations, and spicy fried foods; they were, likewise, annoyed by my refusal to go to church, my outspoken feminism, and my politicized vegetarianism. When I tried to communicate with my stepfather in my expanding vocabulary, he teased me, "What did the white woman say?" My mother (bless her) listened to my new poems patiently but when push came to shove, she could not understand my metaphors. We fought constantly as, much to my chagrin and against my will, I was perfecting the ability to pass for middle-class.

One lonely, pissed-off January night in Cambridge, I snuck out and signed up for the Amazon Slam, a monthly poetry competition then based on the second floor of a popular jazz club called Ryles. I had not yet studied the Amazons so it wasn't until I made it to the semifinal round that I looked around the room and realized that most of the poets, judges, and audience members were lesbians. Somehow, without really meaning to, I had walked into a room full of my people: word-loving, women-loving women. Thrilled and turned on, I offered my most centered, confident performance and won the slam.

By the time I finished college, I had competed in two National Poetry Slams, recited poems in front of Anna Deavere Smith and Cornel West, and shared stages with Saul Williams and Alix Olson. When I introduced myself to strangers, I called myself a poet. I said this word—"poet"—before I said "Haitian American" or "pomosexual" or "playwright" or "performance artist" or any of the other words that make up my identity. When people asked about how or why I started writing, I always told them about Sergo.

By then I was also sharing an apartment with my current partner (another regular at the Oak). When Sergo found out I was in love with a woman, he loudly disowned me. He lost his eloquence and called me a *madivinez sal*, "dirty dyke" in Haitian Kreyol. Shouting through a telephone from Port-au-Prince, he insisted he would see me in hell. "You are dead to me," he said.

I am a poet anyway and very much alive. I craft personal-political stories for social justice, for the planet and people I love, and yes, even for Sergo. If he could see me now—one hand punching the air with my fierce, feminine, feminist fist—perhaps his heart would sing. If he could hear me now, singing protest songs in our *langue-lakay*, I think my crazy, troubled uncle would be so proud.

we live up here

roxy has a secret and i know it.

roxy—fresh
from the dominican republic—
lives on the first floor
and me—a haitian talking
american—i live
on the third. she's twelve
years old
and i'm nine but we're friends cuz
neither of us is allowed
to go outside. there is no play

for the daughters of immigrants
who rest under project ceilings.
we are our parents'
only investments.
in their dreams, we birth
second-story houses in the suburbs, strong
fences and theft-less streets, jewish
neighbors walking well-groomed
dogs, graffiti-less
two-car garage doors.

there is no room
in our parents' fantasies
for the brown
folks of our dreary daily lives
who work or loiter
or die around us. who don't know

coconuts and guava, mango
and kenepas. who don't muse over
lost motherlands and ancestral languages
the way we do.

here we are kept
away from the dark
men who grab
their nuts, blare
boom-box blasphemy and deal
medicinals that never heal. i say,
there are great expectations
and no play
for the daughters
of immigrants.

so when roxy and i get in from school
or church, we poke protected
heads out of our respective dense,
scraped windows and watch
hood rat games of tag, ambulance
arrivals, dss departures, welfare
check elation, various evictions
and arrests. we watch our people
who are not our people
from the safety of our homes.

roxy's english is still
thick with spanish
and mine's so thoroughly bred
in cambridge, massachusetts, that we avoid
speaking to each other. instead we communicate

by lifting bored brows, frowning or rolling
our eyes. sometimes she asks me
what curse
words mean—*slut, asshole, screw*—
and when i tell her, sometimes she smiles.

but most times roxy hates me
cuz i am her
mirror: trapped and also brown.
i throw down
the drawings i make of her.
she winks
up at me, fellating
bananas
and in this way, we
are close.

roxy has a secret and i know it:
while her parents are asleep or out waging
their undocumented minimum,
roxy has a white boy
climbing
in and out of her
first-floor window.
he's irish and athletic, in high
school and cute. he
brings beer.

roxy sticks sepia
arms out—pulls
him through her plastic pane,
into her prison

which i imagine is painted pink and stinky
with perfume, cluttered
with neglected porcelain dolls, purple
diaries plastered with stickers of fake
locks and keys
that probably never get used.

for hours, i wait, missing
the top of roxy's head
as i imagine moans and firm
bananas going mushy
on her thighs, inside. eventually,
it is time for him to leave and i spy
his lean body withdrawing
from her bedroom, his tongue
fast-knocking the roof
of her mouth. she says,

te amo and he whispers
también like
tom-ben and she giggles
like the girls do
in the movies and me and roxy
rest rapunzel-like
elbows on our sills—palms
crushing the faint chin-hairs
we will later pluck to feel
more american. we become

women as we study
her boyfriend's flat butt, fleeing
our end

of this broken world, back
to his house in the 'burbs.

one day my mother says, i'm so glad
we live up here. and that's how
i guess roxy's secret
is out. i hear noises
through her window
now: an aging mother hailing
mary loudly, a father
weeping then breaking
things, beating her.
and when she finally hangs her head

out of the window again i say, *hi*
over and over then ask *where
is your boyfriend?* to which she replies,
screw you, asshole. and i think
slut but dare not pitch it.

these days, roxy wears
the sweatshirts the missing
boyfriend gave her
to conceal the swell of her
belly. these days, roxy
wears headphones, repeating
the standard inflections she hears, trying
to sound like the new
american daughter
she's expecting in the fall

loch ness monsters

after patricia's face
was dragged across
the parking lot of pete's
grocery store and gasoline
stop on buffalo street
in ithaca, ny, one late afternoon
during rush hour traffic in july
2002's brutal, blatant sun

after a white man held her down
and two white women kicked her jaw because
they claimed—although they sat innocently
in their parked pickup truck—
this stranger/black woman—
patricia—just had to go and look
at them funny so they had to get out and try
to put her in her place

after their fists and their spit
after their tired word nigger

after ithacan would-be witnesses
filled their giant grape slurpee cups—filled
their unleaded tanks—filled their ears
with the predictable weather forecast—their ears
with an international report on terrorism—
their air-conditioned ears turned off to screams,
turned on to britney spears' overplayed number
one hit *hit me baby one more time*

after bystanders sat
in their jammed cars, unmoved, someone
inside the grocery store
called the cops and,
late, the cops
handcuffed the assaulted
twenty-year-old black woman
first because—

though her stunned skull thumped
with bitter bewilderment and her broad
nose bled from the burden of meeting
her tears on three dog shit shoes —
since patricia was shrilling *cracker* and flailing
her bruised arms uncontrollably, the ithacan
cops thought she seemed
menacing, not molested

after the ithaca times
reported the incident four days
late, the local liberal whites simply
could not believe
it happened here. *here?*
in ithaca? my god,
they said, *that's just*
incredible. are you serious? here?

and i wonder how some people can keep their minds
open to the possibility of a loch ness monster
open to extraterrestrials, open
to the crazed fantasy of a so-called king of rock
and roll resurrected, somehow

sighted alive; how people will
nod *of course* to a headline that guesses
angelina stole brad from jennifer;

tarot cards, ouija boards
tea leaves for spiritual guidance
people will bribe invisible grim reapers
with age-defying dreams and potions
people will encourage their children
to write letters to santa claus, share
secrets with jesus and keep appointments
with philanthropic tooth fairies

but the sun we can all confirm and agree upon
will shine down on one black woman—
patricia—getting her ass kicked
by three epithet-wielding whites—
her spirit and features evidently crushed
by their hate—the rage in her
gut, the insistence of her fists
obviously outnumbered

and some people just cannot
see it.
and some people just don't
believe it.

Daphne Gottlieb

Lost and Found

THE MOST IMPORTANT READING I HAVE EVER DONE wasn't a reading.

And I wish I'd never needed to write the piece I read there.

I went back east from California, where I live, to help my mother die. It was impossible that she was dying. She was supposed to have lived. She had had a third of her lung removed in November, done chemo. We were assured it was all going to be all right. And then, suddenly, nothing was all right. The cancer had spread. Terminally. It had attacked her everywhere. The battle was over. My sister, a medical resident, said to come home. Fast. My mother was going. Fast.

Within the day, I took a leave from my day job, and found someone to cover my teaching shifts. My wife would take care of the cats until she too flew to upstate New York, and then we would have a friend look after them. My sister was already at my mother's house, having taken a leave of absence from medical school to come support her, handle her medical care. My brother, an attorney, arrived when I did. He would be handling the estate. With the estate and her medical needs covered, I told my mother I felt out of place, useless. "My baby," my mother said, patting my face, "you and I, we have art."

My mother owned an art gallery. It was eclectic and elegant. Jewelry, pottery, and paintings, mostly by local artists, all found a home there. She was a champion of the undiscovered, the overlooked. I was her daughter, the undiscovered, overlooked writer, whose books proudly sat for sale on the gallery counter. I had two books of poetry in print as well as a number of essays and poems. The year prior, I had received my MFA in poetry, but I didn't make a living at it—most poets don't. I did administrative work to pay the bills and support my poetry habit. My sister was studying to be a doctor. My brother was a lawyer.

My mother was supportive and proud of all of us, a confidante to each of us. She talked to my sister the most, soothed her through difficult times; she relied on my brother, eager for his insight and expertise; she and I, we walked hand in hand, fought toe to toe, and sometimes toe against toe, about racism, classism, sexism, homophobia. She was my best friend, the kind with whom you can have table-thumping arguments, then laugh until your eyes are all teared up. The kind of friend who always has the words you need, even if you're a poet.

After my mother's death, what was left of my family—my sister and brother and I, my wife, my aunt and my uncle—staggered around like zombies to prepare the memorial service to be held at the city's museum. Pictures: my mother at all ages for the slide show. Music: Eartha Kitt and Stan Getz. I did not know what I was doing there, what we were doing there. My brother prepared to deal with the estate. My sister was without a patient. I retreated.

When my brother asked when I wanted to speak during the proceedings, I told him, "I'm not speaking." He looked at me, surprised. "I can't," I said numbly. There was nothing that I could say that was big enough, beautiful enough, to memorialize my mother. I could not stand up in a room and tell a roomful of people who she was, what she meant—that was hers to do and she had done exactly that, for all of her sixty-four years.

Later, my sister chose her place in the memorial lineup and asked when I wanted to speak. "I'm not," I repeated. "I can't." If I spoke, I would break down midsentence. I would choke on my own tears. I would make a mockery of her memory. I would dishonor her. I couldn't.

But that night, when everyone was going to bed and the house was quiet, I got on the computer and my hands could not keep still. I had a lifetime of thinking through my fingertips, and now, words for my mother poured through me in a torrent, a poem about the woman whose skirts and hair were always shockingly short, whose earrings were as big as her smile; the woman who—anything I said was incomplete, insufficient. But I tried to conjure her, remember her, invoke her. My training wasn't in medicine or the law. It was in words. And it was then that the bittersweet realization came: This was my purpose in being here. To explain who we'd lost, how much was gone, who my mother was, to a roomful of people who came together to share our love for her. And so I tried, tentatively at first and then rushing headlong and heart first into the piece. I described how she loved art, how she loved her afternoon tea, how she couldn't sleep on bad news, how the dictionary has seven definitions for lost and, in excavating each, word by word, and over and over, I finally discovered my loss and I found my mother. I also found the hardest word of all to say: Goodbye.

She had said, "Baby, you and I, we have art." And we did. And it was for her, for art, for us, that I stepped to the podium, feeling it impossible to try and perform this piece or even just read it. It turns out I didn't have to—the poem and the grief and emptiness stumbled over my tongue, struggled out of my mouth, and my heart went raging out to the room, to the ears of people who also adored her, also had lost her.

And then the memorial was over, and a swarm of people told me over and over, "You're your mother." In my reading, they had witnessed her heart, her soul. Whatever it was that they knew of her, they recognized in me. Or perhaps they simply hoped to—after all, I was living, breathing. I was still here.

"You're your mother," they said.

"No," I told them. "But I am my mother's daughter, no question."

And my mother and I, what we will always have, is art.

But was this art?

No.

I didn't perform. I testified. I used a poem—not a great one—but it was all I could write. Testifying makes for poor art most of the time—it is passionate and urgent, but lacks refinement. It lacks craft. Art is CSI: Miami. Testifying is a coroner's notes. At the podium, I shook and tried to keep my skin on.

That day, I had five minutes in a roomful of people to help them remember my mother. I tell my students to write like their lives depend on it. Most of the time, it doesn't. But once in a while, it is not your own life that depends on it, but the memory of someone else's. When the only way you can conjure someone is through words, when the only life someone you loved can embody is through memories you give voice to, you give it. And you give it with all you've got. Not as entertainment. Not as rah-rah cheerleading. But as the only thing it can be: a valentine filled with blood and thorns.

somewhere, over

My mother is in her bed, in two worlds. She is watching movies
on the ceiling. There are ants and chipmunks. "I want to go
home," she says.

"You are home," we tell her.

The tumor has bloomed like poppies, has spread to her liver,
streams through her blood, is rooted to her lungs. The tumors
are in there with my mother. "Who's that?" She asks. "Who was
just here?" There's a man in the corner that only she can see.

"I need my coat," she says. "I have to go home."

"I have the earrings," she says. She's holding two Ativan in her
hand, small pearls of peace. "There's so much to do," she sighs.

Sepia tones and Auntie Em—this is a real, truly live place.
Some of it wasn't very nice. But most of it was beautiful. She
sleeps in a field of poppies; a red halo on her white pillow, all her
hair fallen like a red rain from her head and she's in the movie
now; she's no one's mother.

"Things don't make sense." "I get confused." "Sometimes I'm in
the movies," she says.

The yellow brick, the bedroom. She's smoking a technicolor
cigarette that only she can see, drinking from a glass only
she can hold. What are you drinking? "Chateau La Monde,"
she says, rolls the glass under her nose for its bouquet, sips
deeply. She's drinking from the house of the world today.

"Is it good?" we ask. She nods and smiles. Yes. Very.

I had this dream that wasn't a dream. If I ever go looking for my heart's desire again, I won't look any further. I'm drinking Chateau La Monde.

The power to go back to Kansas, with pills for pain, pills for sleep, pills for function, pills to alleviate secretions, pills for pulses and blood pressures. Pills in two places at once, earrings. "I have to go home," she says.

Somatic death, the death of the body, involves a series of irreversible events that leads finally to cell destruction and death. Here come the flying monkeys. I'll get you, my pretty.

"Can you help me sleep?" she asks. We have pills for sleep. "No," she says. "I don't want to wake up. I want to go home." She wants the Asian coat, she says. And her shoes. "Where are my shoes?" she asks.

Click your heels together three times.

Physiological death is preceded by an irreversible cessation of all vital systems. "I'm crazy. I might as well be crazy," she wails. She pulls the pillow over her head, sobbing. All I kept saying to everybody was, "I want to go home." I'll get you, my pretty.

One at a time, systems shut down. Poppies close in the dark. The dying person turns to the light. Blood backs up into the lungs and the liver, causing congestion. As for you, my galvanized friend, you want a heart. You don't know how lucky you are to not have one.

A dying person turns toward light as sight diminishes. Glinda floats down in a bubble, chases chipmunks on the ceiling. And they sent me home. Doesn't anybody believe me? All I kept saying to everybody was, "I want to go home."

The heart becomes unable to pump strongly enough to keep blood moving. Hearts will never be practical. Blood backs up first throughout the heart and your little dog, Toto, too.

My father, she says, will be home soon, even though he's been dead thirteen years. Those magic slippers will take you home in two seconds.

Now?

Whenever you wish.

Stay with us, Dorothy. We all love ya. We don't want ya to go. The body surface cools. "I'll never get home," she cries.

She's planning menus. There's so much she needs to do. She's in the movie, at work, she's throwing parties. She points out where the bar will be, where the hors d'oeuvres go. She's working so hard. Oh, Scarecrow. This could never be like Kansas. What am I gonna do?

She forgets how to eat, stabs bread with a spoon, doesn't want food. She wants scotch on the rocks. She drinks one, then another, then nods out in the poppy field.

She opens her eyes and says, "Thank you for the party. I had a wonderful time."

Hearts will never be practical until they can be made unbreakable.

Those magic slippers will take you home in two seconds.

"Thank you for the party. I had a wonderful time. But now I am very tired and have to go home."

Now?

Whenever you wish.

This is my room—and you're all here! Oh, Auntie Em, there's no place like—

Overnight, the wind picks up, rattles through her chest.

It's the tornado, going, going—

death drive
(a transfession)

"We are rebels because those who govern us, often—
blindly, no doubt—betray us."
                              —Nance O'Neill, *lover of Lizzie Borden*

18/19/20XX

Dear Mother/Daughter/Darling/God/Guns/To Whom it may
  Concern,

I'm sorry it's been so long since I've written.
I'm sorry I've been out of touch.
I'm sorry for what I did.
You'll never hear from me again.
There are a few things I wanted to tell you.
They're going to kill me.
This is all your fault.

You wanted to know the truth:
It happened on the hottest day of the year
      /when I was fifteen
      /because I was pregnant
      /in the shipyards. They called me "seagull" because

I flocked around the sailors
I had food poisoning
I ran away from juvie
I crawled into my stepfather's lap
I just wanted him to love me
I pretended I was asking for directions

I shoved the girl into the car
I thought we were going to get married, but

he sent me this letter
he touched me when I was fifteen
he was the man of my dreams
he touched my son
he said marry a nice guy
he said act like a nice girl
he had money
he gave me junk
he killed himself by pointing the gun between his legs and
    shooting
he was shooting up
he liked to fuck virgins up the ass
he wanted my sister
he wanted to videotape it
he said he'd marry me if I didn't have kids
he said he'd kill me if I didn't—
he'd steal my stash
     —if I didn't do it

so I shot him in /the sitting room/the court room/the church
    parking lot/the hot tub/the shipyard with
       an ax/tranquilizers/kerosene/
          with no other choice/with all my strength/with all his
          money/with/love
they were asleep in the back of the car
they were waiting for me
they found me not guilty
they found the videotapes
they sentenced me to life

they were going to kill my baby
they found him not guilty
they found him in the bulrushes
they ripped open my mouth, my cunt
they were sure I did it but

      there was no blood on my clothes
      there was no future for them, but maybe for me
      there was a river nearby
      there was blood everywhere
      there was the ax in the basement
      there was the sound of the car slipping into the water
          /into my vein
          /into unconsciousness
          /into hotels with sailors and ripping
        /off their wallets
            /their clothes
            /my body

I left home
I left fingerprints
I left the headlights on
    /the door unlocked
    /the baby at
    /the river bank
I lit the match and ran out
I said a black man stole my car
I said, "His head on a platter"
I crawled into his lap
I was sure no one would get hurt
I wanted his money
I wanted him to pay

I put the car in neutral and pushed
I watched it sink

I burned my dress
I never confessed
I'll get you for this
I pray God forgives me
I'd do it all again
I know God knows the/guns/God
I know God knows the truth:

I settled down
I took a lover
I took /God/guns
I did it for him
I'm doing life
I'd do it again if I had the/God/guns
I'd shoot him again if I had the chance—

You wanted to know the truth.
Here it is:

I got blood all over the seat but kept driving/my blood stuck me
to the seat and I kept driving/bloody/driven across the border/
here now the signs say God/Guns/God/Guns/God at fifty miles
per hour/the signs/say God/Guns/God/at sixty miles per hour the
signs/say God/Guns/when I go/I go fast/fast enough I can make
them/the signs/the blood/I make them/say it fast/I just say/
Go—

Natalie E. Illum

On Mothers and mothertongue

THANK GOD SHE CAN SPEAK. IT WAS THE FIRST
thing I clearly remember my mother saying about me, to friends, doc-
tors, and curious strangers. For Mum, it was a mantra of sorts, a
declarative that language could ballast anything, even her disabled
daughter.

Growing up, my physical "uniqueness," known as spastic cerebral
palsy that was caused by a lack of oxygen during my premature birth,
was not necessarily celebrated. While I knew that my mother loved
me unconditionally, I was acutely aware that she wanted me to be
safe, easy, normal. In her heart, my mother yearned for her legacy to
include words like *proper, debutante, and elegant;* certainly not *palsy,
spastic, performance. Thank God you can speak, Natalie. You can
prove you are intelligent. Maybe they won't focus so much on your dis-
ability. It's such a shame.* In my mother's mind, I was fixed in my body.
Broken, period. The trouble came from having to deal with it and live
in a world we both assumed was whole in the first place. But I always
believed there was a grey area, some breathing room between *disguis-
ing* and *dancing.* I don't know where that notion came from—but I

started searching for a way to bridge the gap between the way people saw me and the way I imagined myself. What would happen if I pushed myself? Found a way to blend into the able-bodied world?

I began to use words every day, until I felt more like a dictionary than a child. By the time I entered kindergarten, I could read at a fourth grade level. I loved books and the journey they took me on, the lives that were not my own. I loved seeing a new word for the first time in elementary school and defining it based on context. Vocabulary gave me a sense of comfort, control. Outside of school, my life was not so ordered. Our home was a verbally chaotic one; survival was often measured in screams.

I learned the word *mitigate* early. I tried blending. I traveled to Moscow like it was the most accessible place on earth. I spent my whole childhood chasing ableism like I already knew how to balance in it. I think I was afraid to fully accept my disability, because it felt like a failure. So I faked mobility, bravery. In the back of my mind was the hope that one day our family's karmic debts would be paid in full, the collectors would leave, and each of us would wake up whole. At the bottom of every conflict inside our house was a deep regret that we weren't perfect and we couldn't find the language to forgive ourselves. I decided I would be the first to break that cycle, because the alternative seemed too bleak.

So when my defiance arrived in the form of words, it wasn't intentional, it was organic. I suppose I had simply tired of convincing the world I was normal. I didn't know what to call myself, but I settled on *queer* and *liminal* because they seemed to be the most open and ambiguous. I didn't know what to tell my mother. She knew that I had weird friends and that poetry didn't pay the bills.

Soon after my post-college move to Washington, D.C., a friend convinced me to go to a poetry open mic, sponsored by the all-women poetry collective mothertongue, and signed me up to read, secretly. In college, I had fastened myself to feminist theory and analytical research, and while I loved words, I would never have identified as a *poet*. When my name was called, I was shocked, but I figured I could take a risk. It was only one poem, one night. The room was packed, unfamiliar, and everyone was trying to move out of my way at the same time. I was terrified that I would trip over someone's coat, body part, or backpack. I started repeating, *don't fall, don't fall, don't fall*, a mantra I reserve for those times when I feel the potential for social disaster and injury are at their highest. I imagined the shock on people's faces as I started my descent, papers, crutches, and limbs all akimbo and flailing. There was a distinct possibility that I might not make it to the stage at all, poet or not. But I didn't fall that night, I rose.

It was in that moment of tripping, adjusting, introducing, and apologizing that I realized something about stages: they have the ability to hold up our lives. For the first time, people were staring at me out of openness, not abnormality. The audience was encouraging. They shouted out phrases like "Yeah girl" and "Awesome." There were audible noises of approval I'd never even heard before. Their attentiveness was one of compassion and interest, rather than mockery or cruelty. Even while shaking, standing in the words became as crucial as what I was saying. I know this shift started in that moment. I had spent most of my life attempting to escape my body, be it through drugs, denial, sex, alcohol, or sarcasm. Finally, I was using language to stay inside of it. I wasn't defending my experience, I was clarifying my life, balancing some of the injustices I had felt growing up.

The more I performed, the more I became both present in my body and more committed to accepting myself in it. My newfound art began to transform my experience into something much more potent than mere survival. Even though not everyone has my condition, I believe creativity in any form provides people with a necessary catalyst to change how they see themselves, to engage in their communities, to evolve.

Don't get me wrong—there remains a piece of me that aches for a new herstory, to be the daughter my mother would have preferred. There are days words fail me. But just as the scarring is all I can see when I'm broken, the journey to the microphone is all I see when I'm whole. One's life, whatever the packaging, is a dance. The idea of someone like me dancing still feels odd, but I do it because I no longer believe it's impossible. Case in point: I am joining LAVA, an all-female acrobatic troupe, for their spring show in Brooklyn, New York. First I was asked to collaborate by adding some of my spoken word to their choreography. Then, I was asked to move with them. We are creating a comfortable space for our different body types to move together. If a disabled girl can become an acrobat (even temporarily), I know anything is possible.

The courage to take risks with LAVA started with the trust I found within my own creative community. One poem on one stage in one night created an alchemy in my body, a momentary shift toward peace. I believe poets carry an elixir that can change the course of history, just by using the stage and our voices, again and again. Over the last eight years during my work with mothertongue, I have witnessed countless other women returning to themselves, writing themselves forward. I wish I could give my mother that feeling. I wish she could see the way I smile when I am onstage, or the way others see me. Mum, every performance undoes the disability a little and, from the stage, it's not so bad. And when it is, I can usually find my way back through practice, memory, poetry. After all this time, I know I can speak.

I am from, third cycle

I am from the ocean,
sea salt tangled in my hair.

I am from an ancient lineage
of seers, shamans, and crazy women
believing in scattered prophesies.

I am from the cast out and the called in.

I am from a broken womb, a dead landscape
of swollen tissue, spastic limbs, a falling down
I cannot control. I am from the lexicon of *cripple*.

I am from a dirty secret
of my grandmother's mother's mother,
a mixed dialect, a faulty bloodline. A girl
no one would claim.

I am from the wanderlust
of rock stars, from those fantasies spun
out of guitars. I am from the chords
of Joni, tethered to my bones.
I speak in requiems.

I am from a lover I couldn't hold
on to. A woman I can't forget, a man
who traces my body, whose fingerprints
form my smile.

I am from the fragmented Zodiac,
the manipulative sisters. I am from
tattooed skin over scar tissue
and the sound of glass breaking.

I am from a story I wrote once,
A pen I won't put down. I am from
the exhausted scribes of teenaged angst
and track lines. I am from survival songs.

I am from the way you see me
in afternoon light, in shades of darkness.
I am from the ocean; salt and bone
entangled. The pulling tides and I
are whispering.

What we learn in one night

Am I your first tranny?

He says this after a bottle of scotch
and the longest house concert I've ever
performed in. He says this inside my mouth
and it takes me a minute to distinguish his thoughts
from his body. *Yes, I say, but not for the lack
of trying.* But mostly, we are strangers, passing

through this. *Am I your first disabled fuck?*
This somehow stings, he stumbles into
No, wait, I didn't mean.
It's OK, I say, *It's not you. It's just*

People like us overexplain, he says. We settle
back into each other, slow
eye contact, more kissing.

But there is a curiosity factor
I can't ignore, some equation
I've been waiting to solve and chose
this one night in Atlanta to push myself
directly onto his cock and I'm not
unfamiliar with the idea. I am
unprepared for what happens after

the restraints and the fisting and the daylight.

I covet my body most when reduced to a primary
structure, when the firing squad of the nervous system

sleeps. While his body becomes the safest temple
he knows to build from;

We could read maps by each other's scars. We could do this
without the undress of last night. We are already exposed
as poets.

The trouble is getting up again. My feet,
which had somehow found an anchor hours before,
now resist the angle of sock or shoe.
This happens every time, regardless

of quality or partner, the disability creeps back
in like shame. Until I'm standing there, naked and fully
dressed and he can sense my rage and says, *Climbing*

back into ourselves is always
disappointing, but worth it.

Aya de León

Lyrical
Self-Defense
and the
Reluctant
Female Rapper

I NEVER INTENDED TO BE A HIP-HOP ARTIST.
I was just trying to defend myself.

I'd been resisting my role in hip-hop since the age of fifteen, when I wrote my first rhyme. I was gonna be an actress, a novelist, a poet, a solo performer, any traditionally female artist role, *anything but a hip-hop artist.*

I was glad enough to be a hip-hop fan in the eighties, wolfing down beats and rhymes by PE and BDP and De La and of course Latifah. I boycotted hip-hop, though, during the gold rush gangsta invasion of the '90s, when the recording industry appropriated the art form from the creators of hip-hop, stole our flavor, and sold it back to us as a modern minstrel show. This new hip-hop "style" was replete with angry Black buck stereotypes of African American male violence and danger, along with slavery-era sexualized Black women as objects. During my boycott, however, I still longed for a connection to rap music, thirsting for positive, or at least misogyny-free, lyrics. When hip-hop found me again, in 2000, I was listening to gospel rap, for God's sake—*I tried to resist.*

That same year, my friend Juanita encouraged me to check back in with hip-hop, to give it another try. At her urging, we went to see Mos Def headline a hip-hop show, part of the Lyricist Lounge tour, at San Francisco's Maritime Hall. We rolled up in the place, mostly Black and twenty- or thirtysomething-age Bay Area hip-hop heads milling around to the thump of the piped-in music and video loop. We pushed toward the front, past fellas in designer athletic gear and women in Clothestime hot-girl chic. I had on jeans, a halter top, and a Puerto Rico hat—I *had* to represent as an African American/Boricua on the West Coast.

I didn't catch the name of the opening group, some cats from out of town, I think. I was open to them, though, since I had seen Mos Def at various political benefits and knew he was a positive, conscious cat. Bahamadia was on the bill, too, a strong, up-and-coming independent woman emcee, so I expected the opening act to come correct. The big box of a hall didn't have great acoustics, and the music was loud, so I couldn't really grasp their lyrics. Let me tell you what I know for sure: There was a lot of leering, dick-grabbing, and humping gestures. I could have sworn I heard the word "bitch" as well. I was like, *What?* Wasn't this supposed to be a socially conscious hip-hop show? I didn't pay money to see Mos Def and Bahamadia so I could be subjected to this kind of disrespect.

Retreating to the ladies' room, I discovered another fifteen women crammed into the small lounge outside the toilets, like a female refugee camp. I squeezed into a spot on the arm of the couch next to a young Black woman in a backless top and an Asian woman in a minidress. But the sexism was so thick while those cats were onstage that one brother felt entitled to walk in there and try to get at us. Yes. He came into the *ladies' room* and tried to hit on the women.

I was like, forget hiding out, shrinking doesn't solve shit; I'm a poet. So I pressed my way through all the bodies in the hall, back to my previous spot on the floor. I leaned over to my friend Juanita and dropped my own lyrics in the voice of Elmo from *Sesame Street*:

this is a hip-hop show, not a porno flick
and you misogynistic rappers, you can suck MY dick
hahahahah!

But how could I take just one shot? I mean, there were several cats onstage shooting off rapid-fire sexist lyrics. If the folks onstage weren't going to respect me, I would create my own space, filling the air with powerful words to protect myself and my sisters. Yeah, I kept up the volley.

A lyric fragment from the stage: "I was killin that cat . . . "

I blasted back, louder still:

I'm at the Mos Def show
it's the opening act
I'm expecting conscious hip-hop
but instead they came whack . . .

Then, another brother on the mic: " . . . *had to hit it from the back . . .* "

I reloaded and fired again.

After the show was over, the lyrics kept shooting off in my head. They wouldn't stop until I wrote them down, and a few months later I performed the resulting piece at a poetry slam at the Justice League in San Francisco. I wasn't performing as an emcee, but rather as a slam poet *imitating* an emcee, using my feminist rage to fuel the performance and playing a character that I didn't think was me. Was it my fault that the in-house band spontaneously dropped a beat and I rocked the mic and won the slam? Seemed like coincidence to me. I still told folks I was not a hip-hop artist.

Later that year, I found myself performing in the hip-hop capital of the world, New York City; this was the city that wore graffiti proudly like tattoos, where you could still hear echoes of old-school emcees and DJs in the traffic noise, and feel the ghostly breeze of breakdancers windmill by you on the street. In New York, my cousin played me *Black on Both Sides,* a Mos Def CD on which he explains that hip-hop's trajectory follows wherever it is that *we* are going. In other words, hip-hop is us.

Ultimately, I was forced to question why I had been resisting my hip-hop calling. Did I feel as though I were not Black enough? Not ghetto enough, or aggressive enough? If any young man with the willingness to disrespect his mama, while waving some jewelry around, could call himself a rapper, *why couldn't I?*

How had my feminism failed me, encouraging me to settle for the traditional female role in hip-hop? After all, for years, seduced by the lush sensual thumping of the beat, I had been the hip-hop-head dancing at the club, the party, the show, only to have the word "bitch" punch me in the face. Finally, I had protested by staying home, but my body had still craved the beat. In retrospect, I see that I was waiting for the right hip-hop artist to come along, like a knight in shining armor, and make the kingdom of hip-hop safe for me again.

Suddenly, I was tired of being the damsel in distress. I had not been placed upon this fine earth to manifest helplessness. It finally occurred to me that the right hip-hop artist, the rescuer, might very well be . . . *me.*

Let *me* be the one to provide the sisters with some dope lyrics to affirm, not assault, them:

> *this is a poem for the fat girls, like me*
> *cuz anorexia ain't sexier*
> *& bulimia ain't dreamier*

Let *my* words paint new visions:

If women ran hip-hop
the only folks dancing in cages would be dogs & cats
from the local animal shelter
excited about getting adopted by pet lovers in the crowd
If women ran hip-hop
there would never be shootings
cuz there would be onsite conflict mediators
to help you work through all that negativity & hostility
If women ran hip-hop
men would be relieved because it's so draining
to keep up that front of toughness & power & control 24-7

I must speak for every woman who has ever felt violated by hateful lyrics hiding in luscious beats; I must speak for every man who has ever watched a sleazy rap video and felt turned on and repulsed at the same time:

We cannot let the industry use our bodies to betray us—
There are thieves in the temple!

Originally, I was just trying to defend myself. Now, I proudly pledge allegiance to the flag of hip-hop and to the truth-telling artistry for which it stands. In the tradition of Lyte and Roxanne and Latifah and so many other strong female emcees, I am grabbing the mic in my own hands.

Cellulite

Sell-you-light/that's right
they try to sell you lite beer/lite cake/lite cookies/
pepsi lite/99 percent fat-free
but who's trying to be fat-free?
certainly not me
let me see your thighs jiggle
they're jiggling, baby
go 'head, baby

This is a poem for the fat girls like me
don't tell me I'm not fat
that's like saying I'm not Black
yes *technically* my skin is brown
but I say I'm Black because I'm
down with the Blackness
like I'm down with the fatness
because fat is health is life is fertility is womanly
let me see your belly jiggle
it's jiggling, baby
go 'head, baby

It's the way women's bodies are built—we jiggle
even really thin women jiggle a little
unless they work out to have a body of steel
but who wants to look like that? get real!
This poem is a thank-you
to the big bodacious mujeres de Cuba
who taught me by example to know no shame/
show no shame
to the big-body women of the West Indies

who know how to wind/wind/wind at
Carnival time/time/time
let me see your hips jiggle
they're jiggling, baby
go 'head, baby

a sick society
turns women's bodies into problems to be solved
cuz anorexia ain't sexier
& bulimia ain't dreamier
Therefore next time you count calories, don't forget to count
    the thousands of years that women's suitors have thought
    that cellulite was quite all right & were ready to embrace
    abundance

So next time you're working out on your nordictrack
don't forget to savor the sensual feeling of sweat
sliding down the rolls in your back
& next time you're working out in step aerobics class
don't forget to enjoy the bounce of your ass
it's jiggling, baby
go 'head, baby

Special thanks to LL Cool J for the sample
"Cellulite" has been an Off-the-Scale production

Grito de Vieques

*This poem was the winner of the Burning Bush Publications
People Before Profits Poetry Prize in 2000.*

My name is Vieques.
I am a Puerto Rican girl.
My stepfather is the United States.
He comes into my room at night to do his business.

My name is Vieques.
I used to dream that Spain, my real father, would come back and
    rescue me.
But he's gone for good.
I have only the faint and echoing voices
of Africana and Taína ancestors telling me that
I can survive this.

My name is Vieques.
When my body started to change,
my stepfather dressed me in a clingy, itchy dress.
"Smile," he told me. "Smile at the nice foreign military man,"
    and pushed me toward him.
The military man was not nice.
His skin was pasty. His breath smelled.
I couldn't understand his language.
He came into my room and did his business.

My name is Vieques.
Sometimes my stepfather sells me to whole groups.
He calls them allied forces.
I fought back the best I could with chains and live bodies and
    fishing boats.

It happened anyway.

My name is Vieques.
I am still fighting back.
I am bigger and stronger now.
I have put a church, an encampment,
a struggle up at my bedroom door.
My stepfather can't get in.
He has not been able to do his business for months now, longer
than I ever dreamed.

My name is Vieques.
Without the shock of constant bombardment,
the numbness is subsiding.

I look at my body and see the devastation.
Lagoons, like self-esteem, have dried up to nothingness.
My womb is wilting with radiation
from illegally used uranium ammunition.
Where my skin was once lush and soft, I am scarred.
Old tanks, like cigarette burns, dot my flesh.
Unexploded bombs, like memories, may detonate in the future
when chosen lovers touch me in the wrong spot
or without warning.

My name is Vieques.
The numbness is subsiding.
Tender shoots of grass push up toward the sky.
A lizard sneaks back to sun itself on a chunk of shrapnel.
A butterfly alights on a rusted-out jet.
Fish slowly make their way back toward my shores,
no longer reverberating with shockwaves of violation.

My name is Vieques.

This is *my* body.

It may be worth eighty million dollars a year to you, Yanqui,

but it is priceless to me.

My door is barred.

I have burned the clingy, itchy dress.

The encampment grows stronger.

The lizards, the grass, the fish, the butterflies stand with me.

I'll never be the same,

but I'll never be yours again to do your dirty business.

My name is Vieques

and I will be free.

Leah Harris

A Mad Poet's Manifesto

MADNESS IS MY LEGACY.

I am the daughter of two parents who were diagnosed with schizophrenia when they were young. My mother had been a poet, an artist, and a crazy visionary but, like so many young women and men in her generation, she had been brutally repressed for her rejection of the middle-class suburban paradigm in which she had been raised. In 1968, at age eighteen, she ran away from suburban Milwaukee to join the San Francisco counterculture, which greatly distressed her family. Soon afterward, she was picked up off the streets and diagnosed with "schizophrenia." Thus began her life as a perennial mental patient. She was relentlessly bombarded with mind-numbing psychiatric drugs and hospitalized dozens of times. If she was not mad when she was first hospitalized, the brutal experiences she endured as a patient slowly drove her insane. Yet even in a Haldol-induced fog, my mother wrote. She wrote small, sweet poems about struggle, survival, and love for her daughter, and she sketched simple drawings of flowers and faces. She tried valiantly to persist creatively in the face of the unremitting psychiatric assault on her mind and body, until she died at the age of forty-six, in large part from complications arising from her "treatment."

The rampant stereotype of the crazy woman poet has been made famous by poets like Sylvia Plath and Anne Sexton. I identify deeply with their tortured paths, and I'm sure my mother would have as well. While my mother did not stick her head in an oven (like Plath) or commit suicide via carbon monoxide poisoning (like Sexton), she did refuse a medical treatment that she knew would have saved her life. While I will never know for sure, it is my theory that this act of denial represented a suicide of sorts. In addition, like my mother, both Plath and Sexton received psychiatric "treatment" that probably caused them much more harm than good. The oppressive environment of the mental hospital is a primary theme in Plath's famous autobiographical novel *The Bell Jar.*

I was once a suicidal mental patient, headed down the same path as my mother, but today I cling to life with the same tenacity with which I once pursued death. It has been a long and painful road for me, but my recovery is due in large part to the power of creative expression, combined with political activism on the issue of psychiatric oppression and a commitment to healing my wounds using holistic, alternative methods such as yoga and meditation.

Most of my adolescence was spent in and out of psychiatric institutions. From the age of fourteen, I was forced to take a series of harmful psychiatric drugs that drove me from depression to an obsession with self-injury and suicide—which I acted out on more than one occasion. This created a vicious circle of hospitalizations and further despair and hopelessness. Today it is public knowledge that Prozac and other antidepressants can trigger suicidal behavior in young people, but back in 1988 when I first took it, this was a secret well guarded by its maker, the giant pharmaceutical corporation Eli Lilly. Thus, my suicidal behavior was seen as a worsening of my "symptoms" rather than the ugly side effect it actually was.

The psychiatric ward was an incredibly authoritarian place. We were expected to comply with absolutely every rule without question or complaint; dissent was viewed as a "symptom" of our illness and could result in additional time being added on to our "sentences." Quickly I learned that in order to get out, I would have to play their little game—to hide my authentic self and suppress my true thoughts and feelings. I became a very good liar. In the psych ward, and even at home, I did not feel safe keeping a journal because there was no secure place to hide it—I was always under surveillance. Also, as a young woman, I became accustomed to words being used against me, in my chart, written by psychiatrists and mental health workers who made no effort to understand or sympathize with me as a human being. Words were weapons used to diagnose and to pathologize me without my consent.

At eighteen years old, upon leaving my final institution, I made a decision to reject their drugs and their diagnoses and to strike out on my own—a noncompliant, crazy girl. Perhaps it was my fear of ending up like my parents did, but I was determined to chart a different course for my life. I hazily remembered that I once loved to write. Before I was locked up, I had written poems for many class assignments and had dreams of becoming a journalist. My high school English teacher, Mrs. McAuliffe, had wanted to groom me as newspaper editor but, because of my long-term "treatment," I was never able to realize that dream.

Once I was free from the psychiatric system, I felt creative longings but I was terribly afraid to let that side of myself come out. My mother had been the only creatively inclined person in my family, and I was terrified that my artistry would come with the price of a similarly debilitating madness. But, perhaps like my mother, I found it more painful *not* to write. When I was twenty years old, following my mother's tragic death, I began to put pen to paper again in order to cope with the enormity of my grief. I started with small scribbles that might have been poems. I expressed myself, uncensored and raw, on pages smeared with tear-stained ink. At first my writings were mostly self-centered, dealing with the slow and messy process of rediscovering my spirit. Many of my poems explored a nascent, female-centered spirituality that would ultimately be a great source of refuge for me. I began to join writing workshops and nervously started sharing my stuff with other writers. Eventually, I hesitantly admitted to myself that I might just be a crazy artist! Words were slowly working their healing magic on my spirit.

Over the next few years, I moved beyond an insular exploration of the self and, in the hopes that my words might connect to others, began to feel a pull to perform my work publicly. At twenty-five, I first read a poem in front of a small audience at a local coffee shop open mic; my whole body trembled but I felt more alive than I had ever felt. The exhilaration of that experience kept me going. I had finally found a healthy outlet for all the years of pent-up rage. My vehicle of expression would be spoken word: loud, angry, in-your-face, unapologetic spoken word that transformed my rage into self-empowerment, while combining art and activism.

Yet, even among my close poet friends, I remained underground about my past, my mental health history. My poems dealt with political subjects that felt relatively safe to me. Although I occasionally wrote privately about my madness, I didn't feel comfortable busting out with those themes at readings. Deep down, I was still ashamed, still hiding my true self, still living out the legacy of self-stigma.

Then, in an issue of *Off Our Backs* (for which I had guest-edited a special edition on women and psychiatry), I came across an interview with Chrystos, a Native American lesbian poet whose work eloquently and powerfully addresses her psychiatric oppression, connecting it with colonialism, genocide, and race, class, and gender oppression. Chrystos's poem "No Public Safety," about the psychiatric oppression of an elderly Native American homeless woman named Anna Mae Peoples, gives voice to the experience of not only being bodily assaulted with drugs and forced "treatment," but also of being assaulted with words—experiences my mother and I had learned so vividly. The last lines of that poem read, "Nowhere in the six column article/is one word/that Anna Mae Peoples has to say." Another poem, "Interview with the Social Worker," in the form of a dialogue between Chrystos and a condescending social worker, is a powerful portrait of speaking truth to power.

As opposed to my history of words negating me, Chrystos's words finally granted me consent to be myself, in all my messiness and beauty. They granted me permission to talk back to the system that had oppressed me and my parents. I knew I had to gather up my courage and stop being ashamed of who I was and from where I had come. I became active with the psychiatric survivors' movement, a small group of "mad" activists taking on psychiatric oppression and proposing instead a vision of humane, noncoercive, nonauthoritarian alternatives. Simultaneously, I kept writing, composing a series of essays that are now taking shape as a book-length memoir about my experiences in the mental health system. I continued to produce more and more poems that addressed the subjects of psychiatric oppression and personal struggle and liberation.

Throughout my twenties, I became more and more "out" about my experiences as a crazy person, and began to give workshops, talks, and performances at conferences around the country. "Revenge of the crazy wimmin" is a poem that I wrote for a National Organization for Women conference's panel on women and psychiatric oppression. When I sat down to write it, it burst forth from me like a dam breaking loose, a culmination of my creative and political development. I felt like I had channeled the fierce love, hope, and strength of all of the generations of women who had been locked away, murdered, raped, and driven insane for being different or defiant, or disillusioned with the status quo. My mother's spirit helped to guide my pen as I told the truth as I understood it in that poem.

Performing "revenge" is a spiritual experience every time, and it has often been met with tears and hugs and applause from audiences. The poem encapsulates my shamanic journey towards healing, reclaiming my spirit from the Other Side. I am no longer a powerless crazy woman refusing treatment. I am now a Wounded Healer, and my words are the elixir that I have to offer my society. Young women and girls have written to me to tell me that my poems and workshops have encouraged them to tell the truth about their own lives. That alone makes all the pain and struggle I've endured, as well as my mother's sad journey, somehow worthwhile.

In my activist work, I am part of a movement of mental health consumers and psychiatric survivors who are creating a new language and new policies to empower people who use mental health services. We use the word "person" instead of "patient" or "case." We vigorously promote the idea that all people can recover, versus the idea that mental illness is a lifelong sentence. We seek to abolish forced treatment and forced psychiatric drugging. We promote freedom and choice over compliance, and we believe that holistic, voluntary mental health services should be available to anyone who wants them. We view meditation, yoga, acupuncture, and creative/artistic expression as fully valid modes of healing emotional distress. We do not work for a new and pretty language to dress up old oppressions, but for a fundamental transformation of the mental health system in order to uplift rather than crush the human spirit. Most importantly, we believe that it is people who have been through the experiences of madness, emotional distress, and recovery themselves who are best equipped to understand and to help those currently living those experiences. If these principles had been in place when my mother and I were in the mental health system, perhaps our journeys would have been very different.

Today, I look down at the crisscross of pale, jagged scars on my wrists, inflicted by my mentally tortured fifteen-year-old self, and I wonder how I will explain them to my one-year-old son if and when he asks about them. When he is old enough to understand, I will read him my poetry and hope it tells him everything he needs to know: His mama was once without hope, but words gave her new life. As my mama taught me, words have the terrible power to dehumanize and destroy, but they also have the tremendous power to heal and rebuild that which has been destroyed.

revenge of the
crazy wimmin

the man's always had a plan
to slow down the velocity of woman's journeys
to lower the volume of woman's voices
saying hush now honey be calm be still
the powers that be saying
there's an appropriate level for your grief and
there's a healthy range for your rage
and when woman exceeds
the emotional speed limit
society put on the brakes

and the more things change
the more they stay
the same
they use the same tactics
but they just change the names

back in the middle ages
they burned unruly women at the stake
and out of the ashes of their bones and flesh
rose the Enlightenment and Reason fresh
and the white men declared
there's no such thing as witches
they're just crazy psycho-bitches
but we certainly can't let them run free
lock 'em up and throw away the key
yeah they said: lock 'em up and throw away the key

cause there's nothing scarier than a woman mad and/or

aware of her own magic
tragic how much violence is done
in the name of science
to ensure our silence

in Victorian times they located suffering in our uterus
in the blood in the soft internal organs
took our pain our righteous rage
they called it "hysteria"
and then Dr. Freud ignored women's horror stories
herstories of abuse and rape and
took a justified hatred of the penis and called it
envy (he sold more books that way)

what they call paranoia
we call reality hitting us hard
when we name the forces all around
conspiring to keep us down
when we deny the diagnoses of our masters
when we refuse to be sick, defective, diseased, disordered,
     disturbed
when we dare to proclaim our humanity
when we accuse *them* of insanity
they call it "lack of insight"
into our condition

but we got an insight that'll blind you

we know something about our conditions
and how we came to be confined:
our husbands our kids they wanted our house our money
yeah it's kinda funny how it goes down

we were visionaries who shared our visions with the
　　wrong people
we were too poor too butch too ugly too far-gone on the
　　mean streets
we seen shit nobody should ever have to see
we got raped got beat got tortured by strangers and
the ones who claimed to love us
and when life comes apart at the seams
when the castles of our dreams implode
we chase the needle in search of the next high
put on a skirt, fuck who we have to just to get by
and when our demons chase us till
we break up
from the pure exhaustion of being alive
and you're lucky if you survive, honey
yeah, you're lucky if you survive

first: there's a diagnosis for every tragedy
then they sign the forms lock us up put us in solitary
shame us call us names tell us we won't amount to nothing
wrestle us down to the ground with their male arms
"treat" us—like shit—tie us up naked bruised and shaking
dope us up with their drugs so we can't stand
can't write can't paint can't think can't speak
wrap us in white sheets (when we ain't dead yet)
take our babies from us
lobotomize us sterilize us electroshock us
rape us kill us
saying this is for your own good
this is for your own good
this is for
your own good

this is for all the mamas daughters sisters lovers friends
who ended up behind bars
and this is for every woman who died alone
in a locked cell
this is for every woman who's ever survived hell
and emerged to tell the tale to her sisters

our voices thick with saliva and blood speaking
truth my sisters truth my fellow witches unreasonable women
yes we are "acting out"
cackling at the scourge of normalcy
as defined by the men waging endless war à la *1984*
we diagnose them with "mass destruction disorder"
and write out a prescription for the maximum dose of
justice

and out on the horizon
gather the storm-clouds of our retaliation
in a collective conflagration
we are rising up
picking up the scattered pieces of what shattered
building and birthing out new visions for the generations
    to come
with our rage of the ages
the force of our breath
we are shaking off death
and taking in life

the crazy wimmin gonna have the last laugh someday
and it's gonna be
loud

Take refuge

In one thousand versions of the same ancient wisdom
Maps of higher consciousness, tools to
Break down your internal prisons
Find solace in timeless knowledge
From the Amazon to Babylon
Esoteric truths now revealed
So this mother earth wound can be healed;
No matter how bleak these days
Of aggression and oppression
We know our fates are not sealed.

In this year 2005
Take refuge in whatever makes you feel alive
And stay afloat in this sea of toxic culture
eatin' at our souls like vultures
dance round the holy fire inside,
the human heart-drum beating in your chest
How blessed to have a precious human birth
Take refuge in cool earth and
Hot DC concrete pulsating
Under your feet

We've got to take refuge in everyday poetry
Word formations dripping from our lips
Piercing through the veil of inanity
Humanity deserves more than the insanity
Of what's projected on ABC, CNN, and NBC
Be the regime change you wish to see
Swim hard going up against this stream
Act out the themes recurring in your dreams

Embrace the extremes you find
Take refuge in the visions whirling in your mind
Tornadoes of love tsunamis of rage combined
How much harder to be *kind*
Than to fight blindly
Wrap yourself in the blanket of our shared history
Be still, be silent
And feel the mystery of this holy minute
While you're in it

Take heart cause the intentions incantations
And vibrations of your voice
Resound profound
Around the world long after your
Sound fades
Cascading through the universe
A rising tide, a harmony
Our lyrical dissent, a gorgeous cacophony
Higher frequency than the dull one size fits all
Monotony, bloody drone of
Our ailing dinosaur society
Held hostage by our shared
Unexpressed vulnerability and
Collective delusions of scarcity

Take refuge in the interplay between dark and light
Take flight like the phoenix rising from the ash
Take refuge in impermanence,
Knowing this, too, shall pass
Grasp for a sky fulla stars never out of reach
Learn and teach, teach, teach and learn
Never stop yearning, burning, churning, turning

Towards Truth with a capital T
Don't let George W. steal liber-TY
And freedom from our collective vocabulary

Reclaim liberation
Reclaim liberation
Reclaim liberation
And when your soul is most hungry
And your heart is most empty
take refuge in the everyday extraordinary poetry
that is our living, loving, evolving, revolving
community

Meliza Bañales

The Dirtiest
Word You've
Ever Heard

I'VE SPENT MUCH OF MY LIFE AS A DOUBLE
agent. The youngest of four children in a working-poor, very brown
Mexican family in Los Angeles, I was born with, and grew up with,
my Scottish mother's good looks, my father consistently mistaken for
my gardener. In a word, I grew up looking white while the rest of
my family's skin, except for my mother's, told a different story. I was
also raised with my mother's desperate desire to be middle-class. As
such, almost everything about my childhood pertained to maintaining
an image that we weren't as poor or as brown or as migrant as we
seemed. According to my mother, *we* were different. *We* were never
on welfare or food stamps. *We* were not "immigrants." *We* came from
a family that held dual nationality in Mexico and the U.S., our family
tree driving straight from the border, *la frontera*, the line my *abuelito*
used to say, "We never drew anyway." And then there was me. I guess
you could call me my family's great white hope.

Growing up, I was surrounded by people urging me, both sub-
tly and directly, to use my privilege whenever possible to get ahead
and stay ahead. My parents would state that my race was "white" on

all legal forms, and my siblings and I were forbidden from speaking Spanish at school. My teachers promoted my studies while discouraging those of my darker-skinned brothers, who were both pretty quiet kids, especially in front of adults. As a result, my teachers presumed that they didn't understand English very well and even suggested to my parents that I help "tutor" them. This type of racial profiling led to my brothers being held back in school and even put in ESL classes. Meanwhile, I was placed in advanced classes. It was in these classes that my teachers recognized that I had a natural writing talent and, by high school, they had made it their personal goal to help me hone this "gift." Though I'm sure some of their intentions were wholehearted and sincere, I sometimes wonder if I also served as their little project—the white-looking person of color from the barrio who just needed some good old-fashioned white guidance to help me out of my "circumstances."

Nonetheless, my writing career began to soar. I started winning national honors and scholarships. I received the National Council of Teachers of English Achievement Award in Writing, presented to only twenty high school students in the country. As senior year approached, I even had a man in a grey suit from Brown University come to my neighborhood, solely to convince me to go to school there. Due to our racialized history (histories), I don't find it a coincidence that, even though my brothers and I attended the exact same public schools, I entered the university system, while one of my brothers ended up in gangs and eventually in prison, and the other one went into the military. Each of us institutionalized for all the wrong reasons.

In the fall of 1996, I entered the University of California, Santa Cruz, and within a year, I'd become the youngest student admitted into the very competitive creative writing program. I don't know if it was the redwoods or simply being young and driven and having way too much time on my hands, but I did spend the majority of my college years writing—all of the time. And through my poetry, I really began to explore my complex racial and working-class background, searching for a language to explain someone like myself to myself, and to others. Unfortunately, though my teachers claimed to be "hip" to it, they also told me that "that kind of poetry" had been done before, and encouraged me instead to explore abstract work, maybe even write about nature. I once had a professor in one of my writing workshops call my poems "too ethnic."

Upon graduating in 1997, after hearing about "slam poetry," I attended my first slam event at the Washrock in Santa Cruz. Simply put, it was a twenty-four-hour laundromat with a coffee bar inside. The "stage" was a small piece of floor near the doorway, and the only "seats" were laundry-folding tables or washing machines. For the first time, I witnessed poets who didn't have countless awards, publications, or elite university educations. Instead, they were ex-cons, former drug addicts, sex workers, college students, mothers, grandparents, poor, upper-class, dark, light—you name it, slam had it. I didn't understand the scoring, but I was used to open mics so I signed up, performed a poem, and completely surprised myself—I won—marking that evening as my entrée into the now popular slam poetry movement.

By 2002, I had been on three national slam teams and had won my first slam championship, claiming the title in Oakland, an area renowned for its talented and highly competitive slam scene. I was also the first Latina on the West Coast to win a slam championship.

Within forty-eight hours of my Oakland slam "triumph," my name was on the lips of countless veteran slam poets, and I was being contacted by Websites, zines, and radio stations; three popular newspapers in Santa Cruz, a town I hadn't lived in for many years, wanted to hear from me. Suddenly, being the center of attention wasn't very strange anymore. The focal point, however, seemed to be about my identity, particularly my race. The most common questions were, "How does it feel to be the first Latina on the West Coast to win the slam?"

and "How do you think this changes things for Latinos in slam?" As a child, I had been trained not to disclose my race but, abruptly, my artistic life now centered around placing my racial identity front and center. I had no idea how to answer the questions. Overnight, I was expected to represent a community *I* didn't even fully know.

After all, the personal Latino reality represented in my poetry was quite different from the West Coast Latino slam stereotype. I grew up in the United States, in an urban area, while typical Latino slam poetry addressed immigration, farmworking culture, Catholicism, traditional family dynamics, and heavy nationalism. My life, and thus my poems, was vastly different. I grew up mixed-race and my parents didn't marry until I was nine. They were spiritual, celebrating Christmas and lighting candles on Day of the Dead, but they didn't trust the church. There were no customary family dynamics (aside from my mother having the final say on everything), and my *abuelitos*, proud labor organizers, had taught me to "love and serve people, not governments." Furthermore, the standard Latino slam scene generally promoted heterosexuality and heterosexist ideas of sex, love, and relationships. As an openly queer artist, talking openly about lesbian sex and relationships, I was not always welcomed by predominately Latino slam audiences. In fact, some of my lowest slam scores were a direct result of performing "out" poems.

I refused to let these cultural differences, however, deter me, and in some ways they prompted me to be even more vocal. I suppose I was stubbornly driven to disprove others' misconceptions about me, and also to demonstrate the diversity of Latino culture. When the word "diversity" is brought up in Latino circles, it's often a dirty word; in the U.S., it has a history of dismissing us as people or chalking up our collective differences as "other" or "not normal," "normal," of course, being white. For example, I learned growing up, and especially in college, that "diversity" was often seen by most people of color as "teaching the white, normal people to politely deal with the not-so-normal people of color." Through slam poetry, however, I realized that the key to unlocking my diversity and complexity—my unconventional past, my struggles, my search for a language to describe how I made sense of myself—was giving myself permission to circumvent what was expected of me as a Latino artist.

Thus, one of my priorities as a spoken word artist, especially as a Latina, queer, working-class woman, was and remains exposing the multifarious nature of Latino culture. For too many years, history has attempted to erase countless instances of Latinos beautifully resisting stereotypes and expectations, from Frida Kahlo's bisexuality and socialist beliefs to César Chávez's participation in one of the earliest gay and lesbian rights marches in San Francisco. When I take the stage, I'd like to see myself as *that* diversity. It's important that each of us embraces our distinctly unique, complex self; that, in itself, is a common thread, a place from which community may flourish. For me that is how diversity moves from being a dirty word that separates us to an activity that helps us understand one another.

Do the Math

The equation goes something like this:
one white mother plus one brown father divided by two
    different worlds
equals a daughter.
Give or take a decimal the American dream turns out to be:
two half-white children, two full-brown children,
one small house in LA,
four jobs divided by two high school educated parents
The quality of life is high though the means is low.

The numbers vary from memory to memory. Like three.
Three times a week I clean houses in rich neighborhoods to
    make my way.
Folding sheets is difficult. Every house has one rich white lady
    with two dozen sheets times four beds which equals ten ways
    to fold the sheets so that they're
perfect.
Learning to fold sheets at least three to six ways
means I can clean three to six houses a week
which equals rent, tortillas, and lettuce for the month.

Going into one.
One night a week I go-go dance in a cage in a Hollywood
    nightclub.
Ten dollars an hour plus tips.
I'm only eighteen back then and already I know the equation for
    lust:
One bare ass in face gets a twenty, one crotch-drop earns a fifty,
one tongue licking cage bars while slowly gyrating hips
equals I am the first in my family to go to college.

Then there's five.

Five times a day I prayed through my seven-year-old body
that my father would lose his Spanish accent.
I was convinced that if he did he could get a better job and we
    wouldn't be poor anymore.
I was convinced he just wasn't trying hard enough to say
"signals" instead of "singles" or "video" instead of "bideo."

Five times a day I sent my other prayers, my secret prayers
that I was thankful for looking the most white in a family of
    coffee-colored children. How I prayed that my brown blood
    wouldn't seep through my white skin
so that I could
learn English, get an education
make my parents proud of half-white, half-brown
    accomplishment.

Five times a day times seven days a week plus two small hands
    clenched together in fear and ignorance
equals a lifetime of trying to make halves a whole.

You see, it's all in the numbers.

These numbers that haunt my dreams, make my past into single
    digits
which have no common denominator.

Just once I'd like to write an equation for all the things I could
    never write about.

For the three times my father took off work from three
    different jobs to see me in the school play.

For the first and last time my sister told her abusive ex-
    husband that she didn't need him anymore
and meant it.
For the hundreds of times I saw my parents laugh
until the tears rolled down their cheeks,
even in a neighborhood of drugs and gangs.

For that one moment,
I did see my father cry
when I, the first in my family, received my college degree.

I'm writing a formula for all the numbers that have fallen on me.

Fifteen sunrises in three different states,
eight million breaths in one kiss,
185 poems in eight years—

I am writing an equation.
Using the universal language of numbers to describe ten
    thousand ways
that something can mean everything.

It's just all in how you do the math.

Generations

Before men and women were going on strike,
standing on the frontlines with César Chávez screaming,
"*Si se puede!*"
Yes We Can
my great-grandfather was starting his own revolution,
teaching himself to read and write by rummaging through
    schoolyard trashcans
for used spelling books and old newspapers.

Great-Grandfather came over from Michoacán, Mexico, to pick
    cotton in California.
He even helped build the Kansas City Railroad
but ended up being too Mexican
to ride the trains that flew across the tracks of his hard labor.

And who would have thought
My father, little brown hands picking grapes in the Fresno heat
would be the first in our family to graduate high school
and end up building satellites for NASA.

And still
you, Mr. Landowner,
can sit
the owner of lives
and tell me
that we are replaceable.

That somebody's gotta go out there and pick that fruit
because there is a cake that your mother is baking
that needs the perfect sized strawberries.

That we don't deserve more than a fifteen-minute break a
    day because
money doesn't grow on trees,
money
doesn't grow
on trees.

Well neither does blood.
Neither do brown hands.
Neither does strength, neither does courage, neither do
    weaknesses.

You ask me,
the third generation of the brown blood gone white
if I am ashamed of this heritage and I can tell you Señor,
I don't hear shame calling me in my sleep.

I don't hear shame in 3 AM phone calls to my father,
"Papi, I'm working three jobs and I just can't take it anymore."
"Papi I get down on my knees every day not to pray to God
but to clean up after people's shit, and I just can't take it
    anymore."
"Papi, I'm not gonna make my rent again next month
and I am livin' just enough for the city,
and I just can't take it anymore."

I don't hear shame when my father tells me,
"*Mija*, haven't you learned by now that there are fields
    of *soldados*,
soldiers swimming through your veins."
"*Mija*, there are fields of reasons
why the universe only gives you as much as you can carry."

"*Mija,*
there are fields of things that your heart already knows."

And this I know:
I have crawled across the backs of men and women
just so I could climb back into the womb of a mother country
so that I could be reborn and say to you,
You do not plant these seeds.
You do not own these roots.
Your government does not birth this fruit.

So don't tell me
how I don't understand the taste of the sweetest red grapes
on a sunny August morning because trust me
They are filled
with the blood and sweat of three generations of Aztec warriors.
And I've come to know what the truth
tastes like.

Karen Garrabrant

Slam Ma'am

SLAM MASTER IS THE TECHNICAL TERM FOR the person who runs the poetry venue, but I prefer to call myself a "slam ma'am." I fancy the idea of being a verbal madam, keeping details organized behind the scenes, the patrons happy, and the show in the parlor going strong. I'm currently the ma'am of Atlanta-based Cliterati, a twice-monthly, feminist-queer reading series, featuring both local and nationally touring writers and performers. As the "slam ma'am," I am most rewarded by introducing poets (and their work) to one another.

Three early Cliterati friends, Lucy Anderton, A. J. Geil, and Kimberly Simms, are collectively responsible for leading me down this path. A. J. hosted the first slam I ever attended. Then, in 2004, Kimberly enlisted me to host the women's reading at the first Individual World Poetry Slam in Greenville, South Carolina. Later that year, at the National Poetry Slam in Saint Louis, Missouri, Lucy and I managed and hosted an evening of competition. These three women created opportunities for me to witness and play a role in the behind-the-scenes world of slam poetry, often nudging me and prompting me to coach a team. By the summer of 2005, after helping to found Art Amok, a collective arts series, I had become determined to lead an Art Amok team to the National Poetry Slam competition in Austin, Texas, in August 2006.

In order to participate in the National Poetry Slam, local slam venues must be open to all poets, regardless of age, size, color, sexual orientation, class, et cetera. Teams are chosen after seven months of competition consisting of many rounds of three-minute original spoken word performances, each poem scored by five randomly selected audience members. Art Amok went through this process locally, ultimately culminating in the first all-lesbian team in the National Poetry Slam's twenty-year history. In general, all-woman teams are rare; only one other all-female team competed in that year's slam, in a field of seventy-two teams.

Our team ended up including Theresa Davis, teacher and mother of three; Dr. Madelyn Hatter, a recent LSU graduate; Jessica Hand, a budding MFA student; Stacie Boschma, a satirical blogger; and PhoenixYZ, a YMCA social worker and caregiver. We encountered many challenges in the pre-National summer of rehearsals, gigs, and scrimmages, like planning traveling logistics and dealing with dwindling vacation time, demanding girlfriends, and nontraditional family schedules. Each poet also came to the slam table with different motivations: Theresa simply wanted to experience the fun of it, Stacie wanted to flex her writing muscles, Phoenix wanted to expand her storytelling skills. Jessica wanted to try something different than her traditional orientation of poetry-on-the-page, while Madelyn was looking to further her spoken word career.

I decided to initiate group writing sessions, both as a way to bring the poets together and because group pieces are often popular and successful at the national level. At first, poetry lines circulated around the room, quivering with the possibility of collaboration. Then, insecurities stepped in. Jessica worried about the quality of the writing. Madelyn refused to be in a group piece, offering only one or two words. Phoenix waited for everyone else to finish before synthesizing her own lines. Theresa worried about telling the other women what to do and so she held her tongue. Stacie felt time would be better spent on individual work. I had never met poets so reluctant to write, but I was not willing to let go of the idea of seeing the whole team onstage at once.

Subsequently, Phoenix, Stacie, Theresa, and I decided to simply select previously written individual poems for the group to adapt. We divided and rewrote lines over dining room tables and rehearsed in living rooms. Meanwhile, Jess and Madelyn worked together on new, individual pieces. When it was time to compete, we were prepared.

By the day of the National Poetry Slam competition our group had realized that our strength was our shared affinity for poetry, as well as our shared, but simultaneously varied, identities as a coalition of radical queer women. During the competition we all sat around the same table in our bouts to support each other's work and each woman's solo moment onstage. As the slam ma'am and a "behind-the-scenes herstorian," I probably felt eyes were on us more than they actually were. In fact, other poets seemed to accept us simply as a team, rather than "the lesbian team."

I held my breath as Madelyn approached the stage, exhaling as the crowd laughed in the right places. Her score put us in first place, ahead of Austin's home team, for a gloriously electric minute. Renowned Southern poet Buddy Wakefield and many others screamed, "Go Georgia!" as Phoenix, Theresa, and Stacie took the stage with "Rock Star Poet," a comedic mockery of stardom and ego. This second round opening created enough of a buzz to land us in a showcase before a semifinal bout.

Ultimately, we came in sixteenth in the competition. Not bad. But most of all, I think we began blazing a trail. I hope someday, all-female and all-queer teams will be innumerable, and hopefully we have created an opening for many to follow.

A Sylvia Plath Sliver

Life is horrible now,
but things turned horrible long before this.

There were marches of men over asphalt backs
sometime in history like a forever
constructed so we would have permanent
amnesia.

She looks like a portrait of amnesia
in dated photographs,
her thick hair band
holding her head together.

She was the one who said
women love fascists
and from the news, it might appear true.

She looks beautiful and ordinary
like a killer,
like the girl next door,
like the kind of normal
that says beware
of women with guns and knives.

She and these tools
were never as dangerous as the ovens
or the squalling children
banging on tables with spoons.

Was the making of meals

and the slow and steady accumulation of
dough rising,
burnt cookies,
and pies launched
from baker's rack tongues
assisting countless others with her
to a grave dark, crisp?

How did any woman escape with her wits
from the maws of cranky, creaky stoves?
With gaping yawns of ceramic sinks,
where was the time
to do anything like form
a creative sentence?

Somehow she managed to write
between the soapsuds,
the clothespins,
the hostess smiles
and the grocery bills.

Our battles are different now,
the same as they ever were.

They are the battles of the flat and grainy
—but let's not forget—
an immediate and instant—
digital photo generation.

Our different battles could sit
framed next to the black and white,
where it's easy to feel guilty for

a lack of small mouths to feed
or husbands who have all the luxury
to do everything
except dishes.

It's too easy to congratulate ourselves
in color with how far we've come
while we slip
further behind the progresses we've made.

Her beautiful face stares back
from a postcard on my bookshelf,
as though she's just read a poem
really quickly in slam way before slam
for one of her friends of Ivy League ivories
whose teeth chewed her up.

From this postcard on a shelf,
she has the hint of a smile,
like the peripheral view of a solid object
from the corner of an eye,
as if she asked at the end of the poem
if it was any good
and this time
for once
she actually knew the good enough in it.

I wish I could reach back pinwheeled arms
of time and place,
from color back to black and white
and infuse it with an escape,
the big hand on the clock in an

oven mitt
for the pan of melted breath and puddings
which used every one
of her parts.
Where would we go if we had her now?
Where is she among us, lingering?

Air Ego Balloon

for Sonia Tetlow and Cliterati

We don't really believe we should be here.
We apologize for taking space,
being loud,
in your face—
Dis
or lack
of grace.
Poems don't have to rhyme
but it's about time . . .
it's about
our time!

Words get caught in my throat some*times*
like there's a finger or a fist
in there somewhere—and
it still surprises me
how I let too much talking
and being cut off in conversation
silence me,
turn my mouth into an echo chamber,
and my head stale
with unexpressed vowels, ideas—
unsent tenses
of *sentences*
written with invisible ink.

Or how about this one—about how
you tell yourself
she

looks *so* pretty
and doesn't even know it, never knows it.
Her hair is rivers and oceans,
and *her* face never ends.

When we call out to each other,
Her name is made of poem letters in
ice cream shapes my tongue licks, lavishes
so she doesn't run, run away
—*she* won't melt, melt away . . .
but *she* never liked me anyway.
I never had a chance . . . . .

II.
Fumbly. Mumbly soft boys
write lyrics lodging
glowing alphabet splinters into my ears
inspiring me later, even though
I wish I'd written them myself.

They play the happy contrast
with the devastated sad
like a slow-moving shuffle,
like overexposed, yellowing curtains.
like angry on reserve and leaking out
through close-together teeth

like *a girl* . . .
but they're *not girls.*

I think of brothers of my friends in
basement jams,

of Rush,
of Yes,
of over and over again riffs and chords,
of whack-off going nowhere noise
for days
into years
making walls
sweat socks,
sweat

Boy.

The instruments broke from the solo-not-solos
of their going nowhere
Pretty graffiti,
splotchy wallpaper music

But going nowhere road music
takes for granted
a having been there,
a where
in the first place . . .
being *safe* with thumbs out.
Over the shoulder bags
and pockets barely full are *all okay*
and *safe*
on their boyish good looks . . .

I see their quietude,
like mine,
like girl—like soft on my inside
not on my outside.

I always felt a *belonging* with them—
in skins like theirs . . .

but even in their shy, correct brilliance,
and *softer than me–ness,*
in frayed military cargo clothes,
thrift store cool shoes, concert shirt castoffs,
fashions of shabby shy
unraveling,

they sting with the reminder that
I'm not a boy.

Going to any open mic in town or around
I've never heard a one
apologize
for being there
for opening their mouths too wide—
only for not quite knowing the chords to the just written, new
　　　song—

Maybe.

I hear them rotate on and off open mic stages
All declaring to be the *one*—
They are *the* one, the furtive understanding
One and only One.
They *know* they are the one and only . . .

They are *so entitled.*

It's why I even like the girls with guitars

playing softly—
"Just don't
just don't
Just *DON'T*
apologize for being there,"
I say in an emphatic prayer.

As she tunes, I whisper in my head,
"Launch into it girl,
rip it apart
break a nail
break a string
just don't break."

Somehow, through years,
we have learned to have
egos of water balloons
so heavy with water weight
so squishy and fragile—worse than glass, really—
because at least glass is hard and
gritty from sand.
When I line up and list the women to read
I book them pleadingly
in whispers under my breath of "pleasepleaseplease,"
always feeling like I'm in a field
with knife-bladed grass
and I am running to
gently catch the rain
of tear-shaped, not tearing,
water-rubber-air egos,
waiting to bust
open insecure

of "please don't kick me off the stage"
holding on to it like the edges
are a life preserver
and the audience
—like me—looks up
and hopes
to preserve her

Beth Lisick

Stumbling In

I NEVER FELT PARTICULARLY COMPELLED TO TELL
people what was on my mind. In school, I was a good but quiet stu-
dent. To me, it seemed like you were only "qualified" to speak up
about a topic if you happened to know a whole lot about it. The idea
that someone might possess a valid, albeit subjective, opinion on
things, or that the process of learning was really a bunch of stumbling
around, was lost on me for quite a few years.

I felt similarly about art and artists. People bold enough to
put themselves out there creatively must obviously have known
exactly what they were expressing and why it was important.
Otherwise, how could they be so confident? Why else would they
assume anyone would care about what they had created? On the
other hand, was it possible that some of them were full-on phonies,
bluffing their way through? I mean, sure, I took dance classes as
a kid, wrote some poems in the third grade, and loved making my
own Halloween costumes, but to proclaim myself, publicly, an art-
ist? The relationship between experimentation and art had truly
never occurred to me. Luckily, I did a little stumbling of my own,

literally, into a San Jose bar on open mic night, and that scene altered my life forever.

Who in god's name were these funny, smart, tragic, observant, confused, dirty, bewildering people? As each one seized his or her five minutes onstage, I became absolutely mesmerized. Of course some of them were awful, or too drunk to enunciate. But I loved them, too. I loved that the words they were speaking emanated directly from their brains and inhabited the air in that time and place, and that we, in that bar, were the only ones on earth fortunate enough to witness the spectacle. It was a powerful and chaotic collision of global politics, fucked-up childhoods, sexual encounters, workplace drama, thieving roommates, most embarrassing moments, and every type of discrimination or injustice in the known universe. You name it, and there was a rant, poem, or story about it. It seemed, surprisingly, that as long as you had some words, you were deemed "expert" enough to get onstage and spill your gut of "knowledge." I had to get in on this.

I had been somewhat of a secret writer for a few years, if that's what you can really call someone who eavesdrops on conversations and transcribes them into a notebook. Mostly, I wrote down things that made me laugh. I would overhear a car salesman tell a prospective buyer that a car was "loaded like a King Bong" and finish the rest of the conversation on paper. I wrote sarcastic tributes to sham orthodontists and my brother's ex-girlfriends. I'd embellish a trip to Kinko's for comic effect. My scribblings were a way to pass the time on public transportation or to jar my memory later when recounting the day's events to a friend. Not until that night in San Jose had I ever felt the urge to make any of my writing public.

The next week I came back with a three-minute rant about the anorexic girls I had known in college. The piece was just a collection of little snapshots, part fact and part fiction, but I felt pretty good about it. Besides, it seemed as though there was always someone falling off the stage or riling up hecklers, enough to take the attention off me.

When my name was called, I climbed up onstage and kinda let loose. All those notions I'd been carrying around for years about how or when or why you should express yourself short-circuited and disappeared into the air with my words. I might only have been talking about tanning parlors and mini malls, but the fact that I was reading something I had written was suddenly enough. Not worrying about being smart, informed, polite, or truthful enough was instantaneous freedom for me.

A few important things happened after that reading. I discovered I wasn't nervous speaking in front of people; I have a pretty loud voice and I definitely employed it in its full capacity. Also, the crowd seemed to dig my poem. But what I mostly remember was a nice round of applause and some laughs, and afterward meeting a lot of the other writers. And I kept coming back, for the simplest reason on earth: because this was just super fun.

When I moved to San Francisco, I plunged right into the spoken word scene and its furious energy. Each week at every venue, dozens of people showed up with new pieces to perform. I did notice that the scene was male-centered, but it didn't bother me too much since the women onstage were kicking so much ass: Dominique Lowell, Jane 69, Michelle Tea, Bana Witt, Eli Coppola, Jennifer Blowdryer, Danielle Willis, Pleasant Gehman. Michelle Tea and Sini Anderson's notorious group Sister Spit held a weekly open mic by and for ladies at a bar in the Mission. I read there often and became exposed to a whole new crew of amazing feminist voices. And there was Jennifer Joseph, the publisher of Manic D Press, who ran one of the most popular open mics in the city.

When Jennifer Joseph asked me to collect my pieces so she could look over them for possible publication, I was utterly embarrassed. Just as I had previously never thought to read the stuff I'd been writing, I had certainly not considered publishing it. Everything I had created up to this point was meant specifically to be read aloud in a smoky bar between the hours of 9 PM and midnight. What I had was a mess, decipherable only to me.

Around this time, a very pregnant Jennifer Joseph sent me in her place, along with two newly published Manic D poets, to a writing conference in Birmingham, Alabama. The three of us did a reading at a conference-sponsored cocktail party attended by some fancy writers and publishers. Afterward, James Tate, who had just been tagged to guest-edit a *Best American Poetry* anthology, expressed interest in including my poem "Empress of Sighs" in the collection, but added that previous publication was a prerequisite. Fortunately, *Clockwatch Review* editor James Plath was standing right there and suggested that he publish my poem in his upcoming issue; Tate could then pull it from *Clockwatch*.

Up until this point, I had not called myself a writer. When James Tate called my thing a poem, though, and put it in a book called *Best American Poetry 1997*, I realized that there were obviously not a lot of rules in this literary world. Apparently, "being a writer" was something you could stumble into by accident. Nonetheless, it still took me a while to feel as "qualified" as anybody else. But I finally came to feel that what I loved most about writing was how my voice became part of an enormous verbalized mix, and that I had never, not for one second, heard anyone read a poem or a story and thought, *Wow, that person is really unqualified!* Even when I'm not passionate about a particular content or style, I always appreciate the very act of someone writing, and the fact that all voices contribute to the mélange. That may sound feeble, or too generous, but I can't really fault someone for loving to do the same thing as I do. In the end, I was able to transcend my insecurities by seeing myself as part of a community that I stumbled into and now cherish—a community that, ultimately, only wanted me to be myself.

Empress of Sighs

Mom says getting to the new home is a snap. "As easy as a cake falling off a log on a bicycle." Just take a left on Palm Canyon until you reach Desert Falls, bear left at the fork of Indian Canyon and Canyon Plaza taking Desert Canyon to Canyon Sands. This is where you will find Rancho La Paz. Click on 2 for the gate, the guard waves you past and you're on Avenida del Sol where you continue on crossing Vista del Sol, Plaza del Sol, Vista del Monte, Sunny Dunes, Camino Parocela—make sure you heed the golf cart crossing—and then Thousand Palms, Emerald Desert, Desert Isle and Palm Desert Greens. Left on Sagewood, right on Sungate, left on Palo Verde, and ending in the cul-de-sac of Casa La Paz.

"I just love it," Mom says.

"You love it?" I say.

"Yes. I love it!" Then she calls to Dad who's enjoying himself on the eighteen-hole putting green located just three feet outside the kitchen sliding glass door, "Don't we love it, hon?"

He tips the brim of his white cap, a cap he would have seen on someone a year ago and called them a fag and says, "Love it! Another crappy day in paradise! Ha! Ha! Ha!"
Mom clears her throat a little and sighs. She is the Empress of Sighs. "Well, yes, it's still a little funny."

Same funny tax bracket, same funny year-round tans, same funny cathedral ceilings. Same politics, same stocks, same paranoia and medication. The same leather interior, glossy exterior and liposuctioned posterior.

Here comes your neighbor driving up in a luxury sedan just like your luxury sedan except he paid extra for the little headlight wipers and the gold-linked license plate frame—and you didn't. You thought they were useless, extraneous, a little much . . . and now your neighbor comes rubbering by, waving real slow, doing the grown-up equivalent of "ha-ha!" which is basically "ha-ha! I am worth more than you."

And Mom sighs and admits it doesn't feel like home yet. This mom, Empress of Sighs, Empress of afterschool treats and frumpy sweaters and marathon tickling and the 52 Casseroles cookbook, doesn't feel at home.

So I map out a plan. I make a list on how one feels at home here. I say, you need to play bridge, throw a party, plan on some tennis and it'll feel like home. Polish the silver, throw out old photos, balance your checkbook, it'll feel like home. Start eating more fresh fruit. Get your armpits waxed. Drink six eight-ounce glasses of water each day. It'll feel like home.

Squeeze all your blackheads, clip toenails in bed, watch thirteen straight hours of television. Complain about what trash they show on television and begin writing a letter. Stop writing the letter cause it makes you think about yourself, yell at your mother instead, quit drinking. Threaten to deport the gardener.

Go on a crying jag. Consider rhinoplasty, blepharoplasty and a tummy tuck. Forget to water the plants. Buy plastic plants and forget to dust them. Buy books and pretend you read them.

Start a collection. Start a collection of something that might be worth something someday.

Now turn off the lights, sprawl out on one of the matching earthtoned leather sofas and pick a very high number. Start counting backwards. You're in the middle of the desert, the wind picks up and when you run out of numbers you will find that it feels a lot like home.

Monkey Girl

Oh, Monkey Girl! Oh yeah, Monkey Girl!
Gung hay fat choy!
I was born in the year of the monkey

So I'm walking around the Chinese New Year parade
drinking a warm beer I have my paycheck in my sock
when this old lady asks me what year I was born

1968, I say, the year of the monkey
Oh! Monkey is naughty, she says
Monkey is sneaky. You are naughty monkey, I know

Well, oh yeah Monkey Girl
Gung hay fat choy, Monkey Girl
I know all about you

And then this guy, the kind working for the environmentally
    conscious
energy corporations in between getting his bachelor's and his
    master's
approaches me his gigantic hand extended
Hi. I'm Steve. I'm a rat

Oh! Rat is clever, the old lady says
Rat work hard. Rat make good mate.

Why don't we blow this teriyaki stand and get a drink, he says
Teriyaki is Japanese, I tell him
Mr. Stanford Rat Boy is not so smart after all
Yeah, I'll let you buy me a drink

STUMBLING IN

So I go along with this for a couple of months
and I can't even think of my own excuses why
at this point I just keep thinking
well, monkey is naughty

But he's a rat and I have to keep reminding myself of that

I have two recurring nightmares
One about my dad's '77 Pinto and another about rats

I'm naked in my bed and there are big lumps crawling
        underneath my skin
They're rats that have burrowed there except there are no
        entry or exit wounds
They're just crawling up my thighs, up my stomach
busting out right here where my collarbone breaks
and their hideous yellowtooth faces look a lot like mine

The last rat I saw
before this guy
was in an East Village garbage can
snorfling through a bag of used Pampers
The rat before that crawled up my pajama leg
as I slept in a smelly drafty studio in Santa Cruz

Then there was Pippin
the only pet who was ever all mine
She choked to death on a tennis ped I gave her to sleep in
while I was away at a family reunion in the Ozarks

Oh gung hey you you fat choy
You were born in the year of the rat?

ny horoscope and if I don't like it that's okay
am the self-involved Cancer, the brooding

go-lucky Sagittarius
deeply believe in this rat thing
dar business

...ust be all that advertising about the mystique of the Orient
Ancient Chinese secret, huh?

So give me a horse, 1954, 1966, I will gladly swat the flies from
    his butt
Or a snake, 1965, I have no problem sucking poison
Rooster, '69, I've been known to enjoy a cock
Dragons, tigers, oxen. Cool
Dogs, pigs, rabbits, sheep. Cute
Kind of '80s country kitchen suburban wallpaper material
but cute enough

This monkey girl just wants to go to the monkey bars
Hanging upside down until all the blood pools inside my head
And I think I'm somewhere else
Somewhere far away from Pintos and tennis peds,
family reunions, the Ozarks

And this dirty, clever, hardworking rat
With the six-figure income
Who only wants me
because I'm naughty

Genevieve Van Cleve

Page for a Day

"She was an American girl/Full of promises"

—*Tom Petty*

THERE'S A FUNNY PICTURE OF ME WHEN I WAS a kid. I had been chosen to be a "page for a day" in the Texas senate. Nothing could have been cooler. My favorite shows were *Quincy M.E.* and *M*A*S*H*. I was interested in good government and fair play. I was down on the Man, and into the power of the people. So, mom dropped me off at the capitol with my monogrammed sweater, red espadrilles, and disastrous perm. Lloyd Doggett, my state representative and a dead ringer for Abe Lincoln, wrapped his arm around me and I grinned from ear to ear. I was a good citizen and I loved my country.

Growing up in Pflugerville, Texas, was a mixed blessing. Sure, there wasn't a lot of street crime, but between the oppressive religiosity and accompanying sexism, I spent a lot of time dreaming about a bigger world that was free of such parochial sins. I refused to join the Panthers for Christ club. I refused to be bullied by young men who felt quite free to put a bighearted, thinking girl like me back in her place. These rejections culminated in my reputation as a trouble-maker, someone who ultimately was not to be trusted. My freshman year, I had been elected class president. By the time I was a senior, I'd run away from home, gotten a job, hooked up with a college freshman, and accepted the first scholarship out of town.

College brought the larger world right to my doorstep, and it caused me great sorrow when I began to understand that the larger world was infinitely more screwed up than even a hometown could be. Forget the sins of Pflugerville; what about America's sins? I despaired. I was reckless. Once again the optimism and expectation of academic success and friendship of my freshman year was long forgotten by the time I'd reached graduation. Other people were going to be nurses and attorneys. I was going to be nothing, because I felt too much, had too much to say, and didn't know what to do about that.

So, instead of choosing a clear career path or graduate school, I found myself filing and answering phones in the office of a good ol' Texas politician. I hated it. The pretty girls worked in the front of the office and moved up quickly. The rest of us were in the back. The day the candidate walked up to me and said, "You know, I been huntin' with your daddy," was the day I quit.

I got a job as a temp at Apple Computer. I was broke for the first few months. "Bagel Fridays" turned into "Bagel Saturdays, Sundays, and Mondays." Apple Computer had a free medicine cabinet in the break room. I sampled freely. Sitting in my cubicle, I began to write angry crank letters to government agencies and corporations. Every letter began the same way: "Dear Sirs . . . Not since Hitler's Germany have customers/citizens/consumers been treated so poorly." I also began to write funny sketches and stories about my life. A friend from college, Juliette Torrez, was running the spoken word tent for Lollapalooza and became the Johnny Appleseed of poetry slams all over the country. During a visit to Austin, Texas, for SXSW, she encouraged me to enter my first poetry slam.

Juliette and I walked into the Electric Lounge, a popular '90s indie rock watering hole and one of the first homes to the Austin Poetry Slam, and I signed up. I met intellectual misfits and would-be rock stars, bar girls and feminist performance artists, computer programmers and grassroots activists. All of a sudden there was a whole room full of people I wanted to not only speak with, but tell something to. I began to discover my voice and it was loud, calculating, and sharp. I vented about abortion, my hometown, isolation, rock 'n' roll, sex, sexism, alcoholism, cheaters, liars, and all the other things that broke my heart. I was hell-bent on setting the record straight. I attacked the stage. I was breathless, red-faced, and pissed off.

The poetry slam rewarded my writing and energy. I was applauded for my aggression and sass. The stage was my friend. I had the opportunity to host the poetry slam at the Electric Lounge, tried my hand at stand-up, and joined an improvisational comedy troupe called Monks' Night Out. I cowrote a screenplay, like everyone else in Austin at the time, and managed to have it considered for production by MTV. They turned us down because they didn't want to make a "chick film." They made the world's most forgettable Gen Xer movie, *Joe's Apartment,* instead. On several memorable trips, I was the guest of the happening Danish government: Danish artists and their government patrons requested a gaggle of English-speaking poets to introduce slam poetry to Copenhagen audiences. I even lived in Bristol, England, for a period of time toward the end of the '90s, realizing my dream to be penniless and artistic somewhere foreign.

I wasn't happy, though. I finally found a fantastic therapist and went every time I could afford it. Anger can become a habit. Anger is so big and loud, it's easy to ignore all the sadness that had set me on the spoken word path. I gave up writing and performing for several years. It made no sense to continue if I was simply cranking out the same type of pieces, with the same energy, over and over again. I wanted to write love poems, and to do that, I had to figure out how to be in love. I wanted to write about my family in a way that was forgiving and redemptive. I wanted to write about the world and instead of being overwhelmed by it, I wanted to effect change. I wanted my work and my life to be powerful, not just frenetic and bellicose.

I guess the difference between now and then is that I have uncovered a powerful joy in my heart and rediscovered hope. I walked onto a stage and into an art form not just to cleanse my soul, but to make sense of myself and the world I live in. To quote my great friend Susan B. Anthony Somers-Willett, I no longer "stay up all night just to spite the moon." I have realized that joy is not just a good joke or fair weather. Rather, joy is offering compassion in the face of rage. Joy is pitching in and fixing your community. Joy is the blessing of good food and the survival of sweet romance. Today, I write with an eye toward the things we've gotten right: love, the health benefits of a high-fiber diet, Bill Clinton, and, although I'm not a religious person, the teachings of Jesus. The Christian Right hasn't cornered the market on goodness—gigantic hairdos and illicit love affairs, maybe. But goodness? Not so much.

I'm sporting the mid-thirties uniform now. I've got a cool jacket and a groovy haircut. I've got a husband, stepkids, and poetry gigs. I volunteer for pro-woman causes, testify in front of committees, work at the polls, and teach people about how to write and perform poetry. Of course the world continues to beg for change, and I aim to be a part of that good work. Maybe being a "page for a day" is just not enough for me. I want a lifetime. I want two.

In the last ten years, the slam community has saved my life and introduced me to friends and places I never would have found on my own. Spoken word has made it possible for me to find, hone, and celebrate my voice, while listening to those of countless others. I feel as though it is now my time to give something back to the community and art form that have fostered me. I still carry that very eager young citizen with the disastrous perm and monogrammed sweater inside me. However, that giddy kid is now a beloved resident in the body of a fully functioning, fire-breathing adult woman. What could be better?

A Quick Thank-You Note
to Anne Sexton and Sylvia Plath

Slam Intro: In the beginning, there were sweet lady poets.
How do I love thee? Let me count the ways . . .
And if it were up to some people, we'd still be counting.

But these polite words were eventually run over by the Mack
Trucks of modern poetry, Anne Sexton and Sylvia Plath.
Without them, women on the slam stage would be as rare as a
baby changin' station in the Texas legislature.

So here's to you ladies . . . In fact,

Thanks Anne for being so nuts
You told 'em what you had to say
Then you got crazier
And killed yourself

And even though you won the Pulitzer
And even though we flocked to see you

Somehow you didn't measure up
Except to those crazy feminists
Who weren't even fashionable
Hairy Hysterical Whiners

Fee-Fi-Fo-Fum
Now you're broken
Now you're numb

Addictions

Abortions
Abusers

Didn't exist before you

So, smoke, sister
Smoke

You and Sylvia
Got right down to it

Hysterical Bitches
Maternal Failures
Sex Crazed Frigid
Housewives

Smith sister, Plath, patron saint of nutty white chicks
    everywhere
Head in the oven
Tried to win the war at home

Sylvia wore white gloves in the women's magazine ghetto
Until she was so sopping wet sad
Mad and shocked
With a stick in her mouth and a weird ass song to sing

You do not do, you do not do
Barely daring to breathe or Achoo Auch Tung Daddy I'm
    through with you

You two shrews let it be known
Far and wide

To hell with structure and meter
Confession demanded the entirety of your lives

The grateful mother
The perfect child
The humble wife

All myths that we have left Mses.
As flowers on your celebrated
Self-made graves

Staying true to the seedy secrets of pin curls and tweeds
With tragic results
Left the rest of us free to concur

That cutting and purging is no way to survive

And while it's never too late to start huffing gas
In the kitchen—Sylvia
In the garage—Anne

It is better to stick it to
The big bastards that beat us
The illicit kisses and unwanted caresses
The pills and institutions created to control

We are free to fill up our pages
Apply bandages
And leave it if we don't like it

Nothing's perfect
It's you two ladies made that fact abundantly clear

But even in our darkest hours
We know now that there is beauty
You saw to that

Altar Call
(I Want Jesus Back)

Their hands reach up to the sky. Spirit Fingers, y'all. Tuesday
night Christians pray hard, poring over little King James
nuggets, their path to Heaven certain because they only read
that one Book. Hallelujah. Amen.

"We know you're up there Jesus. We're waitin' for you Jesus.
We praise you!"

Their simple glazed gazes cast about the little strip mall church,
adrift in the Jezebel Sea. They're all looking for Him as if He
might be standing in the center of their circle, enjoying all those
songs about Himself.

They're all lookin' up toward Heaven, like a bunch of thirsty
turkeys, finding holy evidence of Him behind every fluffy cloud.
Look, there's his beard!

Well friends you're lookin' in the wrong place. You wanna know
where Jesus is?
Jesus stands in an eight-hour line with black voters while
the members of the Christian Coalition waltz in and out of
white suburban polls in minutes. He sits alone in an empty,
undelivered FEMA trailer, waiting to welcome the weary home.
He was never the Lord of Bullies and Bigots, y'all.

Jesus kneels in Guantánamo Bay comforting enemies both real
and imagined. He was never the King of Preemptive Strikers,
Lord of the Torturers.

I'm a little suspicious of all this personal salvation. Jesus didn't suffer and die just for you. You've got your Jesus all dressed up in a Tom DeLay suit and tie, wrapped in gold. Replacing reason or wisdom, you simply point to your statue over and over again. Proclaim like a jealous girlfriend—tube top strainin' to hold her bounty, can of beer in one hand, baby in the other—"He mine, you can't have him."

Where's Jesus? Jesus walks with a broken-down old drunk, ten-day sobriety chip in one hand and a bottle in the other. He's in the alley where dignity and addiction do business.

I have no interest in your happy, clappy Christ and I am not afraid of the cynicism and secular orthodoxy of my liberal brethren. Don't bore me with your personal testimony. Don't slow me down with your lack of faith. Just like Jesus, I'm busy. Stomp my foot, start singin' like a funky Mother Mary, "Ain't no body gonna turn me round."

I'm working on a path to joy and justice, y'all.—Opening my arms to all that I fear. That is the call of faith. Not prosperity. Not piety. Not judgment.

And if tomorrow is that Great Wakin' Up Morning, let us find our rest, soiled and scarred by the wages of love and courage and a little bit of sin. No matter how hard you pray to that golden idol Jesus of yours, you never gonna get eternity. You've been given a life to use right Here and Now. This is your reward.

Let us pray.—That you don't waste it merely on yourselves. Hallelujah. Amen.

Cheryl Burke

Making a Name

SINCE MY BEGINNINGS AS A PERFORMANCE POET, I have gone by the moniker Cheryl B. and people have always asked me what the *B* stands for. My typical answer has been that it's simply an abbreviation of my last name, Burke, but the story behind it is a bit more involved.

I grew up in Staten Island and New Jersey. My parents were blue- and pink-collar workers with little interest in or time for intellectual pursuits. In our house, watching *The Benny Hill Show* was considered a cultural experience. Luckily, I was a naturally proficient reader at an early age and easily found an escape in books. My yearning for intellectual stimulation led me to spend a lot of time at the local library, where, unlike in my family's house, I would not be accused of "using big words."

As a fat little girl, who grew into an anorexic-then-obese-again teenager, I was well aware of the power of words, particularly derogatory names. I was called everything from "chubby" to "disgusting" to "fat fuck" and some other things that to this day upset me to type. As I grew older, the more obnoxious and sexualized the comments became. Those words destroyed me. I dreaded social situations, refused to eat in public, and avoided speaking, as I also had a slight stutter. I made myself as invisible as possible.

In high school I spent my lunch periods in the school library, where I wrote poems about suicide and my obsession with Sylvia Plath. At sixteen, I made my first big escape to attend a summer arts program in New Jersey, where I earned the respect of my fellow arty teenagers as I continued to bang out depressing yet humorous poems. I gave my first public reading that summer. I survived the reading and got a good reaction from the audience. I think this early experience gave me a bit of confidence to draw upon when I began doing open mics a few years later.

Growing up in the tri-state area, I'd always idealized New York City and thought it would be the perfect place for me to make a more permanent escape. In 1990 I left home to attend NYU and major in dramatic writing. By my junior year, I had lost fifty pounds thanks to a combination of walking everywhere, having a limited food budget, frequent late-night dancing in gay bars, and most importantly, finally being in a place where I felt accepted. As I lost weight, I came to acknowledge that I was a worthy sexual being, and I came out of the closet. During this incredibly transformative time, I began composing prose monologues reflecting the rage I felt over my treatment as a fat teenager and my fascination with my newfound sexuality.

In the summer of 1993, I began attending the open slams at the Nuyorican Poets Café with the intention of reading my work. I remember feeling a rush of excitement whenever I walked in—a rush so intense, it made the thought of performing or even just signing up for the open slam terrifying. Once, I even signed up with a false name, then pretended not to be there when it was called.

One night I made a pact with myself to not chicken out, and showed up at the Café with my rant "Fat Girls Don't Wear Spandex," about the indignities I had suffered as a teenage fat girl. After nervously pacing outside the Café for half an hour, I determinedly marched to the front of the bar, where the host was writing down the open slam list. When he asked for my name, I said, to my surprise, "Cheryl B." I had never called myself that before, nor had I thought much about taking a pseudonym. In that moment, I inadvertently re-created myself.

I didn't win the open slam that night, but "Fat Girls" went over well. Even though I didn't take my eyes off my pages, and I was later told by friends that I swayed from side to side as I read, I heard uncomfortable laughter from the audience at all the right times. I felt as if I had just discovered a hidden superpower, an ability to make the audience simultaneously laugh, think, and squirm. I was Cheryl B. from then on. Taking a stage name, however close it was to my real name, gave me a sense of control, something I'd never had as an adolescent.

Over the next few months, I continued to do open mics, slowly becoming more comfortable onstage, and eventually I was asked to do a Friday Night Slam. As you had to be invited to participate in the Friday Night Slam, this was a big deal. The show's theme was "Valentine Love/Hate Slam," and, for the first time, in the February 1994 *New York City Poetry Calendar* (which I have kept all these years), I saw my new name in print. For the slam, I wrote a love/hate poem about the state of New Jersey, the site of my teenage turmoil. The poem, "Another Brick in the Mall, part 1," involved beer, marijuana, Burger King, Sylvia Plath, and cunnilingus while driving on a New Jersey highway.

The week leading up to the show, I practiced my work nonstop. I had anxiety dreams in which Madonna, one of my idols, was a judge and absolutely hated my poems. When I arrived at the Nuyorican on the big night, I spent a good amount of time in the bathroom dry heaving before the slam. But when I finally took the stage, I looked out at the packed house, which earlier in the evening I was sure would make me faint, and I felt calm, at home, like I belonged. The audience went quiet, waiting for me to begin. Something was happening that I never thought would be possible for a shy, former fat chick with a slight stutter: People were paying attention to me, wanting to hear me speak. That reading was the first time I felt the heady, powerful rush that only comes from connecting with an audience: a mix of flirtation and adrenaline, one big serving of sex with a side order of drugs. I left the Café that night after winning my first slam feeling a bit postcoital and completely energized at the same time, sort of like the way you feel when you first fall in love.

Spoken word, in various forms, has been a constant presence in my life ever since. I've been a touring performer, a storyteller, and a curator. I kept my real name a secret, but as I've matured, Ms. B and Ms. Burke have come to coexist. I've been publishing under my real name for the past few years and still continue to perform as Cheryl B. Maybe someday I'll change the whole thing to a symbol, probably based on the letter B.

Motor Oil Queen

Time: Late 1980s
Place: New Jersey

Tina speaks to her friend on the phone. She speaks almost
breathlessly, without pauses and with a tri-state-area accent.

So, it goes like this: Amanda went to the garage over on Union,
and she was like waiting there for a while in her car, no not
the Caddy, that's her brother's car, you know her car, the 1972
electric blue Monte Carlo with the white leather upholstery, the
dice, the circle of unicorns around the door handle, yeah, the
one with the eight-track player, you remember, you been in it.
She gave you a ride that night, that night down in Seaside with
those guys. Those Puerto Rican guys from Queens. Remember
Christina was like freaking out because she thought she was
pregnant because that guy came on her stomach? And Jen's hair
caught on fire. And Jean, that fucking skank, she was all over
that guy, the one that I liked, she knew I fucking liked him, that
blow job whore, walking skank pond. I'm right aren't I? The
girl looks like she's covered in sexually transmitted diseases.
Anyway, Amanda was at the garage and you know how she is
is, she's flirtin' with the guy, he's helping another customer,
eventually the other customer drives away and they're like
there by themselves, a beautiful Saturday spring day and
there's like no one else around. She says there was something
wrong with the steering wheel, the suspension was off, I mean
the car is as old as we are and he was in there checking it out
and one thing leads to another and before you know it they're
on top of the workbench fooling around and of course he wants
to fuck her and you know how she is, she's always looking to get

her piece of the action. So anyway they don't have any rubbers, and Amanda being the fucking moron she is, don't get me wrong, I love her, I love her, she's one of my best friends, she's like a sister to me, but she's an idiot. She's always buying those *Playgirl* magazines. I'm looking through them going, "These guys, they're a bunch of fags, they don't wanna do you, they wanna be you." How many guys do you know wear hot pink bikini underwear? None, right? My sister Annette is a lesbian and she lives up in the Village so I been exposed to that sort of thing, I speak from experience. Anyway, what was I talking about? Oh yeah, Amanda, that fuckin' idiot, so like they don't have any rubbers, right? So instead of just going across the street to the 7-11 like a normal fuckin' person she has—wait, wait, you can't tell anyone, alright—she lets him fuck her up the ass right there in the open, on the workbench, in the middle of the day, right out on the highway. Yes, I was stunned. So she says they did it and he uses some sort of lubricant and the deed is done and over and a few days later, Amanda's feeling a little weird down there so she goes down to Planned Parenthood and she finds out she has an infection, in her butt. She tells me this and I'm like, "You're lucky that's all you have, you fuckin' idiot." All right, I didn't call her a fucking idiot right to her face, but I was thinking it. I mean in this day and age you gotta be careful. So hopefully the infection will go away. But wait, there's more, the other night we were out at Danny's club and the second we walked in the whole place went quiet, it was like time stopped or something and they were all just looking at us. The entire night we heard everybody buzzing about Amanda and motor oil. They were saying names like Pennzoil Girl and Motor Oil Queen, I mean these are her fucking friends, right? Well, apparently that guy, the ass fucker from the garage, was going around telling everybody that he used motor oil as a lubricant.

I don't know if it's true but I guess it makes sense. Amanda was just totaled. I drove her home and we sat outside her house in my car and she just wouldn't stop crying. And the entire time I sat there consoling her I couldn't help but picture her as the Tin Man in *The Wizard of Oz*. You know, with the can of oil? Yeah, if she only had a fuckin' brain, right? (*She laughs, then catches herself.*) It's not funny though, we shouldn't be laughing, I worry about her. Really I do. She's like a fucking sister to me. So anyway, I gotta go. What are you wearing tonight? Yeah, yeah, that sounds great. Okay hon, I'll see you there.

Jones

I am addicted to this city, having seen Houston Street high
   on substances;

The marijuana causes much headiness

On speed the lights flash electricity—the word "Katz's" burns
   itself to the insides of my eyeballs

Tequila brings heightened awareness on Ludlow Street

From the corner of Stanton I begin to negotiate how I am going
   to cross Delancey

It's a Saturday night
I'm home watching *America's Most Wanted*
And I'm writing a poem about addictions, perversions and
   debauchery proper
A poem about New York
On the TV, a cop wrestles a guy to the ground
Apparently he was cooking crank in his bathtub
A baby toddles out onto the lawn where her daddy is flopping
   about like a fish

When my father died, I fought for his fishing trophies, his
   fisherman statue carved out of wood and the humongous striped
   bass that hung in the garage, still smelling like the ocean

I remember the trip to the taxidermist and helping my father pick
   out the watchful glass eye, it was green and cloudy and I swore
   I saw it move once when I was in high school and on acid

In the end, my brother packed up my father's car, with my
   father's electronics equipment, his statues and trophies

My mother and I stood in the driveway and watched my brother
   drive away before we went back inside to finish the thank-
   you cards

I once wrote an essay about my father, how when he taught me
   how to swim, he taught me how to treat the ocean

I told my mother not to touch the fish

I was going to rent a truck and drive it away, along with my old
   books and journals

I was going to hang it on my kitchen wall so I could smell the
   ocean as I drank my morning coffee

When I returned to her house the following week, the fish was
   gone—in the garbage or maybe at the Goodwill, she couldn't
   remember what she did with it

So, it's a Saturday night
I'm single and this time I'm not drinking
All I can do is reminisce
Like when I pass by the Polish bar as someone swings the
   door open
And the beautiful noise of drunken chatter, the rhapsody of
   secondhand smoke and the familiar strains of "Sympathy for
   the Devil" escape
I am reminded of the quarts of beer served in Styrofoam cups,
   beer nuts that I later find trapped in my bra

And for some reason my pants are in the kitchen in the morning

I stopped drinking when I woke up one day with a man I did not
    know, snoring next to me on the bed
I stopped partying when I didn't want to wake up anymore

This city is full of madness and I am addicted to this city

Having seen First Avenue on mushrooms and a bit of magic
It began to snow
I said to my lover "this snow, it looks like snowflakes,
    stereotypical snowflakes the kind you cut out of paper and
    see in cartoons"
"I feel like they're kissing my face," he said
On the train ride home to Brooklyn, he said "honey, I may not
    be able to perform tonight"
And I said, "that's okay, I just want to touch your chin"

This city is full of escape and I am addicted to this city

In the tiny bathroom of a way-off-Broadway theater, five of
    us crowd around a full-length mirror we have just removed
    from the wall and balanced on the toilet. On this mirror we
    vacuum up powder and caked-on dust through cutoff straws
    into our noses. We return late for the second act but stand at
    attention in the back, feeling the dialogue as if it is our own.
    Later we form a circle on the floor of someone's apartment,
    a lazy Susan sits and spins in the middle, a pile of white is
    distributed evenly amongst us. Our fourth walls display their
    ability to break down.

This city is full of promise and I am addicted to this city

Then there's the ecstasy, oh the ecstasy! When have I not felt
like jumping from rooftop to rooftop, singing a punk rock
version of "Rose's Turn," wrapped in satin sheets the color
of the night sky? Kicking in you feel like jumping out, that
tiny explosion that turns complacency into elation, enemies
into friends, friends into lovers, lovers into mythological
creatures with unimaginable, near embarrassing talents.
Through a kiss you can reach their soul. Your fingers never
felt so good, a furnace of sensation burns between you and
the person you are sitting next to on the couch and you are
both eaten by the flames.

This city is full of freedom and I am addicted to this city

Having seen Sixth Avenue under the influence of abstracts,
that moment at a party on Twenty-Fifth Street with a
friend you almost lost to jealousy and nonsense. You sit on
the couch, cry, embrace, say "I love you, I miss you." You
walk the thirty blocks to her apartment, holding her hand
wanting to hold her all night. Later, you both stand in her
doorway, raccoon-eyed, feeling closer to her than you ever
could to a lover.

All roads lead to the walk of shame, sex-funky and subversive,
awakening to a new day in a new place. Early in the
morning I roam amongst people who deliver newspapers,
walk dogs and jog. The most I can do is thank the goddess I
remembered my sunglasses. In my vinyl pants and sparkly
tank top, I am a yesterday person in the land of today. I
ignore the stares and my strappy platform shoes continue to
cut ribbons into my feet as I hobble along, not enough money
for a taxi.

The summer sky is a sight. At dusk, the buildings bask in an
orange glow. I have seen this from a sloped roof on the
Lower East Side, my fingers walking a precarious trail down
my lover's arm. I lie on my back, my head hangs over the
side of the building, the world is upside down. I can see a
candle burning in the window across the street. A woman is
rinsing a shirt in the sink, the water drips down her arms.
She notices me watching and we smile at each other. I close
my eyes and think of the ocean, when my father taught me
how to swim, the waves broke into tiny ripples at the shore.
He held me by the waist, dipping my lower half into the sea.
I could taste the salt water in the air, feel the sand in my toes
as my father taught me how to keep my head above water.

There are days now when I wake up and can't believe he's gone.

There are days when I wake up and I can't believe what's past.

My father told me if I learned how to float, I could always save
myself. I learned how to float and I can carry myself to
safety.

And this is me, not the drugs talking. This is me trying hard to
be better.

A Choir is
Born

I WOULD LIKE TO SAY THAT IT WAS MORE THAN
spite for, and the desire to disprove, an ex-lover who had little faith
in my writing ability that got me moving, with literally furious speed,
from stage to stage. But isn't it just like heartbreak to bring a person
closer to G-d, the bottle, or some sort of new hobby. Me, I took on the
whole trilogy: I prayed that I wouldn't pee in my pants onstage, drank
to calm my nerves, and picked up the microphone for verbal release. I
mean, Hallmark can give it a try, but nothing really says "I'm a cow-
boy-loving Jewish transsexual looking for love in all the wrong places"
like spoken word poetry.

This was in 2003, during the end of my tenure at the University
of Georgia, where I had also met my best buddy, Rocket, through our
rugby team. Rocket was a fellow trans-man and, after realizing that
we shared not only a similar political perspective but analogous writ-
ing and performance styles, we became a team. Together, we began
performing at poetry open mics throughout Athens, Georgia, and
rapidly our presence began gathering all of the transsexuals below
the Mason-Dixon under one roof, along with the street preachers

and beatboxers. Soon, Rocket and I became the Athens Boys Choir, a quirky name derived from being stifled by such a religious environment, as well as a nod to our newfound trans-identities. We began performing our fifteen-minute set at a local gay bar.

During one fireside night in my backyard, and after a few too many Southpaw Lights, Rocket and I began discussing "our future career" with the slurred judgment of dreamers. We decided to send our "demo," a rusty ten-poem CD we had recorded with a microphone held up to a tape player, out to several indie labels. Thankfully, the next day we remembered the plan and packaged up a bunch of demos. Those stamps changed my life. Less than forty-eight hours later, Amy Ray of the Indigo Girls, founder of the indie record label Daemon Records, was calling my house. To be honest, I barely remember what she said—something about digging our social politics and being interested in signing us as Daemon artists; they were looking to add spoken word artists to their label. I do remember dancing with my dachshunds and drinking champagne before ten in the morning. I looked all over for Rocket to share the news, and finally tracked him down while he was on a date, in his underwear.

I quit my sandwich-making job quicker than you can say "turkey on marbled rye," and Rocket and I hit the road on a tour reminiscent of our spoken word stylings: a sort of hard-hitting, fast-paced, underhanded egg-toss across the country. We cobbled the dates together by contacting queer bars throughout the country, and by checking out other spoken word artists' and musicians' archived tour dates.

There were definitely highs and lows in that first tour. On the East Coast we sold out our first show at All Asia in Boston, primarily because a good friend spread the word and got people out. At the end of that run, we had made four bucks each. On our first West Coast tour, our Greyhound bus was stranded in the snow and we had to spend the night in a high school gymnasium Red Cross shelter somewhere in northern California. In Seattle, we did a show with burlesque dancers, drag kings, and a bunch of writers from Bent and Oratrix; we sold out the Re-bar and found a whole new family in the Seattle artist community. We performed at a sports bar in San Jose and had to wait to go onstage until the football game on TV ended and the poker game in back became quiet. We were so uncomfortable and nervous that we decided to hit the stage with a piece called "Mighty Sodomight." It was our defense mechanism, kind of like a skunk spraying and clearing the air.

That fall, we released our first CD, *Rhapsody in T*, on Daemon Records. Our buddy Brian did all of the beatboxing and me and Rocket recorded in a room smaller than a jail cell. *Rhapsody in T* was met with myriad reviews. The folks who loved it dug its "unapologetic edginess," while those who disliked it struggled with our transgender identities. One review said something along the lines of, "the Athens Boys Choir is not a choir, they're not even boys." Quite honestly, though, no negative review could have dampened our spirits. Rocket and I had never felt more loved than during that tour. Countless people provided places to sleep and the comforts of home for a couple of wayward poets. We repaid them with kickass shows. We learned that a lot of strangers out there are ready to catch you when you fall. Our community is definitely one hell of a parachute.

Since that time, Rocket has moved to the west of the Mississippi. I miss him but try to keep that whole romantic "alone on the road" notion rolling. I have self-released two more CDs, *Rose Cuts the Cake* and the most recent *Jockstraps and Unicorns*. I have opened for, and performed with, some of my musical and literary heroes: Ani DiFranco, Ivan Coyote, the Butchies, Amy Ray and the Indigo Girls. I have learned, via trial and error, the finer points of booking, promoting, and full-time touring.

Since those auspicious beginnings, the road has now become home. I know the quickest route from my house in the foothills of Georgia to the best pad thai in Oberlin, Ohio, without looking at a map.

I have found family in the rockabillies in Tennessee, and I can tell you where to find the most beautiful turf ever to line a Little League field in eastern Kentucky. When the metaphorical potholes along that road appear, I have a quick pick-me-up—I listen to the words of my favorite poets and wham, bam, thank you ma'am, I'm healed. Seriously, it's better than any tent revival you can imagine. And I aim to bring my own personal brand of revival to others for a long time to come. Through my work I intend to honor the women in my family, my struggle as a trans-man, and give a shout-out to the roads going south, which hold my heart tight in their kudzu embrace.

So I guess you could say, with some thanks to that ex-lover, I have finally found my calling.

Nothing Generation

I once heard that my generation was to be called the
Nothing Generation.
Children of the '80s, Nancy Reagan told us to
"just say No!"
Hell, I love saying no, it's the spirit of protest but I'm
thinking good ol' Nancy had something more like drugs or
sex on her mind.
Guess that's another thing me and the former first lady
have in common see I often have sex on my mind . . .
but back to nothing.

It's not that we're content with nothing.
We graduated college in the year of the
Nothing economy,
Nothing job market,
waiting for a president with nothing between his ears to do
something.

White collar.
Blue collar,
and we got stuck with ring around the dollar.

We're children of the '80s,
Post-millennium.
Post-9/11.
Post-Saddam,
His statues now long gone and back in America we've
learned to get on with
Less shifts,
Less hours,

Less man-power because desire's not for hire for the
Nothing Generation.

Overqualified,
Underquantified,
Not satisfied in unemployment lines,
me thanking the divine because spitting rhymes paying for
my dining,
my boarding,
hoarding poetry like calories waiting to fatten me up in the
winter.
Storing lines like pennies hoping to cash in my jar because
the Nothing Generation appreciates art.
We know there's nothing like artistic expression to get you
through economic recessions.

We're children of the '80s.
Post-integration.
Waiting for the end of segregation.
Not sure how to react to affirmative action, we got our
wheels spinning but finding little for traction.

We survived the New Kids and other group dancing. We
Kris Krossed and gave you Hanson.
We are still romancing world peace.
Yeah, I want a ceasefire before I retire.
I'll take Medicare instead. I want my free scooter-chair
before I'm dead.

We played Oregon Trail.
It taught us survival.
Remember we shot deer with that stupid computer rifle?

We bought tapes before CDs,
saw the *Challenger* on TV,
watched hippies hit their fifties
and HIV become mainstream.

This is not-nothing,
a double negative representative of something. Something,
a presence,
a reference to essence,
the existence of resistance,
and a generation resilient with Nothing. To. Lose.

Oh, you want nothing? We'll give you a whole lot of nothing.

Nothing to deny the fact that we are a generation of voters.
Nothing to keep us off the streets fighting for equal rights
'cause it's an endless fight when you've got nothing to call
your America.

No comfort in a 9/11 commission.
No faith in an enduring freedom mission.
No trust in the stability of a Supreme Court decision.
No lack of insistence of historic revisions.

Nothing.
A lack of.
An absence of substance.
The abundance of twenty-somethings expected to do
nothing?

But need I remind, there's nothing more dangerous than
desire and free time.

Taken in Like Oxygen

1980 was the year I appeared, C-section from within a woman
who worked pregnant till the day I was born on a computer that
filled a large room and whose radiation killed her before my
second decade zoomed by on this earth.

Birthed too late for a seventies drug-induced procreation
mistake . . . and too soon to fill my room with toys from the
electronic-learning boom.

I skipped across Miami streets. On my feet, KangaROOS with
colorful twos of fat laces and traces of Cuban and Yiddish accents
on my tongue, a mixture of plantains and Jewish Wisdom.
Arroz con pollo and pico de gallo settled a Manischewitz
hangover after every Passover.

I identify as Polish and Jewish
Polish and Yiddish
The Kiddush . . . I dished it
World peace . . . I wished it
Gefilte . . . I fished it.
The last five years of synagogue, I skipped it
My parents' idea of what I'd become, I nipped in the bum before
my adolescence could come.

The roots of my family tree have been lost to poverty in my
ancestry and Poland's Nazi infestry.
My grandma was born on a dirt floor.
First saw the American shore at eight.
At eight, my parents moved up from middle-class, tried to prove
to me the grass was greener on a cul-de-sac.

My grandma's back and bones are weak from a lack of nutrition.
She relies on strength from within,
a survivor's intuition,
love without hesitation,
and a seventh. Grade. Education.
She has seen much transformation in this world . . .
Saw bricks laid till tall buildings made green lands into
  grandstands . . .
saw world wars open old sores,
Vietnam and a country torn,
Korea and a Desert Storm,
still prays for peace each president sworn.

Mourned for her parents. and siblings. and husband. and
partner.
Questioned her belief in God when she lost her daughter.
So she reminds me she loves me over phone lines designed in
her lifetime like calculators, A-bombs, and limos to gay proms . .
. saw in black and white and civil rights.
Death Camps.
And Jap Camps,
And working ladies in long pants.
She loves babies and weddings, calls me her "Sweet Liz" in
letter headings, "love forever" she reminds me each Hallmark
card ending.

Bending, she teaches, is key.
Hopes can be bent without breaking.
Hearts can find joy at the end of the aching.

I take her words in like oxygen . . .
Life givin'

Life driven
Been in this shit for eighty-two years and still kickin'
Seen life change like a drum rhythm
Seen the world split like nuclear fission
Seen a government take a women's decision
Seen prohibition and failed NASA missions,
Lost some of her hearing and most of her vision
And still can envision a world without love restrictions.

I listen.
Place myself in her position.
Realize that women in my family are strong
My grandma passed that strength to my mom and while I know
I don't totally belong, the trait carries on in me . . .
An independent sense of reality, and a destiny nudged by the
kick-ass women in my *kick-ass* history.

What I
Remember

IT'S WHAT I REMEMBER. A RED—BONED AMAZON—
size 12 top, 16W on the bottom, white starched blouse tucked neatly
into elastic-waisted denim A-line skirt. More salt than pepper long
swinging braid, hanging half way down her back. Left leg supporting
all the weight, right arm bent and hand balled in half fist on her hip, left
index finger pointing like a scold from the reflection in the mirror. Me,
her granddaughter, three-quarters her height, standing right next to
her. My white button-down shirt tucked into blue jeans, size 6 top, 12
juniors on the bottom, emulating her exact stance. Shifting my weight
to the left with exaggerated mimicry of finger pointing at mirror.

"Hold your head high," she commands, "and look right in that mir-
ror. Now repeat after me: ''Lias! 'Lias! Bless de Lawd.'" She sounds like
a preacher. Maybe that's where Daddy gets it from. I repeat her words
in my high-pitched third grade voice: "Lias Lias bless de Lord."

She continues,

Don' you know de day's erbroad?
Ef you don' git up, you scamp,

154

Dey'll be trouble in dis camp.
Tink I gwine to let you sleep,
W'ile I meks yo' boa'd an' keep?
Dat's a putty howdy do
Don' you hyeah me, 'Lias—you?

I imitate each line, each movement, each intonation, each expression and undertone.

My grandmother would take care of me on Mondays and Wednesdays, or maybe it was Tuesdays and Thursdays. These details escape me, but I remember it was because Mom was in graduate school and Dad had to work late. But mostly I remember that Grandma and I had this alone time twice every week. And the day I came home with the Langston Hughes poem "Hold Fast to Dreams" and my elementary school assignment to "learn it for Black History Month's assembly" was the day my dreams changed forever. I didn't understand the intention of the poem, what it meant to "hold fast to dreams." Grandma said that was because I was mumbling, trying to learn it under my breath. "You can't feel a poem just by reading it—you got to speak the poem, act out the poem, then you can know its true meaning."

And there in the mirror, watching her perform "In The Morning" by Paul Lawrence Dunbar entirely by memory, that's when I realized that my grandmother was magic. She had secret powers to transform from an old woman into a larger-than-life superstar. That's also when I first understood the poem I was to learn: "Hold fast to dreams/For if dreams die . . . " My grandmother had dreams that would never come to fruition. Most importantly, this was my spectacular introduction to spoken word poetry.

We would practice for hours and when my mom, or maybe it was Dad, or maybe it was both, would get home we would be in the kitchen cooking or sitting in the living room watching TV. They would ask us what we did that day and Grandma and I would say in unison, "Nothing." And that was good enough for them; as long as nobody got hurt, all was well.

My private performance poetry lessons continued all the way through the eighth grade, when I learned how to use poetry to silence my enemies—spouting off to the bullies in the hallway, "You may write me down in history/With your bitter, twisted lies,/You may trod me in the very dirt/But still, like dust, I'll rise." Or to the mean, snotty girls, "Pretty women wonder where my secret lies./I'm not cute or built to suit a fashion model's size . . . " I went on to win oratorical contests all through high school and minor in theater in college, all the time studying and writing, perfecting performance of words begging to be spoken.

When Grandma died, I lost my voice. I went to the funeral, heard people tell strangers all about what they thought they knew about her. I couldn't speak. I couldn't tell them that she was a legendary performance poet who had saved her granddaughter's life with spoken words. They threw away her journals, or maybe they were poems she had written, I can't remember. I couldn't speak to demand that they give them to me. I wouldn't recite poetry or speak in public forums for seven years after that.

It's cold outside, severe snow threatening postponement of the fifth annual Gwendolyn Brooks Open Mic poetry competition. I'm standing in front of a dressing room mirror in a white blouse, pulling up my denim jumpsuit and zipping it up over my size 10 top and size 14 misses bottom, elastic in the waist accentuating my family's legacy. And then she comes over me. I hear "'Lias! 'Lias! Bless de Lawd." I think I see her in the reflection, but it's me. I think to myself, *I look like her.* I wait to hear my name announced. I have not performed in seven years. I am nervous and can't seem to grip the intent of my own poem. I have never performed it live, only read it and submitted it on paper for publication, and this is the one that has been picked for the finals.

I walk out onstage, spotlight in my eyes. Gwendolyn Brooks is in the front row. I hear, "We real cool. We/Left school . . . " Try to shake Gwendolyn's poem from my mind, try to focus on my own words. There is a glare and I can't see the audience past the first row but I hear them rustling in their seats—there must be two, maybe three hundred people. I hear, "Hold your head up, look right in that mirror . . . " She merges with me and we shift all our weight to the left leg, plop that right hand on right hip, lift that left finger, point at the reflection, and ask the question that will go down in an all-time highlight moment of my career: "What is it that you misunderstand about these hips?" It is the tribute that I wrote to my grandmother, the greatest spoken word performance poet never known. It is why I perform poetry and what I remember every time I take the stage.

The Herstory of My Hips

What is it that you misunderstand about these hips?
my hips?
These are my hips—
these forty-six-inch hips
attached to this twenty-four-inch waist
are my hips and they tell herstory

Perhaps you question the size of my hips—
the second largest continent in the world sired these hips
of course they would be as large—

The oldest civilization on earth gave birth to these hips
of course they would be as wide—

For these were my great-grandmother's
and my grandmother's
and my mother's hips
and now I am heir to this throne—my crown?
these hips, of course—
and I would proudly pass them on to my daughter
for her dowry, would you say—

These hips are pyramids—
no blueprints modern technology
no cranes and chains erected these hips
blood sweat and joy created these hips—

My West Indian "fadder"
loved my Dominican "madre"
and they mixed up the spices

to create the recipe for these hips—

'Cause my hips are hip—
they swing a jazz tune
they bop a blues beat
they talk a rap rhythm
they dance a drum solo—

These are hot summer days
cold winter nights
spring into action
make you fall in my lap hips—
These are my hips—

No aerobics
no treadmill
no run a mile—
these hips are for you to snuggle
for you to cuddle
for you to sink into and dream—
for you to get lost in all your fantasies—
wrap yourself around and let me squeeze you hips
lock you in and yell "si mommy" hips
draw you deeper so you can scream,
"*dame a bueno, dame a bueno,*" hips
shake with ecstasy, "what's my name," hips
rock your world and swing from chandelier hips
when you want to hold a woman's hips
when you want to feel the difference between you and me hips
when hard hips want to be soothed by Charmin hips
these are my hips—
so let the legacy live on.

Warning

Lipstick and lace make me suspect
to women who say
women like me
set the feminist movement back
one hundred years
They watch from hard chairs
through blank stares
try to judge what they see
like
I once did strippers
who teased men
and some women
with revealed flesh
I try to cover—
Until I saw, she
was me who magnified
all my insecurities
and I was not embarrassed
for her
but for me
who could not dance free
from blind barriers and opaque obstacles
prescribed at birth
when a doctor pronounced my sex
confined my potential
to a check box
with low ceilings and brick walls
squared off from flying—
I see my sistahs
stare at me

a life-size Barbie
would be—
Flashing curve and breasts
adorned lips and neck
thinking
"She needs to stop—
this is what we fought hard not to be!"
But,
we interrupt this poem with a special announcement.
An unidentified black female
has infiltrated the system
and all
We Repeat
ALL
national security defenses are at risk

Cause this is a warning warning warning!!!
There's a person passing as woman
Warning warning
Passing as straight
Warning
Passing as fake
Passing
Passing
Passing
The way my brighter and light
great great mother
passed
sun-kissed field workers
quick fast
on her way to the big house
Passing

turned noses
snubbed shoulders
judgmental stares
Cause she was the chosen one
for the good life
for the nigga wife
who hid a kitchen knife
in sweet potato pies
weaved escape routes in quilts
then helped twenty to freedom—
Saying prayers on her back
massa riding her front
cause one more sistah
don't need to be
a victim of
This
is a warning
to my militant marys
toting handguns and grenades
downgrading sistahs
Whose weapons
are BAs or MAs
some with PhD degrees—
Working in corporate capitalists/man-decision-making
    companies
for the key to the office—
While you're protesting
on the outside
she's lobbying for your rights
on the inside
passing
the key out the window

for you to come through
This
front door
is a warning
for sistahs who preach too much
about war and revolution
then suck their teeth at those
who don't lock their hair
which sometimes
has locked you out
of power positions—
Where you could have
helped another
worked with a brother
schooled a single mother
Yet, you say I'm a sellout
'cause I won't be real
This
is a warning
for if ever
there came a time
when you really walked your talk
made the bed you laid—
Then this
Barbie pin-up
would gladly let the hair
grow from my roots
long under my arms
thick between my legs
hide
amazon sistahs in my bush
and while checking role call

from the guest house
I pass
right by to the white house
don't get checked at customs
They think I've been trained well.
Go in my office
pop off acrylic nails
load them into an ak-47
break my pumps
boomerang them
Past
the man
all the way to the Taliban
Take off my Anne Klein suit
string up my combat boots
strip down like my sistahs in nightclubs
to lace underwear
revealing floor plans
of security codes
Stand naked
raise my arms
release the funk of fumes
that's worse than napalm
Take the extra key
unlock the fence
and we my sistahs will
rage war together
Oh yes!!
This
is a warning
It takes a lot of women
to form an army

It takes all kinds
to win
this
revolution

Alix Olson

Turn it
Down a Notch

IN 1999, I WAS INVITED TO PERFORM MY SPOKEN
word poetry at Portugal's Faladura International Poetry Festival.
Surrounded by national poet laureates, I was one of very few slam
poets flown over, ostensibly to expand a new international poetic lan-
guage. It was the first time this festival had introduced spoken word
to the catalog. Quickly, I realized that I also represented a handful of
women artists, and was certainly one of the only openly queer art-
ists in the mix. My hosts were gracious, but I don't think they were
entirely sure what to expect from my art form.

During my performance, my work was presented on a screen
behind me, translated into several languages. As I peered cautiously
over my shoulder, I was greeted by my American "curse words" filled
in by X's. "We don't have words for those in our languages," they
explained later. The festival had also employed an American Sign
Language interpreter who, desperate to keep up with my motor-
mouth style, began frantically displaying ASL signs for "fuck," "cunt,"
and "dyke." Representing Uncle Sam, I slalomed through my first
European show.

As the weeklong festival progressed, I became acquainted with many of the poets, and we spoke at length about the divide between spoken word and formal poetry. The last evening of the festival, the lot of us gathered at a local bar for a final reception. I slowly became aware of a line of male poets, apparently eager to speak with me about my work.

The first guy cleared his throat, then plunged into a diatribe about how my "feminist art" did not resonate with him. "You see, we do not have sexism in my country, so a lot of your politics went clear over my head." He demonstrated his barely disguised vitriol by flailing his hand above his head. The poet behind him, clearly relieved by the previous man's courage, eagerly agreed. "We do not really have sexism in my country either," he explained patiently, "and so much of your work translates as just incredibly angry." A third male poet nodded, joining the discussion: "Poetry belongs to the page. It should be universal and up for interpretation, not so confrontational and direct. Your style is really more like theater. Perhaps you should consider performing a play or entering politics instead." The first man concurred: "Yes! May I suggest that if you continue in the field of poetry, to consider taking it down a notch? Perhaps being a bit more subtle? My sister, subtlety really is the key to poetry." They all agreed and ordered another round of port.

On the plane back to the United States, I pondered this newfound advice from my international male peers. I reflected upon the notion that there are countries where "sexism does not exist." I considered the roots of poetry, before the time of "the page," when poetry existed solely as a form of verbal communication (i.e., spoken word). Most significantly, I began to digest the reality that these men, clear across national borders, have been raised to be so confident as to attempt to define an entire artistic genre. I speculated about my artistic merit. I doubted, confused, comforted, and motivated myself. It was a bumpy ride.

The next day, I read "Subtle Sister" to myself for the first time, a poem that details, quite frankly, the anger of living within global sexism, the frustration of working inside a male-dominated poetic world, and the correlative naive response to feminist art. It was a pissed-off diatribe, a call to resistance, a personal remembrance of the rape, incest, and aggressive and sexual violence inflicted upon my friends, my community, and the women of the world. It was not, and defiantly not so, subtle.

Since that time, I have refused to remain obedient to the theory that poetry should adhere to the confines of an on-the-page, up-for-interpretation, nonpoliticized prescription. I am forever indebted to those male poets at the Faladura festival for reminding me of the dire need to poet forcibly.

I was also motivated to name my independent production company Subtle Sister Productions. I think of it as a personal tribute to my encounters in Portugal, and I thank those guys for their contribution to that particular stage of my personal feminist evolution.

Subtle Sister

So we've learned karate,
carry knives on our runs
wield words like weapons
prepare glares like hidden guns,
we've deconstructed, demystified
tried retribution, remythologized,
we've been diagnosed with your diseases,
and still tried pleases, tried tears, tried Jesus.

You wanna see what it's like down here
in this pool of someone else's rules, well
jump in, take a swim or just sit in this pit
squishing bare toes in someone else's bullshit,
we do it all the time.

Still we've tried being patient,
collected, calm, nice
trying praying, tried laying you
paying the price,
we've learned to scream
until our throats throbbed
what else do you do
while your cunt's being robbed.

And they say "you've made progress, girls,
take a rest in between"
but see while you're resting,
someone else is progressing,
it's what i've seen.
So i take back the whispers,

the cute mute act,
and the high-pitched giggles, yeah
i take them back,
i won't avoid your stare, evade your step,
nothing of that kind,
won't help you help me victimize
the only space that's mine.

See now i'd put my life on the line just to see them trip,
frown and say "funny love, i never saw you slip."
i say, "my life on the line—"
you say "man, she's jaded."
i say, "maybe control's overrated."
like when we cackled, they called us witches,
now we don't giggle they call us bitches
well I'm cacklin loud, taking it back, full of hiss,
cacklin loud, cackling proud now.

And they're getting nervous with this kissing each other,
scratching their heads,
what's going on brother
and they yell feed your husband, stop feeding the fire!
and we just cackle,
we're a fuckin witches choir.
and we sing "sharpen your knives, sharpen your daughters
steam up the mirrors, bake us some dreams,
cook up some riots, fry up some screams,
and when you're sick of your skirts
slice open the seams
cause they want domestics,
they'll give us needle and thread
for patching their egos.

we'll sow revolution instead."

And i hear you saying
"subtle, sister,
less bite, more bark
you can make your point without leaving such a mark.
subtle, sister,
stop your seething,
i think we got it, i think we're even."

subtle like a penis pounding its target?
subtle like your hissing from across the street?

subtle like the binding on my sisters' feet?
subtle like her belly raped with his semen,
draped in his fuck, funny,
doesn't seem even.

See, sometimes anger's subtle, stocked in metaphor
full of finesse and dressed in allure
yes, sometimes anger's subtle, less rage than sad
leaking slow through spigots you didn't know you had.
and sometimes it's just

fuck you.
fuck you.
you see, and to me,

That's poetry too.

That the Protagonist Is Always a Man

That Cheney's daughter campaigns for Bush's son.
That Bush's son wins a presidency that hates her.

The way Condaleeza Rice called her boss, her husband. That it
was an easy slip.

That the 1960s beatniks are the revolutionary poets. That
seventh-century-BC Sappho is that lesbian poet.

How the Rock and Roll Hall of Fame describes Joan Baez as
"the female Bob Dylan." That she launched his career.

That in "female musician," adjective becomes noun.

How Marge Piercy says "the moon must be female."
That the moon was forcibly penetrated by an American flag.
That plots on the moon are now up for sale.
Because Mother Earth is melting.

How the Security Council of the United Nations has five
permanent members. That all five are the official "nuclear weapon
states." That the United States is the only country to have
dropped an atomic bomb. That it is called the security council.

The way the old philosophers who declared human nature to be
naturally brutish were men.

How that one guy in your women's studies class raised his hand
for the first time in the semester to reprimand that "men can

be raped too." That we respect all voices. That maybe he has a
point. That he is a good guy for being there.

That Margaret Thatcher. Queen Elizabeth. Hillary Clinton.
How anomalies save their ass.

That father with the baby in the backpack in the grocery store.
How exceptions erase us.

That Adam produced Eve. That Mary did not birth Jesus.
How miracles screw us.

The way that a Father, a Son and a Holy Spirit exclude us from
the highest positions of power in the Catholic Church. How
they, condemning women and fags, then don dresses, diddle
little boys, devour the flesh and blood of their gaunt, devout,
dapper, special man-friend.

The way women, denied education, had to pass down our
herstory through stories and poems and dance and music and
recipes. How the Great writers and poets and dancers and
musicians and chefs have not been women.

That my computer spell-checks "herstory."

The way the English language carries us inside Man like his
fetus. That it is only our wombs that are patrolled.

That the members of Jane, helping to provide safe abortions
before *Roe v. Wade*, were criminals.
That the rounding bellies in South Dakota clinic lines are
murderers.

That Emma Goldman was considered a U.S. terrorist.
That they are pro-life. That they take the good words.

That Ann Coulter may consider herself an "us."
That self-determination is terrifying.
That self-determination is what we fight for.

That we fight for our sisters' right to choose stilettos. How
the women in horror films can't run in stilettos. That one drag
queen who used her stiletto as a weapon during Stonewall.
How the women in horror films can't run in stilettos.

The way CNN finally devoted an hourlong segment to the
brutal systematic government-sponsored rapes in Darfur.
How these women fled bombed and burning homes and still
had the courage to testify to Amnesty International. How one
sixteen-year-old had been raped by ten men for seventy-two
hours straight. How pregnant women are not spared. How
women have their nails pulled out. How unmarried women are
considered spoiled.
That the title of the broadcast was "Angelina Jolie: Her
Motherhood, Her Mission."
That she was wearing stilettos.

That the Lesbian Herstory Archives can fit no more material
into its Brooklyn brownstone.

That Focus on the Family headquarters has its own zip code.

That the National Organization for Women. That the Kitchen
Table Press. That the Radical Cheerleaders. That the Feminist
Majority. That NGLTF. That the Third Wave Foundation. That

Planned Parenthood. That the Guerrilla Girls. That Code Pink. That NARAL. That Refuse and Resist.

That.

Is why I am a radical feminist.

Suheir Hammad

In My Own English

SUHEIR HAMMAD IS A PALESTINIAN AMERICAN writer and political activist who recently won a Tony Award for her performance in the Broadway premiere of the spoken word show *Def Poetry Jam*. She has published a book of poems, *Born Palestinian, Born Black*, and a memoir, *Drops of This Story*. She spoke with anthology editor Alix Olson about resistance, translation, and self-identification.

What was the first poem you read out loud, who was your audience, and how did it resonate for you?
The first poem I read aloud, entitled "Dedication," was also the first poem I ever felt I wrote honestly, with my own voice, and for my own personal reasons. I wrote "Dedication" about a young uncle who was killed as a resistance fighter during the Palestinian liberation movement, when it was based in Beirut. I was visiting Jordan, seventeen years old, and trying to learn Arabic before I headed to Hunter College. The first time I read "Dedication" was at a reading I organized. I was very nervous, like paper-shaking nervous. Hunter had a sharp poetry scene, and many

of the poets I looked up to—reg e. gaines, Willie Perdomo, Mike Ladd, and many others—were always coming to our urban campus, usually invited by the Black Student Union. I considered myself an activist, and organizing poetry readings went hand in hand with writing press releases for the student organizations throughout CUNY who were protesting budget cuts and tuition increases. I remember that Audre Lorde taught in the building I first read in, and it was at that reading that many of us found out she had passed. I'd never taken a class with her, but had started reading her work during my freshman year. I've written many poems since then, but never finished college.

For the most part, U.S.-based poets write within the landscape of contemporary American poetry. How have you found your work translates, culturally, in other countries? Have you had your work literally translated to other languages and what has that experience been like for you?

I was blessed with the experience of having the poem "First Writing Since" translated into more languages than I ever dreamed—Italian, Spanish, Arabic, Hindi scripts, Urdu, and Korean. Are the translations exact? I doubt it. I think unless the poet sits with the translator, or the translator is a sensitive and nuanced poet in her own right (I think of Khaled Mattawa), there is a huge opportunity for confusion. I've read my work in many countries, and always in English. When the audience really doesn't understand what I'm saying, that's when I have realized that the entire point of being onstage is to connect, and I figure out how to do that. I sometimes translate my poem before I recite it. Sometimes, "translation issues" have been most acute here in the United States! I remember being in Vermont for my first ever out-of-state author reading, and of the four people who showed up to the signing, not one had heard of "a forty."

Do you write in languages besides English?

I like to think that I write in my very own English. Lately I am fusing

Arabic and hip-hop vernacular in ways I never felt confident enough
to do before.

Do you identify as a "political poet?" What does this term mean to you?
I actually don't identify as a "political poet," per se, but I understand
that when people label me as such, it's because we live in a sanitized
and domesticated culture, one that is force-fed for-profit media/enter-
tainment which insists on polarizing our lives into what is and is not
appropriately named art. So I don't mind it, not at all. To be "nonpo-
litical" is as much a conscious choice (unless you really do live in a
cave) as deciding to use creativity in ways I deem progressive and
compassionate.

**You are often described as "striking" and your "beauty" is often mentioned
in your reviews. How have you navigated "beauty" as a female poet?**
Descriptions of my looks have always been random and have never
made me feel beautiful. I think this is important for young poets to
understand. Like so many artists, I was picked on for being different
as a child, and my looks were fair game to bullies. I was aware of the
attention of grown men at a young age and, in a multitude of ways,
I was told I was responsible for their reactions and their actions. In
my early twenties, my hair was short and I wore overalls and flannel
shirts onstage, because I didn't want the poetry I was reading aloud
to be interpreted as a come-on. While working with *Def Poetry Jam*
(the Broadway production), I was adamant that my costumes never
show my cleavage and that my skirts were never short. This wasn't a
judgment on my part about what my peers were wearing. I was aware
that brown girls, Muslim girls, and immigrant girls who came from
strict parents would hold me up as a role model to their parents that
they too could share their work and not have to show their bodies. You
can't please everyone. My mom is still mad at me for one TV appear-
ance. I think it's a battle, to feel comfortable onstage, representing all

the things people project onto you. Also, calling a woman "pretty" is a way to undermine the strength of her craft. Nowadays, I am more comfortable with myself in general, but it would be foolish to think that the insecurities and vulnerabilities that made so many of us turn to poetry go away because a critic, a hater, or a fan says something.

I know that you struggle with embracing the culturally accepted defini-tion of "spoken word artist," often synonymous with "performance poet," choosing rather to identify simply as a "poet." How were you able to reconcile this negation with your recent tenure onstage for Def Poetry Jam's Broadway show?
I think there is a simple definition for me. My friends who are amazing spoken word artists often leave the stage fed, hyped up, and ready to go back on. They live off it. I have never felt that. I feel fed when I write, alone and with my thoughts. What I get from the stage is another feeling, beautiful and connected, but I only have to see the look in my peers' eyes to know that it's a different energy. Besides, I think spoken word itself needs to come up with a definition that is clearer, but it's not for me to define it. *Def Poetry Jam* on Broadway broke my back in many ways. I received a lot of negative attention from self-proclaimed representatives of the spoken word community about the lack of movement onstage, the monotone, et cetera.

When were you first published?
My first book was published when I was twenty-two years old. I couldn't write those poems again even if I wanted to. But they serve as a record of not only my life, but the people and time I came from. As long as you are true in the moment you are writing, you are being responsible to yourself.

My second collection of poems came nearly ten years later. I often thought, reading the many rejections that came in for the manuscript, that if my latter poems were as nationalist and "young," they'd have been accepted immediately, but there was something about the growth of my voice as a poet that made publishers wary. Even when nearly all the poems had been published on their own, it was hard to get anyone to put them out together.

Have you written work you now regret or disagree with?

I once referred to Barney the Dinosaur as gay—in a derogatory way. I didn't think anything of it until my friend mentioned it to me, years later. I think, however, it's very important for a poet to keep her public work public, so that her readership can follow the arc of her own growth as an artist and a human being. I also think we shouldn't punish each other for insensitivities—never ever through censorship. Believe me, I am offended all the time. I think dialogue is the truest response to something hurtful or ignorant in a poem.

First Writing Since

1. there have been no words.
i have not written one word.
no poetry in the ashes south of canal street.
no prose in the refrigerated trucks driving debris and dna.
not one word.

today is a week, and seven is of heavens, gods, science.
evident out my kitchen window is an abstract reality.
sky where once was steel.
smoke where once was flesh.

fire in the city air and i feared for my sister's life in a way never
before. and then, and now, i fear for the rest of us.

first, please god, let it be a mistake, the pilot's heart failed, the
plane's engine died.
then please god, let it be a nightmare, wake me now.
please god, after the second plane, please, don't let it be anyone
who looks like my brothers.

i do not know how bad a life has to break in order to kill.
i have never been so hungry that i willed hunger
i have never been so angry as to want to control a gun over a pen.
not really.
even as a woman, as a palestinian, as a broken human being.
never this broken.

more than ever, i believe there is no difference.
the most privileged nation, most americans do not know
    the difference between indians, afghanis, syrians, muslims,
    sikhs, hindus.

more than ever, there is no difference.

2. thank you korea for kimchi and bibim bob, and corn tea and the
genteel smiles of the wait staff at wonjo—smiles never revealing
the heat of the food or how tired they must be working long
   midtown
shifts. thank you korea, for the belly craving that brought me into
the city late the night before and diverted my daily train ride into
the world trade center.

there are plenty of thank yous in ny right now. thank you for my
lazy procrastinating late ass. thank you to the germs that had me
call in sick. thank you, my attitude, you had me fired the week
before. thank you for the train that never came, the rude nyer who
stole my cab going downtown. thank you for the sense my
   mama gave me
to run. thank you for my legs, my eyes, my life.

3. the dead are called lost and their families hold up shaky
printouts in front of us through screens smoked up.

we are looking for iris, mother of three. please call with any
information. we are searching for priti, last seen on the 103rd
floor. she was talking to her husband on the phone and the line
went. please help us find george, also known as adel. his family is
waiting for him with his favorite meal. i am looking for my son, who
was delivering coffee. i am looking for my sister girl, she started
her job on monday.

i am looking for peace. i am looking for mercy. i am looking for
evidence of compassion. any evidence of life. i am looking for life.

4. ricardo on the radio said in his accent thick as yuca, "i will
feel so much better when the first bombs drop over there. and my
friends feel the same way."

on my block, a woman was crying in a car parked and stranded
      in hurt.
i offered comfort, extended a hand she did not see before she said,
"we're gonna burn them so bad, i swear, so bad." my hand went
      to my
head and my head went to the numbers within it of the dead iraqi
children, the dead in nicaragua. the dead in rwanda who had to
      vie
with fake sport wrestling for america's attention.

yet when people sent emails saying, this was bound to happen,
      let's
not forget u.s. transgressions, for half a second i felt resentful.
hold up with that, cause i live here, these are my friends and fam,
and it could have been me in those buildings, and we're not bad
people, do not support america's bullying. can i just have a half
second to feel bad?

if i can find through this exhaust people who were left behind to
mourn and to resist mass murder, i might be alright.

thank you to the woman who saw me brinking my cool and
      blinking back
tears. she opened her arms before she asked "do you want a
      hug?" a
big white woman, and her embrace was the kind only people
      with the
warmth of flesh can offer. i wasn't about to say no to any comfort.

"my brother's in the navy," i said. "and we're arabs." "wow, you
got double trouble." word.

5. one more person ask me if i knew the hijackers.
one more motherfucker ask me what navy my brother is in.
one more person assume no arabs or muslims were killed.
one more person assume they know me, or that i represent a
    people.
or that a people represent an evil. or that evil is as simple as a
flag and words on a page.

we did not vilify all white men when mcveigh bombed oklahoma.
america did not give out his family's addresses or where he went to
church. or blame the bible or pat robertson.

and when the networks air footage of palestinians dancing in the
street, there is no apology that hungry children are bribed with
sweets that turn their teeth brown. that correspondents edit
    images.
that archives are there to facilitate lazy and inaccurate
journalism.

and when we talk about holy books and hooded men and death,
why do we never mention the kkk?

if there are any people on earth who understand how new york is
feeling right now, they are in the west bank and the gaza strip.

6. today it is ten days. last night bush waged war on a man once
openly funded by the cia. i do not know who is responsible. read
    too many books, know too many people to believe what i
    am told. i don't give a fuck about bin laden. his vision of the

world does not include me or those i
love. and petitions have been going around for years trying to get
the u.s. sponsored taliban out of power. shit is complicated, and i
don't know what to think.

but i know for sure who will pay.

in the world, it will be women, mostly colored and poor. women
    will
have to bury children, and support themselves through grief.
    "either
you are with us, or with the terrorists"—meaning keep your
    people
under control and your resistance censored. meaning we got the
    loot
and the nukes.

in america, it will be those amongst us who refuse blanket
    attacks on
the shivering. those of us who work toward social justice, in
support of civil liberties, in opposition to hateful foreign
policies.

i have never felt less american and more new yorker—
    particularly
brooklyn, than these past days. the stars and stripes on all these
cars and apartment windows represent the dead as citizens
    first—not
family members, not lovers.

i feel like my skin is real thin, and that my eyes are only going to
get darker. the future holds little light.

my baby brother is a man now, and on alert, and praying five
    times a
day that the orders he will take in a few days time are righteous
    and
will not weigh his soul down from the afterlife he deserves.

both my brothers—my heart stops when i try to pray—not a
    beat to
disturb my fear. one a rock god, the other a sergeant, and both
palestinian, practicing muslim, gentle men. both born in
    brooklyn
and their faces are of the archetypal arab man, all eyelashes and
nose and beautiful color and stubborn hair.

what will their lives be like now?

over there is over here.

7. all day, across the river, the smell of burning rubber and limbs
floats through. the sirens have stopped now. the advertisers are
back on the air. the rescue workers are traumatized. the skyline is
brought back to human size. no longer taunting the gods with its
height.

i have not cried at all while writing this. i cried when i saw those
buildings collapse on themselves like a broken heart. i have never
owned pain that needs to spread like that. and i cry daily that my
brothers return to our mother safe and whole.

there is no poetry in this. there are causes and effects. there are
symbols and ideologies. mad conspiracy here, and information
    we will

never know. there is death here, and there are promises of more.

there is life here. anyone reading this is breathing, maybe hurting,
but breathing for sure. and if there is any light to come, it will
shine from the eyes of those who look for peace and justice
    after the
rubble and rhetoric are cleared and the phoenix has risen.

affirm life.
affirm life.
we got to carry each other now.
you are either with life, or against it.
affirm life.

a prayer band

every thing

you ever paid for
you ever worked on
you ever received

every thing

you ever gave away
you ever held on to
you ever forgot about

every single thing is one
of every single thing and all
things are gone

every thing i can think to do
to say i feel
is buoyant

every thing is below water
every thing is eroding
every thing is hungry

there is no thing to eat
there is water every where
and there is no thing clean to drink

the children aren't talking

the nurses have stopped believing
anyone is coming for us

the parish fire chief will never again tell anyone that help is
    coming

now is the time of rags
now is the indigo of loss
now is the need for cavalry

new orleans
i fell in love with your fine ass poor boys sweating frying catfish
    blackened life thick women glossy seasoning bourbon indians
    beads grit history of races
and losers who still won

new orleans
i dreamt of living lush within your shuttered eyes
a closet of yellow dresses a breeze on my neck
writing poems for do right men and a daughter of refugees

i have known of displacement
and the tides pulling every thing
that could not be carried within
and some of that too

a jamaican man sings
those who can afford to run will run
what about those who can't
they will have to stay

end of the month tropical depression turned storm

someone whose beloved has drowned
knows what water can do
what water will do to once animated things

a new orleans man pleads
we have to steal from each other to eat
another gun in hand says we will protect what we have
what belongs to us

i have known of fleeing desperate
with children on hips in arms on backs
of house keys strung on necks
of water weighed shoes
disintegrated official papers
leases certificates births deaths taxes

i have known of high ways which lead nowhere
of aches in teeth in heads in hands tied

i have known of women raped by strangers by neighbors
of a hunger in human

i have known of promises to return
to where you come from
but first any bus going any where

tonight the tigris and the mississippi moan
for each other as sisters
full of unnatural things
flooded with predators and prayers

all language bankrupt

how long before hope begins to eat itself?
how many flags must be waved?
when does a man let go of his wife's hand in order to hold his child?

who says this is not the america they know?

what america do they know?

were the poor people so poor they could not be seen?

were the black people so many they could not be counted?

this is not a charge
this is a conviction

if death levels us all
then life plays favorites

and life it seems is constructed
of budgets contracts deployments of wards
and automobiles of superstition and tourism
and gasoline but mostly insurance

and insurance it seems is only bought
and only with what cannot be carried within
and some of that too

a city of slave bricked streets
a city of chapel rooms
a city of haints

a crescent city

where will the jazz funeral be held?

when will the children talk?

tonight it is the dead
and dying who are left
and those who would rather not
promise themselves they will return

they will be there
after everything is gone
and when the saints come
marching like spring
to save us all

Rachel Kann

From Inside

I HAVE A LETTER HANGING ON MY KITCHEN WALL.
An eleven-by-seventeen sheet of paper turned landscape rather than portrait.

The left half of the paper is where the message to me is scrawled.

On the right half of the paper is a drawing.

The whole of it, undeniably teenager, undeniably female, undeniably street. There's a sexy woman's head with long, wavy black hair and a fedora. The head's floating in front of a brick wall. There are words and symbols floating all around her too, the mind language of an incarcerated, brilliant child. Melting clocks and question marks.

I commissioned this piece of art from D. to grace the cover of the zine-chapbook-style anthology I was creating for her and the rest of my students at Camp O., an all-female detention center for minors. Although I had been teaching poetry workshops for incarcerated kids for a few years, I had never been assigned to a female camp. I'd begged for one—it just felt strange to not have the opportunity to connect with these young ladies—and finally, I'd been placed at one.

First day at the camp, I tell all the girls who want to participate to bring a chair over and make a circle. D., small and wiry, with a little moustache and her hair close-cropped and combed back in a pompadour, stays on the outskirts, lurking around the edges. I address her by the last name scrawled in Sharpie across her right side, just below the waist of her khakis, like all the other girls. "I would love for you to join us, D., but you're gonna have to sit down."

D. looks at me deadpan and says, "I can't sit that close to girls."

I convince her to come sit next to me, as I, well past eighteen, am technically no longer "a girl." Plus, I tell her I can tell already she is gonna write some amazing poetry, just based on her banter. And I am right. And it isn't just her, it is all of them.

I was floored by their brightness. The intellect, the hunger to absorb and to express. I pondered long and hard; why were these highly bright children in jail? Had the system failed them simply by not challenging them, not stimulating them?

The more I got to know these girls and their stories, the more I realized the harrowing truth. They weren't locked up because being smart got them in trouble; they were simply . . . still alive. Being smart had kept them alive. The fact that they were in jail meant that they were still alive. These were girls who were prostituting as young as thirteen, or mixed up with gangs, or having their lives swallowed by meth. They had made it this far; there was a chance for them. Their stories mattered.

The day of our last workshop, I brought D. her original artwork that we'd put on the cover of the Camp O. anthology. At the end of our workshop, D. came up to me and handed me the artwork, saying she wanted me to have it.

I was choked up on my walk to the car, and when I got in, I saw the message on the other side, which D. had folded in back, on purpose, so that I'd later discover it.

Not only was the letter a beautiful expression of gratitude, it thrilled me to no end to see her use of metaphor. So here I was, my heart breaking with joy and my own gratitude to her, simultaneously delighting in her descriptive imagery. I had gotten through to them!

Sharing the gift of expression through poetry can be an amazing experience. And I am sure I received more from them than I gave. That's true whether I am working with a group of kindergarteners or Alzheimer's patients or anybody in between. But I still put my own art first. I am still most at home speaking onstage. Teaching poetry workshops is my day job, highly intense yet highly gratifying.

I constantly strive to expand myself as an artist, to do whatever is scaring the crap out of me the most at any given time. I'm hard on myself sometimes, and once in a blue moon I'll really go on a self-indulgent bender. I wonder if my art has any significance, if anything could signify to myself that I am making a difference, and what the nature of success really is. And then I go and look at that letter hanging on my kitchen wall. And then I feel great because I know there is big work to do.

This world is bursting with silenced women and girls who have stories that need to be screamed, or whispered, or sang. All I was doing with the girls of Camp O. was tapping a vein that was rushing and thudding with lifeblood long before I showed up.

What matters most about standing up and performing poetry-as a woman is always so much bigger than the woman doing it at any given time. It's still a political act, still so threatening to the status quo. We get to own our sexuality, own our pain, our joy, our humor, our spirituality. When you have people sitting and listening to your words, you are the one receiving the blessing.

montaña de oro

montaña de oro *was written for the girls of Camp O. and for*
my dear friend and inspiration RAC, and for all of us who get
shredded by our own hearts sometimes.

we are the girls with the cheesegrater hearts
wet red nicks inflicted with each involuntary beat

with driveway spikes for teeth
piercing our lips
backing out every word uttered
with oedipal proportioned inevitability

we are the girls
with timebomb tongues
counting down until others
duck and cover
unable to contain the runaway train
of our freightweighted force of nature

with pocketfuls of shiny shards
with palmfuls of question marks
with bellyfuls of crackling chrysalis glittering

we are the girls
anointed in snake oil
we didn't covet

and now are we running
breathless
from screaming at joshua trees

in the rain
to make clean what was tainted
praying to be redeemed:
in/clemency

we are the girls exquisite in our comprehension
of *excruciate*
we spill love
we are leaking transmissions
from each duct

yet
for every breath we
ponder reversing

for every moment insurmountable

we are tenfold beholden grateful
awestruck
at the vast and delicate delectation
of this particular and precious and tenuous existence
we are bursting at the seams
innocent criminals
teeming with rubies

we make way

any helena will tell you
consider the orchid amputated and atrophying in glass
note the skinned bloodball of discarded mink:
it is the nature of our species
to destroy what it desires

to consume
to violate and take
what it deems beauty

we make way

we are the girls trapped in concrete
only knowing there is a snowglobe inside
a memory floating in pale grace

a place where the bottom of the sea
has heaved its own tectonics
and nudged up through the surface of the earth
in all its sedimentary splendor

it is triumph despite the unbearable gravity of being
we make way
with pocketfuls of shiny shards
with palmfuls of question marks
with bellyfuls of crackling chrysalis glistening

glittering

Titular

Now ...

Some of you might not believe this,
'cause its fucking pathetic,
but it's true.
And some of you might get confused
trying to understand
what kinda man
I have been known in the past to pursue—
—but—
I believe
there is a seed
of something wise,
some insight inside it,
if I can find it,
so try and
follow this through.

Before you have a chance to misconstruc the issue,
lemme just tell you
that this is a poem about
a conversation about ...

... boobs.

My boobs.

There's not much to discuss,
we're talkin' A cups,
but they're mine,

and I like 'em just fine.

My boobs!

Thank you.

So,
I'm sitting in a car with my ex,
(now we're just friends, I mean we broke up years ago,)
and he goes,
(mind you,
between crooning the lyrics of "just the way you are" by Billy
    Joel,)

he goes:
"ya know, I like your boobs better
when you're
on the pill and they're all swollen
from the horomones."

Allow me to state at this juncture
that the structure
of this story has not been altered one iota
to fill some quota
for the sake of poetry.
Seriously.
He actually said this shit to me
while singing
"just the way you are"
by Billy Joel.
And, in describing how he liked these titties to be,
he actually used the word "swollen."

This guy, who thinks he's all hippy,
all vegetarian granola earthy,
actually thinks it matters to me
how *he* prefers my titties to be,
and he is suggesting that I engorge them artificially
with the birth control pill
a.k.a. BCP
a.k.a. horomone therapy.
Excuse me?

Excuse me?

So I go,
"Listen, honey,
these titties don't belong to you, they belong to me!
And they are currently protruding from my body
exactly how my god intended them to be!
And—you know what?
These babies may be just A cups—
but these muthafuckas are *perky!*
And they will be, well past thirty!
They stand at attention
24-7 . . .

. . . wait, wait, hold up,
you know what?
That point is *moot,*
'cause my intention
is to mention
that your perception
of my worth physically
doesn't mean *shit* to me!

What?
Do I need more breast meat
like some mutant-deformo poultry
to be shipped to KFC?
Are you kidding me?
Umm . . . I am trusting
you don't want to go too deep into the size discussion,
let's not rush into
that one too fast,
because, uh, she who laughs last . . . "

. . . well, I'll leave the rest to your imagination.
The point of my poetic exploration
of this conversation
is me, venting my unending frustration,
in hopes of imparting at least a partial explanation
of the situation
I am facing due to the limitation
some guy is placing with his dissertation
on my current physical manifestation
and his recommendation
that through artificial fetal gestation
I trick these boobies into swollen and confused
pseudo
food
containers.

It makes my brain hurt just to consider it.

By the way—

Postscript:
While my boobies were all swollen
with the horomones of the BCP,
there was this constant ache
that made it too painful
to touch them,
let alone be playful with them.

And who's that fun for?

Nobody!
Not anybody!
Definitely not me!
Owww!

So, screw you, dude.

And screw your swollen titty fantasy.

My boobies,
my body,
my beauty.

Newsflash:

It's not for you, it's for me.

Me!

Nomy Lamm

Body
Sanctuary

I WAS BORN WITH WHAT DOCTORS CALL A "congenital birth defect" and what I call a little leg. They cut off my foot when I was three, and gave me a fake leg, which I wore strapped so tight around my hips I could barely feel myself. Inspired by my body-hating, eating-disordered father, I began dieting and starving myself at age five, which developed into long-term yo-yo dieting and massive weight fluctuation, until I finally gave up at seventeen and admitted that I was a fat person. I was trying so hard to learn how not to hate myself, but was still years away from being able to start dealing with sexual trauma, abandonment, and the horror of losing a part of my body at such a young age. When I was a teenager I would walk around the neighborhood at night with a baseball bat for protection, cursing the world for making shit so confusing, writing letters and diatribes in my head, trying to harness the consuming anger and sense of betrayal I felt.

I could feel it controlling me but I couldn't locate the actual feeling. I wasn't really myself; someone or something else was always controlling me. Consumed with loneliness and confusion, I didn't understand why I couldn't access my own power. Other people got to be themselves and things worked out for them; they got boyfriends and respect and friends who didn't end up ditching them. I didn't know how to fit into any of the available roles in the world, I didn't want to be a victim, and I wanted to talk about it but couldn't figure out where to start.

It was around this time that I first saw spoken word performed on a stage. Kathleen Hanna and Billie Rain were two local girls involved with starting the Riot Grrrl movement in Olympia, Washington—a network and support system for young feminists in the punk scene. I saw them perform at a fringe festival event at the Capitol Theater. I couldn't believe what they were doing was even possible—like the raging fits in their heads were suddenly scripted and out on the stage for everyone to see. Their words tore me open and inserted their perspectives into the righteous heart of my reality. They were able to take the fury I felt so familiar with—over sexism, abuse, body hatred, systematic oppression—and frame it as something real. They showed that these were issues that could be confronted and changed, that a girl revolution was possible and real and that I could be a part of it.

I wrote my first piece of spoken word for that same fringe festival event a year later. I approached the organizer at a diner and asked if I could perform—he hadn't seen my work (since I'd never done it before) but he said yes. I memorized my piece and stood on the same stage where I had performed musical theater as an adolescent. Performing in musicals was all about being good enough; I was happy to be onstage even if I had to hide my fake leg and couldn't get romantic leads because I was too fat. This was completely different. As a spoken word performer I could dramatize the crazy shit in my head, make it bigger than life instead of downplaying it, and that was what made it good. I talked about trying to feel beautiful and free and connected but always getting interrupted, either by external forces or by my own demons. I slapped my own face onstage, calling myself an ugly monster, then cradled and comforted myself saying it didn't have to be that way. Afterward several people told me I made them cry, and that felt like power to me—I made an impact.

I started being asked to perform more. I lined up my fake legs at a punk show and answered questions. I played a floor tom and sang and opened for Exene Cervenka and Lydia Lunch. I performed at the Omaha Riot Grrrl convention and a queer punk convention in San Francisco called Dirty Bird. To create my pieces, I would ask myself questions like *How do you feel? What are you avoiding? How is it connected to community? Activism? Oppression? What would you like to see happen?* I would spend a few days beforehand banging on my typewriter, practice five or ten times, and then go for it. I was a teenage fat girl with a lifelong disability, trying to come out as queer, still living in the same town I grew up in. There was a lot going on. I was lucky to have an outlet.

At twenty-three I was asked to go on my first national tour—an all-girl spoken word tour, Sister Spit's Ramblin' Road Show. The writers on that tour seemed so worldly to me, and I felt really lucky to be asked to get in the van with them and travel around the U.S.—to have a chance to be seen by so many different audiences and taken seriously as a writer and artist. On my way to meet up with them to start the tour I felt like a little kid going to summer camp. *What if I don't fit in? What if I can't handle it? What if my leg breaks? What if I get sick?* These questions weren't rhetorical: I often felt on the outside of social interactions, I never knew when some part on my leg might break, and I had a delicate immune system that got easily thrown by stress, and when I did get sick I often lost my voice for a week or more.

Of course shit happened, but it was still worth it. The other artists were nice—smart, deep, funny, hardworking, interested in me and my story, and willing to share theirs. I did get sick. I got heatstroke so bad that I got spots in my vision that lasted for weeks. In New Orleans I was so out of it that I chose to drink Gatorade out of my shoe rather than get up and go dump it out. I lost my voice and had my first migraine, a headache so bad I could feel it in my whole body. I remember sometimes crying in the van because I had sores from my prosthetic leg that made it painful to walk, and there wasn't anyone I felt comfortable with to help me deal with it.

Over time, after years of touring as a spoken word artist, lecturer, performance artist, workshop leader, and musician, I got better at it. I learned how to stop a sickness before it got to crisis levels. I learned how to make boundaries around socializing, and focus on creating circumstances crucial for delivering a quality performance—getting enough sleep, stretching, finding a meal with vegetables in it once in a while. I figured out how to cope and keep going regardless of obstacles. One time, in Denver, my leg broke in half on the way to sound check with my band, but we managed to find a prosthetist who frankensteined it back together and didn't charge us, and we still played the show that night.

I worked for a long time to create a life supported by my art, which meant touring, hustling, living without a reliable income. It felt like my calling. There may not have been a thousand people in each town interested in what I had to say, but there was always someone who was affected by my work. I wanted to help build a revolution, create spaces to hold stifled realities and release them into the realm of the known. I wanted to know about the world: what people go through, how they survive, what they're working on, how we connect. And of course I enjoyed feeling like a body image expert and a punk rock diva.

But after a while the excitement of being on the road was overshadowed by the act of taking care of myself, and knowing that I would crash once I got home. I felt strangled by the physical pain, dissociation, and psychic and emotional toll of pushing so hard, but the pain was preferable to numbness. What if I had convinced myself my feelings didn't matter and kept trying to fit into a world that couldn't hold me? I couldn't let my destiny fall into the hands of those who didn't understand it—I saw what happened to my grandma when she went crazy after years of avoiding her shit—electric shock and the loss of all personal agency. Touring and performing gave me a life that was mine, a community that could validate my perspective, a safety net in times of questioning.

But after the culmination of so many days of my own life that I didn't feel like I got to participate in, I decided to stop touring. Once I was back home, I realized I didn't know how to live unless the days were framed by plans for the next project or endeavor. I wanted to focus on my physical, emotional, and spiritual healing, and my relationships with the people I have long-term commitments to, as opposed to those with whom I had only fleeting connections. I also wanted to reinvent my artistic process, since the stage had usurped the place of that empty night with no expectations where creation usually begins. With all the touring, I stopped feeling like I had something to say, something that came from inside me and was dying to come out. It felt mechanical, like pushing and pushing from moment to moment, knowing I could do it, but no longer seeing the point.

Over the past few years my disability, combined with post-traumatic stress disorder from medical and other childhood traumas, has become harder to manage, forcing me to reevaluate my lifestyle choices. I still don't feel like I've written the piece that makes the world make sense. I still don't know if I've been heard. There's no magic word that will release it all; it's my life story, and it won't be told by pushing myself to my limits. It will be told in intimate spaces where I am safe and comfortable and feel at home. I have love. I have my body. Things I worried I could never find. Hours upon hours to go deep places inside myself without the need to protect and defend.

From this new clean slate, I can begin again from that same point where I started fifteen years ago. Alone, with no audience. I turn back to myself, the teenage girl who paced the neighborhood at night. *What were you trying to say?* She stares at me wide-eyed, startled at being addressed head-on.

"I want a real life."

My real life starts every morning, here in my bedroom, painted blue with pink accents, decorated with candles and gold frames, stuffed animals and porcelain dolls, cupcakes and crows, fake flowers and unicorns. My sanctuary, where all of me is real.

Book of Rules:
A Girl's Guide to Doing What
You're Told

Part 1.

you don't get to decide what you are
what happens is, you are nothing, and then you pop out
and the doctor says "boy" or else "girl" and that's that.
for the rest of your life you are trying to be "boy" or else "girl."

if you are very lucky, you will be called a man
and you will feel like a man and everyone else will think
you are a man and you will do all the things that real
men are supposed to do and you will score lots of chicks.
then you will be on top of the world, the pinnacle of success,
a very powerful person. this is a catch-22 though,
because if you are called a man and you feel like a man
and everyone thinks you are a man and you do all the things
that real men are supposed to do, then chances are
you are a fucking asshole and i hate you.

if you are called a woman and you feel like a woman
and everyone else thinks of you as a woman and you do all
     the things
that real women are supposed to do, then you are probably
     miserable.

if, like most people, you lie somewhere in between or beyond,
then you are also probably miserable.
(tough life.)

Part 2.

The First Thing You Have to Do if You Want to Be a Woman Is
    Be Pretty.

this is simple.
To be pretty, all you need is to fulfill at least three of these
    requirements:
(a) a great tan; (b) long legs (two of them); (c) blonde; (d) perky
    tits;
(e) button nose; (f) smooth skin; (g) slender waist; (h) stare
    dumbly;
(i) you are a doll; (j) a shimmery lipgloss; (k) a can of diet coke;
(l) a short skirt; (m) be on television

okay, count your points.
don't worry if you didn't quite make it
being pretty is all in the mind.
do this exercise:
every night before you go to sleep,
look in the mirror and say
"please god, you can take away all my friends and family,
make me into a moron,
send me to hell when i die, just please,
make me as beautiful as tori spelling."
if you don't want to look like tori spelling then too bad for you
because it doesn't work any other way.
when you wake up you will be pretty.

Part 3.

your body is a whole entire beautiful magical universe

of its own, exactly right and perfect.
i know that this is not what you have been taught, but it is
    The Truth.
how could anything so incredible ever be denigrated,
scoffed at, invaded, discounted, spat on, violated, ridiculed?
your body is magic.

what you are thinking now is:
why was i told to look at charts, diagrams, scales
and teen magazines to tell me what is wrong with me?
why wasn't i told to trust myself?
why did they make me feel like a horrifying ugly
pathetic puking loathsome monster,
if the truth is that i am magic?

as woman, you must learn to identify as an object.
you must learn to be objectified, made ugly and disgusting,
but not in a way that is powerful or frightening to them—
you will be made ugly in a putrid, rotting way.
your soul is the first to rot.
then your heart, then your mind, then your flesh . . .
whatever is left is the magical part that will live forever.
this is the part of you that is eternal.
your silicone implants.

There's always this feeling like something's missing

I wanna be a starving child so I can understand what loss
    feels like
I never lost anything!
(reach, grab, hold tight, put it inside
reach, grab, hold tight, put it inside)
I'm rich, and white, and pretty
I have a pink carpet and a ceiling fan, like a Barbie come to life
I'm a pretty princess, I don't know the smell and feel of
    rotting bones.
(That doesn't count.)

I call the police about the swastika written on my door
It's leftover conditioning from officer friendly
I hope for the illusion of protection
When I open my door the policeman looks me up and down
    suspiciously
He asks me three times what I do for a living and tells me
"maybe if you got this place cleaned up
people wouldn't feel like they could come in here and mess
    with things."

I'm a thing.
I dream I'm asleep and somebody came in my house
And covered the walls with het porn
Girls sucking cocks and nasty things about me
Dream cops, who are a part of me,
Come and take notes and tell me there's nothing wrong because
Nothing is stolen.

This is a nice little town.
They're really getting the place cleaned up!
Fancy restaurants on the docks and wine lofts and hair salons
Make the downtown core more shopper-friendly for shoppers
Who want to shop and not be stopped or bothered or deterred
From their shopping by homeless people or street punks
Who want change from them.
More parking! Less crazy people!
The police make sure that our walls stay white
And we don't have to smell people who haven't taken a bath.

Four thousand years ago my people (on my dad's side)
Were slaves in Egypt. As it is said.
Two hundred years ago my people (on my mom's side)
Were slaveholders in the American south.
I'm a direct descendant of Jefferson Davis.
I live here, in the northwest, on Squaxon land
And I don't remember learning about the Squaxon people in
    school
But I had a good education!
I eat food and wear clothes made by people I'll never know
    or see
It's easiest that way.
I've lived here as long as I can remember.

Driving down the freeway I hear a voice in my head say
"soon none of this will be here"
I'm afraid to believe what I know
I wanna be safe but there's no homeland,
It's all colonization
I'm in the middle of it
The heart of the grid

Andrea Gibson

Shaking It Off

WHEN I FIRST TOOK THE STAGE, SEVEN YEARS ago, at the Mercury Café in Denver, Colorado, it was as a twenty-four-year-old queer woman. I was so terrified that I was shaking and could barely keep my feet on the stage. Was it just stage fright? I felt more like a wild animal who, after escaping a predator's chase, will stand and shake until the trauma of the incident has been released from its body. As a woman, I felt as though I were shaking off the experience of being prey to a rapacious patriarchal culture, one that had traumatized me daily since childhood. Somehow, being on that stage, and voicing my distress for the first time, allowed me to stop running, and begin a kind of journey toward freedom. I felt as though my life were just beginning.

I quickly plunged into the local Denver slam poetry scene. I was so excited about the dynamism of the scene itself—the politics expressed, bold poets communicating radical ideas—that it took me some time to figure out what was largely lacking: women and women's voices.

At first I thought this disparity was specific to the Denver scene, but in 2000 I attended the National Poetry Slam in Providence, Rhode

Island, and realized that the majority of the poets taking the microphone there were also men. Men offered a variety of theories concerning the absence of women: the organizers and hosts of most slam events were male, the competition of the slam was intimidating, and my favorite, that spoken word was loud and women don't like to be loud. Women, on the other hand, saw it differently; while the slam scene was in many ways an incredibly liberal space, it still mirrored U.S. culture, a patriarchy that silenced women.

So, in that sea of Y chromosomes, I felt spotlighted, like a woman with a capital W. Every time I got onstage I wasn't just myself or a spoken word artist, but also a *woman getting onstage*. And certainly that was important. It was important to the scene, it was important to our culture in general, and it was especially important to the women in the audience.

Women continued to approach me after my performances that week, and thank me for the topics I was addressing, but what really hit me in the gut was how often they thanked me for just simply speaking. They'd say things like "I could never do that," and "I wish I could do that." It was as if one woman speaking onstage was a collective surfacing for us all. I couldn't think of anything more important than trying to help keep our heads above that water.

One male poet approached me after a performance and said, "I don't mean to be rude, but do you ever write about anything other than the struggles of women?" I replied, "I don't mean to be rude, but take your finger off the trigger and I'll stop." After all, who among us ever wanted to speak about these things? What little girl dreams of growing up to write "rape poems?" About violence? About the muffled voices of women worldwide?

Shortly after my experience at Nationals, I joined Vox Feminista, a passionate performance tribe of radical political women, ranging in age from sixteen to over fifty years old; many of the members had over twenty-five years of direct action experience in the feminist movement. Vox was a multimedia collective, writing and performing shows addressing a wide range of political issues. These powerful and motivated women urged me to become increasingly fearless in raising my feminist voice.

During these years, I was also politically influenced by my position as a preschool teacher. Little boys came to school ready to be big and loud, while the girls came to school in pink dresses, standing quietly behind their mothers. On all levels we excuse this difference: "Boys will be boys," we say. But what will the girls be? Whenever I heard a teacher tell a little girl to be quiet, I immediately felt angry. Already they were being silenced by the world. I wanted to put a microphone on the playground. I wanted to hand the girls megaphones and tell them to *wake up the neighbors!*

Inspired by the combination of my experiences within the male-dominated slam movement, with the women of Vox, and with teaching, I began touring around the country in 2003. I was hosted by university women's studies departments, organizers of GiRL FeSTs and Ladyfests, and Take Back the Night rallies. In light of these feminist events, I would primarily read poems that I had written from the perspective of a woman, addressing feminist issues, such as my poem "Blue Blanket," about sexual assault. In all of these spaces, I was welcomed as a woman.

Over the years, however, I began to question that term: "woman." Something inside of me was shifting. The poems I wrote began to feel increasingly genderless. And that realization led to some critical evaluation of my own gender identity. This year I wrote a poem called "Andrew," the first poem in which I out myself as gender-queer, as not fitting into the formal boxes of he/she, male/female, one-or-the-other options. At first, I was terrified to read it aloud. I was afraid that those in the straight community who had stretched to hear a queer voice would be pushed one step further. I didn't want them to stop listening. I was also afraid of being misunderstood by women and of being ostracized by the feminist or queer communities. If I did not identify "as a woman," per se, it might suggest to them that being a woman was not enough. After all, most of the people who have heard me perform assume that I'm a woman. It scares me to know that by releasing this honesty I might somehow break the sacred solidarity I feel with women in the spoken word scene and beyond.

I recently performed on the same stage where I first held the mic. I was still shaking. Honestly, I'm not sure I will ever stop. But I do know that the spoken word movement has helped me to begin to understand and dismantle my past self-exploration and to continue the work toward creating a current authentic self.

andrew

When I was a kid I would sometimes
Secretly call myself andrew
Would tug at the crotch of my pants the way
Only pubescent boys do
Ran around pounding on my bare chest like tarzan
It's not that I thought I'd grow up to be a man
I just never thought I'd grow up to be a woman either
From what I could tell neither of those categories
Seemed to fit me
But believe me, I knew from a very young age never to say
Hey dad, this adam or eve thing isn't really working for me
I mean, what about all the people in between?

In the third grade lynette lyons asked me
Where all of my barbies were
I lied and told her I got in trouble
So my mom took them away
I didn't dare say: barbie sucks, lynette!
And for that matter tommy, so does gi joe
I wanna grow into something none of us has ever seen before
And gender is just one of the ways
We're boxed in and labeled before we're ever able
To speak who we believe we are
Or who we dream we'll become
Like drumbeats forever changing their rhythm
I am living today as someone I had not yet become yesterday
And tonight I will borrow only pieces of who I am today
To carry with me to tomorrow
No I'm not gay
No I'm not straight

And I'm sure as hell not bisexual damnit
I am whoever I am when I am it
Loving whoever you are when the stars shine
And whoever you'll be when the sun rises
Yes, I like girls
Yes, I like boys
Yes, I like boys who like boys
I like girls who wear toys and girls who don't
Girls who don't call themselves girls
Crew cuts or curls or that really bad hair phase in between

I like steam rising from the body of a one-night stand
I like holding hands for three months before kissing
I like wishing your body was saturn
My body a thousand rings wrapped around you
You wanted to be a buddhist nun once
Last night you held my cervix between your fingers
I thanked gods I don't believe in for your changing

Tell me we'll be naming our children beautiful and nothing else
Tell barbie she can go now
Tell gi joe to put his gun down and find a boyfriend
Or a girlfriend
Of a girl/boyfriend
Fuck it, gi joe just needs a friend, y'all
I mean, he's plastic
And not even the kind of plastic that bends
I want to bend in a thousand directions
Like the sun does
Like love does
Like time stopped
So the hands of the clock could hold each other

And we held each other like I held these words
For too many years on the tip of my tongue
I am my mother's daughter
I am midnight's sun
You can find me on the moon
Waxing and waning
My heart full of petals
Every single one begging
Love me, love me, love me
Whoever I am
Whoever I become

Blue Blanket

still there are days
when there is no way
not even a chance
that I'd dare for even a second
glance at the reflection of my body in the mirror
and she knows why

like I know why she only cries
when she feels like she's about to lose control
she knows how much control is worth
knows what a woman can lose
when her power to move
is taken away
by a grip so thick with hate
it could clip the wings of god
leave the next eight generations of your blood shaking
and tonight something inside me is breaking
my heart beating so deep beneath the sheets of her pain
I could give every tear she's crying
a year a name
and a face I'd forever erase from her mind if I could

but how much closer to free would any of us be
if even a few of us forgot
what too many women in this world cannot
and I'm thinking
what the hell would you tell your daughter?
your someday daughter
when you'd have to hold her beautiful face
to the beat-up face of this place
that hasn't learned the meaning of

stop

what would you tell your daughter
of the womb raped empty
the eyes swollen shut
the gut too frightened to hold food
the thousands upon thousands of bodies used and abused
it was seven minutes of the worst kind of hell ... seven!
and she stopped believing in heaven
distrust became her law
fear her bible
the only chance of survival
don't trust any of them

bolt the doors to your home
iron gate your windows
walking to your car alone
get the key in the lock
please please please please open
like already you can feel
that five-fingered noose around your neck
two hundred pounds of hatred
digging graves into the sacred soil of your flesh

please please please please open
already you're choking for your breath
listening for the broken record of the defense
answer the question
answer the question
answer the question miss!

why am *I* on trial for this?

would you talk to your daughter
your sister your mother like this?
I am generations of daughters sisters mothers
our bodies battlefields
war grounds beneath the weapons of your brothers' hands
do you know they've found land mines
in broken women's souls?
black holes in the parts of their hearts
that once sang symphonies of creation
bright as the light on infinity's halo

she says
I remember the way love used to glow on my skin
before he made his way in
now every touch feels like a sin
that could crucify medusa, kali, oshun, mary
bury me in a blue blanket
so their god doesn't know i'm a girl
cut off my curls
I want peace when I'm dead

her friend knocks at the door
it's been three weeks
don't you think it's time you got out of bed

no
the ceiling fan still feels like his breath
I think I need just a couple more days of rest
please

bruises on her knees from praying to forget
she's heard stories of vietnam vets

who can still feel the tingling of their amputated limbs
she's wondering how many women are walking around this world
feeling the tingling of their amputated wings
remembering what it was to fly to sing

tonight she's not wondering
what she would tell her daughter
she knows what she would tell her daughter
she'd ask her, what gods do you believe in?
I'll build you a temple of mirrors so you can see them!

pick the brightest star you've ever wished on
I'll show you the light in you that made that wish come true!

tonight she's not asking you what you would tell your daughter
she's life deep in the hell, the slaughter
has already died a thousand deaths with every unsteady breath
a thousand graves in every pore of her flesh
and she knows the war's not over
knows there's bleeding to come
knows she's far from the only woman or girl
trusting this world no more than the hands
trust rusted barbed wire
she was whole before that night
believed in heaven before that night
and she's not the only one

she knows she won't be the only one
she's not asking what you're gonna tell your daughter
she asking what you're gonna teach

your son

Thea Hillman

My Longest
Relationship

MY SPOKEN WORD CAREER STARTED WITH SEX. NOT
with having it, but with talking and writing about it. A lot. My dorm-
mates at UC San Diego named me "Most Likely to Bring Up Sex in a
Conversation." When I transferred to UC Santa Cruz, I first wrote for
and then became one of the editors of an "intelligent erotica" zine called
Inciting Desire. Writing about sex gave me the opportunity to inves-
tigate and rehearse different sexual selves and scenarios. I explored,
on paper, my first sexual encounter with a woman, not to mention my
first S/M experience, before either had actually happened.

Editing an erotica magazine allowed me to peek in and then gain
access to the underground world of sex-positive activists and writers
in San Francisco. After graduation, I moved there, and I immediately
plunged into the scene and began reading at open mics around town.
I was featured at events such as WordFuck, Perverts Put Out, and
Poetry Above Paradise, and received invitations to contribute to mag-
azines and anthologies like *On Our Backs* and the *Noirotica* series.
Because I often read material with sexual content, I quickly became
pegged as a writer of erotica.

San Francisco in the 1990s was a hotbed of erotic writing, performance, filmmaking, and parties. I found an audience for my writing in San Francisco's sex-positive community. It was a huge relief, and it felt like coming home.

As I began actually having sex, the title "erotica writer" started to feel strange to me; I mean, most of the time I wasn't even writing sexy material, I was just writing about sex. Real sex: sex as part of dating, part of life, part of being human. People so seldom read frank accounts about sex that they often think anything with sex in it is designed to turn them on. I realized that what I loved about sex writing was its power to make people feel something intimate. The goal wasn't to turn people on, but rather to touch what was alive in them: shame, anger, passion, and indignation. I began writing about sex paired with violence, relationships, breakups, and politics.

Over the next several years, I applied and got into graduate school for creative writing. I tried my hand at poetry slams, toured the country performing with other authors and performers, and then published my first book, *Depending on the Light*. I began to see myself as a writer.

Right around that time, I also discovered an explanation for my fascination with sex. Through a random series of events, which included chatting with my neighbor, I learned that a medical condition I'd been treated for as a child and teenager was called intersexuality and that there were actually a whole bunch of people like me. By initially attending a queer activist conference in Atlanta, Georgia, and then seeking out additional support groups, I met other intersex people who were able to describe the effects of the medical treatment on their bodies, their sexual identities, and their sex lives. These stories provided me with a new perspective on the social repercussions of imbuing a different kind of body, and in particular having different genitals and sexual development. I began to reconsider my sometimes overly generous interest in talking about, writing about, and having sex. Just as I had explored my queerness and relationship with S/M culture, I now began pursuing my new understanding of my body through writing and performing.

In 1999, I came out publicly as intersex at a benefit performance event I produced called Intercourse: A Sex and Gender Recipe for Revolution. It was incredibly scary to come out to an audience filled with friends, family members, and hundreds of people I didn't know. But because so many people in the San Francisco queer community were already dealing with sex and gender issues, my show and my news were received with open arms. Sensing an evident thirst for trans and queer voices, I started producing more events addressing intersex and transgender lives. While intersex issues began gaining attention, mainly by being linked to the growing trans community, there remained a gap in the number of intersex performers, and as one of the few out intersex performers, I began to receive numerous invitations for local and national speaking engagements.

For a long time, I believed that my intersex political activism and my work as a writer and performer were fundamentally at odds with one another. I was convinced that I needed to know a particular audience and talk to them in the language and medium I assumed they would comprehend. I thought audiences would be bored if I incorporated ending the shame and secrecy around intersex surgeries into my spoken word performances. Likewise, I figured I needed to use speeches and more linear, less artistic forms of persuasion to urge academics, doctors, and activists to create a world free of shame, secrecy, and nonconsensual intersex surgeries.

But my reality repeatedly defied my assumptions; it turns out that I was wrong on both counts. Each world both expected and appreciated the delivery and content of the other. In all sorts of venues, from colleges to conferences to festivals, I was asked to "perform about intersex issues" and to "use creative writing and performance as an activist tool."

At an intersex organization fundraiser where I was asked to perform for a bunch of wealthy queer donors, I would have thought that speaking soberly from the heart would have been the best way for me to help raise money. However, it seemed that what truly compelled the donors was my performance, a show that graphically addressed genital surgery and relationships between parents, children, and surgeons. They were entertained, but more importantly they were drawn into my world via art, and thus were viscerally educated. I watched people watch me, enthralled. I could see the horror and pain cross their faces. Tears streamed and they didn't move to wipe them away. My performance at that fundraiser garnered me an invitation to perform the same piece at an international meeting of pediatric endocrinologists—the doctors who diagnose intersex children and offer treatment options to their parents.

When I was asked to speak at universities about intersex issues, students responded to the jargon-and-fact-filled discussions of sex and gender, but they also repeatedly requested performances from me. It has been my spoken word performance that has affected students most deeply and educated them in a more holistic way. I can hear it in the questions they ask me afterward; they are more nuanced and more compassionate than the questions following a more academic speech.

I suppose my one-dimensional expectations for my audiences ("academic" or "literary" or "activist") reflected similarly flat or narrow ideas about myself; in being surprised by my audiences time and time again, my view of myself has also expanded. The more I've performed work about my intersex experiences, the more I've gotten in touch with the parts of myself that have been rendered hurt or vulnerable around sex. I have realized that while it's true I'm pretty fearless about talking and writing about sex, that courage doesn't all come from a shame-free place, or even a celebration of pleasure. Much of my writing process has been about discovering the parts of me that were hidden, even from myself. It is through many supportive audiences that I have been able to see how much larger and accepting the world is than I ever could have known. And it is through these audiences that I have come to know myself as more complicated and layered than I could have imagined.

Starfucking Closer to Home or What Happens When You Reach for the Stars and They Reach Back

Names and genders have not been changed to protect the innocent. All similarity to persons real or imagined is just a big fucking coincidence.

Anybody can lust for Madonna or Keanu Reeves. I like a challenge with a more realistic payoff. I like grunge glamour, the local girls, the stars that shine out of grubby neighborhood bars. The one who stands in the shadows, smoking, who everybody knows, who knows everybody, who has fucked everyone. The musician, the writer, the artist, the activist, the one who everyone sees around on their bike, goes to see them read, recognizes their truck. The one whose name becomes the name, a syllable, even if it's something common, like Anne, because everyone knows which Anne you're talking about. If it wasn't her, there'd be qualifiers like "Little Anne" or "Anne who works at Harvest." The one with her name on fliers and bathroom walls. A name that draws crowds and raises eyebrows. And I don't even have to know any of this about her yet; I can tell it all by the way she stands.

The thing about fucking stars is it's a victory of sorts. Show up with a star and all of a sudden people who have met you nine times will remember your name. But you have to fuck them. Hanging around with them isn't enough. Being their friend isn't enough. You have to have gotten lost in their kiss, made them groan, gotten your fist in, watched their star face contort and strain from the orgasm you've given them. You have to do all this and know that you're getting what others want, and that by association, you're a little bit hotter and a little bit more powerful yourself. Sometimes you can even pass for a star, but deep inside you know you're not.

There are certain rules to abide by when you are fucking a star. First of all, only one of you can be a star. Two-star relationships are tricky. It's unhealthy, dare I say toxic, to have that much ego in one room. It's also confusing. Who wears the hanky and in which pocket? If I wear a hanky to your band's show, do you wear one to my reading? Which brings up interesting philosophical questions: Once you are a star, are you always a star? What if you're only a star in certain contexts? What about being a star just because you look like one? If no one recognizes you, are you a star?

Which brings me to my next point about stars. Looks are everything. Clothes are lifeblood. Grunge Star musts: a Rock for Choice T-shirt, leather pants, very large boots, latex anything. Hair is a very important part of the star statement, as well. It must be fucked with beyond all recognition.
Acceptable product for starhair includes:
1. Bleach
2. Wax
3. Acrylic paint
4. Lube
Conditioner is a definite no-no.

Stars are freaks. The first person I ever fisted was a boy who shared his poppers and his animal porn. Then there's the star who squirted so far when I fucked her that she basically watered her plants from across the room. Or the one who suffocated me and called me bitch and told me she was going to kill me. Or the one who sat on the ledge of her tub, when I was in it, pissing on me and bringing handfuls of piss to her mouth to drink, telling me lots of people do it.

And then there was fucking a whole band. I won a date with the band Frat Boy 51 by being on a dyke dating game. We were given $25 for the date, which was supposed to cover dinner or rollerskating, or whatever else, depending on how the night went. Two members of the band were friendly and pleasant on the date, but L, the only single one, was solely concerned with how we were all going to get fed on $25. We used the money for safe sex supplies. I consoled L by buying her a burrito.

I am constantly amazed by how insidious dyke stardom is. The best was me going to a reading by a locally famous dyke, B. She read this story about an affair she had, lambasting the whole cool-dyke S/M scene. Like a good writer should, she filled her story with lovely specifics of the affair, how the woman had been on the cover of a fetish magazine, how she let her dog fuck her leg, everything from how she smelled to how she fucked— everything except the girl's name. She didn't have to identify her; all the dykes in the audience were laughing in recognition and I got this creepy feeling that B was writing about the very person I happened to be dating just then, Q. In B's story the woman is really into knives and says, "I won't hurt you, I just want to scare you." And that's when I knew: Q had just used the exact same line on me a week earlier.

Strangely enough, some of the most enjoyable starfucking is finding out after the deed that the person lying next to you is a star. You get all the benefits with none of the annoying social-climber hangover. I call this phenomenon blind starfucking. Unlike traditional starfucking where usually the longer you fuck them, the less you like them, in blind starfucking, the longer you fuck them the more starstruck you become. Thus, blind starfucking is a high-risk activity that poses a very real threat to the serious starfucker—there is the potential to fall in love. In fact, I recently succumbed to a disabling bout of blind starfucking that has effectively ended my starfucking career.

I was at the end of a monthlong spoken word tour across the U.S. My traveling partner and I were thrilled to be performing at the quintessential dyke dive bar in the Lower East Side. One could even say that, for a minute, I was a star. Of course, I spotted her immediately: the lanky blonde with fucked-up hair and a ripped T-shirt, slouching in the corner. Only on the way to her apartment, and then in the following months, did I come to find out that she was the publisher of a fabulous underground zine. Then I found out she was friends with three of my favorite performance artists, that she knew my favorite poet, and that her name appeared in two of my most beloved books. Each new aspect of her glittery stardom rocked the foundations of my love-em-and-leave-em starfucker world. But then again, I shouldn't have been surprised. I could have guessed it all from the way she stands.

Miscarriage

I have been a mother many times, but I have never been
pregnant.

There was that one child, older than me. I picked her up in a
bar. Her apartment was small. She leaned back against her
headboard, smug and sexy. Her mouth went slack, eyes soft,
when she pulled down the straps of my bra. She made a noise I
didn't understand yet.

I am the mother she never had. There have been a few of us
in her life, makeshift mothers who fuck away the pain, or cry
trying.

It was only moments, but it was no longer just sexy. She buried
her head in my chest, arms around me. Surprised, I held her
close. *Something happened to this girl's mother,* my head told me.
This girl hasn't had a mother in a long time, my heart told me.

I am only thirty but I have been a mother to many girls. Oh my
sweet girls. I haven't saved a one of them yet.

I hold her. Tell her she's beautiful. Hold her and rock her when
she's hysterical, heaving sobs harder than any I've ever cried
and I wonder, how will I ever hold all those tears, how can I
teach her to let them go, that they are part of an ocean, lapping
a welcome shore? My mother's heart breaks for a baby that isn't
mine and for a child I know I'll have to give up.

I hold many of them longer than nine months. I have never
carried any of them to term. It's funny that miscarriage sounds

so much like marriage, but without the promise, the ring, or
a future.

Poor baby. She is older than me, but I see the beatings in her
young eyes housed in an ancient face. It's the pictures that kill
me, a knife twisting in my mothergut. She shows me pictures.
She hands me her hurt like a beloved headless doll, oblivious to
what it reveals, each year another scar. The baby eyes in the
pictures give way to a hard teenage grin and a glint that makes
me wince. Each year a pristine new dress hung off her, and the
pictures look progressively wronger than the year before, the
boy peeking out from the girl that's getting beaten to death
inside there, by her mother, by her.

I fall for the girl who takes refuge in her brother, in boyhood,
the girl who sees her survival in a square ass and flat chest.
Today my girls wear army fatigues, hooded sweatshirts, and
briefs. Their shoulders curve to hide their chests. They get
mistaken for boys on the street and in public bathrooms, but I
see the little girls, invisible to others, but unmistakable to me.
Bigger than me, they get sirred all the time, but they'll always
be my little girls.

I love their little boy bodies. I love their breasts. I put food on
the table, I hold down a job, I keep the house clean. Each time
I tell myself, this one, this'll be the one, I'm going to save this
one. And she lets me in. She lets me touch her. She lets me
in and I tell her I love her and I tell her how to keep a job, to
feed herself, to succeed in the world. I tell her *I believe in you,
you have something to offer the world, you have a chance.* But
motherless girls don't want to be nurtured, they want to be
mothered. And they'll do anything to not grow up, and not let

go. So with every word of encouragement, I cement her failure. With every hope, every word of support, I build the tower of expectation she's going to fall from. And then with every hurt and disappointment, I seal a future without me in it. For she is motherless, and I will necessarily lose her, she will necessarily grow up without me. I lose another baby. And maybe I will try again, when the bleeding resumes.

Ellyn Maybe

We All Leave Something

AS AN INCREDIBLY SHY KID GROWING UP IN Milwaukee, Wisconsin, I expressed myself through writing early. I scribbled stories about going to California and meeting Barry Manilow, and once a birthday poem for my crush, Paul Molitor of the Milwaukee Brewers. I never imagined reading this work aloud. I mean, I was too timid to order in restaurants or even to ask where the bathroom was. My shyness, in part, stemmed from having a hypercritical father (luckily my mother was loving and supportive), growing up in the proverbial dysfunctional family, and enduring classmates' criticism that I was "an unusual-looking girl."

Luckily, I had enough confidence not to let my introversion overwhelm my future potential. I knew that I needed to seek accepting spaces that made me feel deserving of my creative possibilities. So after one unhappy semester at Pierce College in Woodland Hills, California, and after having seen Woody Allen's *Manhattan* one too many times, I decided I belonged in New York City. Although I recognized that I was too frightened to try acting, I knew I would thrive in a creative environment, so I began contacting theatrical arts organizations and was accepted at the Actors Studio as a general apprentice. At twenty years old, I moved to New York City.

Poetry found me again shortly after moving to New York City. One day, while walking home from the Actors Studio, I saw a mannequin in a bookstore and his inner life came to me in stream-of-consciousness lines of poetry. I rushed to the Ninety-Second Street Y, where I was living, and recorded it. The folks at the Actors Studio had fixed up a prop typewriter for me and presented it as a gift. This is where I typed my first poems. I still treasure it.

From that point on, poems began to come to me in that sporadic form, urging me to convey my emotional landscape. I wrote very surreal, personal poems. But even though poetry allowed me to express myself, I was lonely.

In 1987, I moved back to California—after two and a half years in New York—and decided to pursue this organic poetic instinct. I sought community by attending workshops at the Santa Monica Community Center, which I'd heard about through other poets. To my surprise, both the teachers and the other students at these workshops were encouraging and enthusiastic about my work, recognizing that I had "some sort of natural gift."

And so, like my poetry in general, my first reading happened by chance, one year later, at Santa Monica's Midnight Special bookstore. I was attending an open reading in order to support some local writers whom I knew. They had nineteen readers and were pushing for twenty. A friend, who knew I wrote privately, grabbed and raised my hand and coaxed me gently to the stage. I was nervous, but I suppose at some level I craved to be a part of something larger than myself. I sensed it would be powerful to have people laughing with me, instead of at me. And I knew that my work was funny. As it turned out, the audience didn't just accept my shy and giggly nature, they even seemed to find it charming, and this gave me the courage to perform my work for the first time.

I began signing up at open mics as *ellyn (maybe I'll read)*, just in case I was too timid to follow through, but surprisingly, that never happened. Occasionally, I've encountered a loud environment, or an inattentive audience that made me especially nervous, but this has not been the norm. If it were the norm, I am sure I would have retired quickly! Nonetheless, something in my shy spirit had been irrevocably sparked. I even began to be candid about my fears in order to develop an authentic rapport with audiences.

I also began to locate kindred spirits through spoken word poetry—eccentric people equally passionate about their art and invested in developing artistic community. These people invited me to perform in venues like Bebop Records in Reseda, California (a record store, performance space, and art gallery where Henry Rollins, Victoria Williams, and Exene Cervenka, among others, have performed), and North Hollywood's Iguana Café (a wonderful bookstore and performance area). These were places where people like me found a home away from home, and created many an artistically magical late night.

One of the most personally thrilling evenings occurred while I was doing a reading at the Rose Café's Hyperpoets series. Michael Radford, the director *of Il Postino*, happened to be in the audience and asked the organizers about casting me in his film *Dancing at the Blue Iguana*. Since I was sulking about what I felt was an "off" reading that evening, I figured the organizers were just trying to cheer me up when they told me. Not so! I went on to perform in Radford's film and join the Screen Actors Guild. I even was randomly selected to be on the nominating committee for the SAG Awards.

My interest in film led me to Prague, where I went to film school for two years (2003–2005) at FAMU, the state film school. These years held some of the most prolific writing periods in my life. I wrote some poems about Prague itself, and how its architecture connected me to a different era, but much of that work was about the newly fertile emotional landscape I was nurturing abroad, away from my past. One of my poems, "Being an Artist," was turned into an interactive film in a workshop, and this collaboration nurtured my understanding about the connection between poetry and film.

I'm grateful to have audiences to listen to me, to offer encouragement. In a way, poetry is some tin can line that we talk through and hope somebody out there understands with some sense of clarity, and empathizes with, if we're lucky. There is a collective *Yep, I understand* in the way a crowd listens or laughs that has an eternal nurturing effect. It provides even the most solitary among us a sense of community.

As a little girl, I never thought I would have the courage to order in restaurants, let alone have the chance to eat in restaurants worldwide. But sometimes I wonder, if I hadn't been such a shy and eccentric girl, would I have met the words? Would they have even shown up? Sometimes I think that I was born with this internal language in my mouth, and if I had been "normal," it might have been chewing gum and bubbles I blew throughout my life, instead of words.

Poetry has blessed me with the sacred opportunity to meet the kinds of people I wish I'd met in high school—the outcasts, misfits, and shy kids who would transform into creative swans. Perhaps we needed to be spread around a little so we could spiritually reunite in our coffeehouses and used bookstore performance venues at a later time, singing songs for an alma mater we all knew by heart and wearing the school uniform like vowels. It strikes me that I am profoundly lucky to be an artist, and thus able to find these rare places, cropping up in nooks and crannies around the world.

It's like how a song plays through a noisy room and you always sense the rhythm, like the way people remember how to play "Chopsticks" on a piano even decades after they've last played it. Some things are just in us. It's like a life preserver worn on the inside. We preserve life, we archive the moments.

Poet has become a lifetime badge, an explorer badge, if you will.

I have found that some people are afraid of artists and our abundant sense of wonder. We seem like children to some. Perhaps that's why it's so hard to make a living; people treat us like kids on a lark, as hobbyists. Poets are on the low end of the marginalized arts, sitting between basket weavers and folksingers. Still, on my tax form, I write *poet*; while poetry has a high cost and lousy pay, for me claiming it is interchangeable with claiming "human." It's got a little bit of the magician's cape, mixed with the historian's monocle, the artist's easel, and the cinematographer's breath.

There are always ebbs and flows. I don't get up each day and write a poem, but each day I am ready for one to arrive. I don't know where in the world poetry will take me. I guess we're all a little like lighthouses in a turbulent world, trying to keep the boats from capsizing amid the stormy seas. Life and its serendipities certainly rock. I do know that they will lead me down more provocative roads, where I'll be sure to leave some syllables behind—like verbal choreography. We all leave something. Then we travel some more.

Ball and Chain Record Store

Someone came into the ball and chain
    record store I work at
    and said no bags
    a waste of plastic.

I said yes.
You must be a granola-eating, left-wing,
    dig-gothic, postmodernist, watch a lot
    of Billy Jack movies, Arlo Guthrie type.

He said yes.
I smiled.
I dream of Tom Waits fingerpainting
    lightbulbs on my holiday wreath
    and I'm Jewish, pretty weird huh?
    I celebrate Tiny Tim's birthday
    with a parade of dancing deadheads
    some who never sleep and some
    who never go to the bathroom.

His T-shirt said have you hugged
    a rainforest today?

I said I love the planet
    but it's unrequited love.

He told me babe, you're bringing me down.
When I was born my first word was ohmmm . . .

In kindergarten I organized the pacifists

to demand we didn't have to read
from Dick, Jane and Spot books.
Too generic.

I demanded we get American Indians
　　to talk about what's real.
And I gave them my nap mat
　　cause it's their land and
　　I gave them my peanut butter
　　and jelly sandwich cause
　　the buffalo have been murdered
　　and they need protein.

He blushed with passion and said
　　tell me you.

Well, the first fifteen years of my life
　　I thought Barry Manilow was a sex symbol.
Needless to say I got a sort of late start
　　at being at one with the cosmic heartbeat.

He gave me one of those looks
　　like I better get this girl
　　some Jack Kerouac books to read fast
　　before she suffers the confusion
　　of not knowing there's other existences
　　beside the banal.

I put my hands on my hips and squealed
　　I read *On the Road*
　　and the letters of Allen Ginsberg to Neal Cassady
　　and vice versa.

He said on Monday, Wednesday, and Saturday
    I'm a part-time Marxist.
He took out a beanie
put it on his head
and began to chant.

This definitely turned me on.
All of a sudden he began to sing
    the minimum wage workers' song
    "the walls are full of faces
    the minimalls are full of neon
    the bitter bite the hands that feed them
    the food is a mixture of bone, blood
    and snails
    man is a cannibal."

I said wow! you are the sort of guy
    who says right on and really means it.
You probably only drink the milk
    of socially conscious cows
    who voted Crosby, Stills, Nash and Young
    for president.

He screamed, oh chick, my life changed
    in 1962 when I realized the Constitution
    was written without women, blacks,
    Indians, and poor white men in mind.
That was not okay.

I became the Jackson Pollock of feminism.
I threw paint of outrage everywhere.
I was a man who identified

with Billie Holiday and Ernest Hemingway.
I was a traveler.

So what brings you into this
    San Fernando Valley air-conditioned
    intellectually malnourished record store
    with the exactlys?

We open exactly at 10:00
Close exactly at 10:00
No matter what our karma.
Damn it's so crass,
        you can't even rent *The Last Waltz* here.

He said I'm in a competitive mantra makers
        bowling league.
We have weavers, chess players,
        avant-garde stamp collectors
        and Hell's Angels.
        Inventors all.
We bowl whenever the fuck
        the spirit moves us.
With any luck we'll be playing the
        New Age/lawyers/used car salesman league
        again real soon.

Hippies and New Age people are like
        the difference between Bob Dylan and Bob Hope.

He smiled and said do you want to bowl?
We are definitely into strikes
        for the betterment of the worker.

We need someone who looks
    like she could walk into the woods
    and find incense without getting poison ivy.
You look like Van Morrison
    when you pout your lips.
You could be a part of the father, son and
    the holy ghost meshuganeh athletic league.
Besides I love you.

I started to weep.
    Tears of Bas Mitzvah cake
    and tears of being the last kid picked
    for field hockey in gym class.
Authentic tears.
Nobody ever said all that to me before.
I guess I kind of do have Van Morrison's mouth.
Why hadn't anybody ever noticed?

I said I love you.
But every free moment I moonlight at
    Hairy Krishna Organic Coiffures
    and Tea Salon.
We use
    no chemicals
    no dyes
    no sprays
    no combs
    no brushes
Hell, you look pretty much the same going out
    as going in.

He said what's a nice girl like you doing

living in a Republican administration
like this?

The manager of the record store comes over
    and says
You know the movie *Fahrenheit 451?*
Corporate has ordered us to burn it.
Get to it!
Don't give me your damn whimpering
    Joan of Arc eyes.
Lots of people would love to have your job.

I screamed pig! PIG!
You are giving barnyard animals a bad name.
Cops are Pigs!
Intolerants are Pigs!
Bigots are Pigs!
Everybody who does it and says
    they're just doing their job is a Pig!
Everybody who does it to someone else
    knows what they are.

This is my first day at the record store.
I guess if they want to have a quiet
    complacent yes sir type of employee
    they ought to ask different questions
    on the application.

Like do you conform?
Like do you care that this is stolen land?
Like do you believe in playlists?
Like do you believe in yourself?

Do you mind waking up alone
    rather than being beat up with fists?
Do you see the government is beating us up
      as bad as a knife in our elbows
      as bad as a slur in our ears
      as bad as a rape
      when we just wanted to be held.

And all they ask is
    can you work part-time?
    and what days can't you work?
    and they say whom do we contact
    in an emergency?

I said
    cause you need to ask that
    constitutes an emergency.

The hippie said my name is Hell's Bells
    but you can call me hope.
He said I dug you.
Now I dig your whole being.
It's strange,
No matter how many nights I wake up unhappy
    there is still a possibility of rising
    into a change so easily.
The outlaw lives in a world where
    when he sees a mirror he sees a hero.
And all heroes put their bellbottoms on
    one leg at a time.

Let's face it,

How can you trust money when
    there are politicians' faces printed on it.
Money is sexist.
The only woman on so-called American currency
    which is really Turtle Island to the Indians
      is Susan B. Anthony and they stopped making those real fast.

Good

Is money worth killing for?
Is money worth dying for?

I ran through the store singing
    about William Blake's eyebrows
    and Walt Whitman's bellybutton
    saying everything is alive
    and everything is sort of adorable.

I took paperclips and gave them
    to loving vegetarian families
    who needed someone.

I took the bathroom sink and gave it a hug.
I freed all the rubberbands!
And I said to all the plastic bags
    I will never burden you
    with films weighing you down,
    Perry Como cassettes,
    or even a piece of Jerry Garcia's beard.
Well maybe.

But I will never staple a bag
    for you brought love.

Most people tell me
    it was all the pop tarts I ate.
Some people tell me
    it was because I was a liar.
And I said I'm too honest
    to be anybody's best friend
But at times nobody believes
    this hippie ever even came by.
There are
    no lingering peace signs
    no incense
    no tea bags
    no fuck the fuckers pamphlets
Yet I still can't even believe
    Abbie Hoffman is dead.
So my strengths and pains are in my sense of wonder.

All I know is I don't believe in
    wearing sandals and argyle socks together.
And when I need it most, hope was here.
Change must not be too far behind.

Ellyn Maybe's Dream

Girl . . . poet belongs in 1960s . . . folksinger . . . very Nouvelle
Wave
Guy . . . part Edward G. Robinson . . . loves noir . . . pulp
novels . . . secretly musicals
Gargoyle . . . smart, funny, nice and extremely hip to music

The first two characters live in a tiny Midwestern town where
they meet at Just Like Tom Thumb's Blues Café at the open mic
hootenanny night.
The girl performs some Dylan poetry from *Tarantula* and the
guy sings "Desolation Row."
Bob Dylan is a huge life raft in their metaphoric desert, so
they quickly decide to write a musical about the characters in
Dylan's songs.

They love being different. At the very same time, it's something
that's caused emotional bruises and skinned knees since they
were kids.
Loneliness, precociousness, chance.

They decide to play pin the tail with a map and whatever
country, town or continent they land on, they'll go. While
blindfolded listening to spinning, whirling dervish songs, she
suddenly reached with her thumbtack wand and decided their
not so simple twist of fate.

He says, hey doll, where for art we headed?
She says, smiling and jumping up and down, we're going to
Prague.
He says, wow!

They are both ecstatic she picked some place farther than
Chattanooga or Dallas or Alabama or even Alaska.
She was grateful she was wearing heels that day so she
propelled the thumbtack into Central Europe.
In flats, she would have picked Michigan or some *M* place. She
had that knowledge.

She knew Allen Ginsberg had been the King of May in Prague.
She knew he had been kicked out too. That's what she wanted.
To be Queen and then to be returned to herself.

She related to Kafka, of course, like every Jewish outsider who
grew up on Woody Allen films and gefilte fish. She felt she'd
know Prague on sight like Salvador Dali some night got in her
eyes and the things she'd see . . . the melting Astronomical
Clock, the Vlatava with its lions and circuses underwater.

She saw illuminated manuscripts on her tongue when she
brushed her teeth. On every tooth she saw a saga, a hymn,
something from some other time. She saw the library burning
at Alexandria every night. She felt the books march into her
like a squadron of drowned soldiers asking to be saved.

She reads all the time. Never sleeping. She was the one who
would remember. The books traipsed into her room like she was
some call girl. At all hours, she'd have Dostoyevsky showing up
with a roulette wheel. She had Madame Bovary wet with oceans
knocking in the middle of the night. She saw a room full of bugs
as evidence that Kafka had slept there.

She saw the crazy ink, the melancholy topography of many
scribes.

Suddenly the girl woke up. She had a slightly sweaty forehead.
She told the guy I had this vivid dream, but somehow I forgot it.
I was reading or was I being read to?

When they got to Prague, it was so beautiful. The theaters
looked like cakes . . . gold icing, murals, horses, everything. She
never knew there could be so many kinds of cobblestones.

She had tried to learn Czech before coming to Prague. The first
word she learned was slunce meaning sun. The language came
intricate and quick out of the speakers' mouths. Everywhere
she went, she felt people were talking of philosophers,
musicians, and alchemy. Many were only making a bit of small
talk, but she imagined she was missing out not knowing.

On the other hand, she had spent so many years in America
knowing exactly what people were saying. This was not
necessarily an advantage. All the words with rough edges, all
the endless talk about reality TV, all the eternal chatter like
contemplation was nefarious or something.

The Charles Bridge was beautiful, but she didn't feel compelled
to linger there like others. It was the side street architecture
she felt deep in her marrow. It wasn't just the various styles
of architecture alone, but the sculpture, painting, sgraffito,
ornamentation and most of all the people in their stone state.
They were their own Prague . . . a nation of gargoyles. At
night you could hear their speeches, their music, their litany of
witness.

Others looked like angels. Some held up balconies, their
Veronas, the lovely soliloquies of this magical and haunted city.

Sometimes they held their bodies a certain way, practically
leaning into eternity.

One day she was singing all kinds of songs as she walked in the
night. She felt safe enough to enjoy the way-past-twilight hours
on certain streets. There she would sing and sing. "Tangled
Up in Blue," "Love Is a Four-Letter Word," and "Adelaide's
Lament."

Suddenly someone said Bob Dylan, Joan Baez and Frank
Loesser. She looked around and nobody seemed to be talking to
her or even looking her way. But she looked up and smiling at
her was a gargoyle wearing a T-shirt with a picture of *Starry
Starry Night.*

He winked, that's Van Gogh and a little bit Don McLean.
This was seriously unusual for anyone to get her references, let
alone a gargoyle.
She sang more songs, he knew all the lyrics too.
It was as though he was waiting for her to come to Prague and
walk down this street.
He looked more human than gargoyle like he had just jumped
into the building for her benefit, but he looked like he had been
restored.

He told her how he had once been a composer, a painter, a poet,
a baker, but a few credits short to be a candlestick maker. He
was one of the Renaissance people alive during the Renaissance
who nobody remembers anymore. He was in Shakespeare's
shadow. If not him, then somebody else. Shadows drove him
crazy . . . now he cast his own.

She listened to his psychology unfold and told him that the guy
she came with walked into a hospoda and walked out with a
girlfriend and now he was history, so to speak,
and here they had come all this way to write a musical about
the characters in Bob Dylan's songs.

She started to ask him if he had any time.

She caught herself. He said, look, I don't want a pity gig just
cause I've been on this building since 1348. I was here before
this building was. The building is here because of me. I used to
live in a tree, it can always be done, but sometimes this takes a
toll after one hundred years or so. Suddenly he started to talk
about directors and playwrights and penguins and where the
peanut butter and jelly sandwich was invented and he pulled a
dictionary from his rib.

She was awed by his mystery. His head, which was not bigger
or smaller than other heads, was full of this . . . while others it
seemed were full of that.

Tracie Morris

Ad-Libbing

IF YOU HAD TOLD ME, WHEN I STARTED
writing in my first little journal, that I'd be documenting the journey
of how my poetry led me to a tenure-track college professorship, I'd
have accused you of writing really bad fiction. And to tell the truth, if
I had known, when I first started writing, what an intense and down-
right weird life path poetry would send me on I probably wouldn't
have started writing and certainly wouldn't have started performing.
At the beginning of my career, however, I got so caught up in the
exciting poetry slam scene in New York that I wasn't thinking about
the deep waters in which I was starting to tread.

Until 1991, I had pretty much kept my poems to myself, with the
exception of publishing a couple of them in Hunter College's Black
student newspaper, *The Shield*. The first time I read poetry in front of
other people was at the dusky, funky club CBGB's, during an acoustic
musical evening that happened to include poetry. I was mind-numb-
ingly nervous; however, because it was a political event, challenging
the *first* Gulf War, I felt morally obligated to do it—moral outrage
can be a great motivator. From that night on, I dove into the "perfor-

mance poetry scene," primarily through the multimedia performance venue, the Nuyorican Poets Café.

The big advantage that I had over other writer-performers in the national scene, was that I was acutely aware that I had to understand poetry more, and work harder at developing my art form. I just knew there was more to it than writing down "thoughts." I recalled lots of the poets I'd enjoyed, from Dr. Seuss to Edgar Allen Poe, Langston Hughes to Maya Angelou and obviously Shakespeare. Even recorded poets and orators such as Oscar Brown Jr., Nikki Giovanni, Kahlil Gibran, and the original Last Poets conveyed that some "technique" was involved. At some level, I figured out that to be *really* good at anything, you had to study it. I may have liked my poems to a certain extent, but I knew I wasn't, pardon the pun, "well-versed" in poetry. While I confess that I did get some mileage out of my "charm," as well as from the novelty of doing hip-hop poetry as a woman—which was fairly new in poetry circles at the time—I really wanted to shine as a *writer.* After all, there were too many great writers in New York City for us to succeed based solely upon our personalities or presentations. One way I figured I'd learn more about writing was to go where writers went.

I eventually ended up at the Nuyorican to read at the open mic. What I didn't know at the time was that the open mic took place after something called a "slam," and the week after my first open mic, I found myself winning a slam competition. I had inadvertently become involved in a new "scene" and opened up a new path in my life.

A few of us "new" Nuyoricans began to gather and socialize with each other. There was a sense of this new energy, this new "vibe." We saw each other read and also met some of the more established poets in print and in person. (I even had the good fortune of reading before the great Gwendolyn Brooks at the Nuyorican.) The unevenness of some of our, and certainly my, efforts reached enough of a critical mass that we decided to work on our poems together.

I took a Nuyorican Poets Café workshop run by Steve Cannon, Miguel Algarin, and several other seasoned Nuyorican regulars. These were strong writers who had an extensive artistic range and were very good poetry critics. It was a dynamic scene: We critiqued each other's poems, incorporated multilingual phrases, and copied and stapled our work into a modest, short-lived underground poetry compilation called *The Fuse*. Through the Nuyorican scene, I also came across the chapbooks of other poets, like the great Bob Kaufman (the first experimental Black poet, and the first Black beat poet I read). Because the Café had a range of programming, I became acquainted with the natural interdisciplinary nature of poetry: work that incorporated not only hip-hop, but also theater, music, and a wide variety of other cultural and artistic forms. Although I was grounded in my nascent idea of poetry, the range of arts I was exposed to helped me to see poetry as infinitely fluid, applicable to everything. This understanding, as well as the range of popular poetic styles at the Café, encouraged me to experiment with my voice and follow the *poem's* lead, rather than what I thought I, as a poet, *should* be saying. As a "student" of the Café experience, I began to get increasingly clear about just how much more I needed to know in order to start making baby steps as a writer. I began to study poetry books, and thought more about poems that I'd read and heard and why I liked them. As a result, I was constantly reevaluating my own work. The intensity of live performance helped me to not only crystallize my rapport with an audience but also learn to pay attention to the on-the-spot editing I was doing when words were awkward as I read them aloud.

In 1993, I won the Nuyorican Grand Slam and decided to go on the road and compete in various national slams. I won the 1993 National Haiku Slam Championship on pure luck—I had no real haiku-writing knowledge at the time, but was a decent performer. My national exposure led to more gigs out of town and around the world, as a solo artist, with groups of Nuyorican poets, and later, with my own band.

As a touring performer, I was often asked to conduct workshops. I had no experience leading workshops and hadn't been exposed to any formal, academic workshops. I didn't have the luxury to go and study poetry in school; performing live was my *job*. So I basically had to wing it. I started to work on exercises, inspired by my simple research, that might be useful for the participants' future art practice. As I learned more about poetic form and technique through this "on the job" training, I began to feel more free to experiment with my page poems *and* my performance-based poetry, particularly my sound poems (sound-based experimental poetry) that are improvised.

My informal study began to clarify my relationship with the idea of "spoken word," and I began wondering about my own designation as a "spoken word" artist. I had to make a decision about the type of artist I would be, and my choice was eventually articulated at the 1993 national slam forum. I advocated that the scoring be skewed toward writing and away from performance. I was told that I was "imposing my aesthetics" on other people—which I suppose I was, because I've always seen myself as a writer first and a performer second. Ironically, it seemed as if the environment that had helped me blossom as a poet was beginning to impede my continuing growth. One of the "problems" that crystallized this quandary for me was the decreasing use of the term "poetry" and the increasing use of the term "spoken word."

"Spoken word," as a demarcation, sustains an ambiguity about poetry, at least in contemporary American society, especially for younger people. Poetry, no matter how "orally based" or experimental—and from *any* tradition(s)—is dependent upon certain historical and cultural references. The writer is then able to decide whether to reinforce the "craft" of these traditions or reject them. The generality of the phrase "spoken word" (a.k.a. "talking in public") includes poetry, stand-up comedy, preaching, dramatic monologues, storytelling, forensics, and even hawking jewelry on the streets of Greenwich Village. It really doesn't mean anything specific. "Poetry" gets lost in the breadth of the definition of "spoken word."

I'm not suggesting that there aren't real, and legitimate, reformations of uttered poetry that take performance into consideration. Women poets, poets of color, queer poets, and other marginalized people have often found the slam scene and other venues that focus on performance friendlier than mainstream poetry circles. In general, these forums are more democratic and less elitist. After all, anybody can get onstage and take a shot at an open mic, and often there are on-the-spot sign-up sheets at slams; there is no institutionally sanctioned programming or academic structure to exclude different voices and their messages. In fact, many women on the slam scene in New York have been actors, musicians, and other types of performers who write poetry to present material on their own terms, rather than accept the limited roles for women.

There is, though, a tangible, generation-specific tone and attitude in performance poetry that's influenced by urban culture, particularly hip-hop culture, as the predominant new wave of today's creative orality. There's nothing wrong with this, but *any* spoken creative work has text-based (even if it's not page-based) criteria for excellence, whether it's blues poetry, indigenous storytelling, orature, forensics/public speaking, preaching, acting, or rapping/rhyming. People whose oral *poetry* precedes (or doesn't include) formal writing must still have specifics to determine if the work is fine-tuned and effective. These specifics not only strengthen the poetry in the short term, but help to take the work forward.

"Spoken word" is a sales term, like "roll out" or "bottom line." "Oration" or even the admittedly awkward "performance utterance" are fairer terms, as they have less ambiguity. They clearly mean "speaking" but don't pretend to be poetry or storytelling. The emphasis isn't on a form of writing, and is, therefore, more honest. Judgments about their success is based on *how* the person is speaking. There are great orators out there, but they are not necessarily poets.

It's taken me some time to adjust to the profundity of accepting the term "poet." I am not making a judgment about people who choose *not* to see themselves as poets per se, but I do want to address something that is present but is unsaid, even in everyday life: When someone says they're a poet, they're tapping into a genre of art that has deep roots and holds a different cultural place for people. I can't tell you how many times—in elevators or taxis, at supermarkets, even at political events—when someone happens to ask me what I "do" and I say I'm a poet, the very next question is: "Are you published?" I don't take the question as an insult (most times), but rather as an indicator of how all people, even folks who don't read poetry at all, are expressing a respect for poetry that goes beyond the current popularity of our "spoken word" moment.

Those of us who consider ourselves poets and *also* perform have to convey strong performances, but we are also committing ourselves to writing, no matter what stage of aesthetic development we may be at or level of knowledge about poetry we may have. We go where the work takes us, irrespective of the popularity of a specific style of performance of the time. That's what makes "old" poems endure, and also what inspires us to write poems that build upon, or question, their established place. My journey from self-taught poet to graduate-level poetry professor first started in my journal and continued in those smoky New York clubs and cafés. And it was those venues that really gave me the perspective I needed to take poetry seriously, to work on the art and craft of it, to experiment, and to teach in the best way I can.

Apology to Pangea

I sent you
blue: silk on a peacock feathered eyelet
corona around pupil of the old
Dye with expensive tastes:
red—corpuscles of the dyers.
In the underbelly of current,
coffin canoes heavily down.

And here we be with capes, spandex and big hair
hieroglyphs spelling *superduper*, people who made atoms,
his momma, molecules before mourning.
Dat was me with the buck dance and chicken head.
Me, making Grits gris-gris, wif.
Can I say sorry for dem sweep yo feet, Mam?
Do I throw coarse salt over ma shoulder?

Las Brujitas

Bubble, bubble toil and double
Double dutch too much
Turning into trouble trouble

Tapping time 'til we just can't
Take it. Chanting rhymes
when the moments make it.

Blessed/cursed being double
handed. Leaning to the left
strands deftly commanded

Understudies be understanding
as brujitas switch, be turnin'
Dispel, casting, breaking curses

Through portal dimensions
simple phrases making
mischief not to be phased as

bracelets clink in synch
wink: a be mine phrase
invoking through games:

> "Tell me the name of your sweetheart"
> "*K-I-S-S-I-N-G*"—"*Miss Lucy had a baby*
> *a baby, a baby, Miss Lucy had a baby*—
>
> *and this is what she said! She said*—"
> "*. . . went downtown to get a stick a butta . . .*
> *saw James Brown sittin' in the gutta . . .*"

Even when Ali needed mo' machismo,
He put the dopes on a rope, then a butterfly float
flippant wrists let loose the noose's grip

like we girls did, reworking the kinetics
left turn, right turn, overhand aesthetics
feet thinking double time, meter reason

school's in season, flipping, flouncing
guild lilies dust cloud breezes.
Ten little drummers summon up

those stories. Speak in tongues
old souls got the blues—and browns
round white fronts, tassles flat down.

Keeping up the chatter from the patter in the 'pation
vibes 'verberate teeny-bop intimidation.
Tensile strength makin' a stand

Not still, we grand!
Significadence ain't random,
we clasp our hands in tandem.

Cristin O'Keefe Aptowicz

Working Luck

WANTING TO BE A WRITER IS EASY, THE FANTASY of a writer's life nearly irresistible. You are paid to create stories and poems whole cloth out of your sparkling, witty brain. Your books are published—of course!—to immediate acclaim, after which the money and awards roll in. You create your own working hours, spending your whole day in pajamas, merrily typing away whilst chugging coffee. Sure, you'll likely be dragged out of your house for a book signing, performance, or awards ceremony, and yes, there are the bags full of fan mail to be attended to, but other than that—your day is how you make it. Wonderful. Perfect. Heaven.

But if you are serious about pursuing this illustrious life, a nagging thought begins to penetrate the dream: *That all sounds lovely, but how do you get there?*

For the teenage me, having grown up in a working-class Philly neighborhood called Somerton, the answer was not at all obvious.

Somerton's Little League team was called the Somerton Spartans, and on the weekends, our baseball fields and soccer fields could be found clogged with police officers and construction workers, each cheering for one or several members of their ever-growing brood. The area's major points of attraction were the abandoned Byberry asylum, the Nilla wafer–scented Nabisco factory, and Franklin Mills, the world's largest outlet mall. Pursuing a career as a professional creative writer was not just a foreign concept to this community, it seemed almost archaic—an insane and unrealistic waste of money, talent, and life.

I was the last of three children born to an IRS agent mom and a wastewater-treatment-plant-managing dad. While my parents agreed that I was a funny kid and tolerated my passions for writing, they ultimately shared the community's sentiment about the idea of writing for a living.

Are you crazy? they'd ask. *How are you going to make money? Where are you going to live?*

And even as a mouthy sixteen-year-old, I'd be gobsmacked if I knew how to answer them. All of the books and articles I read on the lives of successful writers indicated that their career paths had hinged on a combination of talent, connections, and luck. Even if I had the talent, I certainly didn't have the connections, and there was no guarantee that I would have the luck.

But if there was anything I learned from my short tenure as a Somerton Spartan—other than that being beaned in the head with a softball could be used like a Get Out of Practice Free card—it was that you never let your opponents see you scared.

Gathering up my tenacity, I decided that if there was no clear path from my neighborhood to that fabled life as a "professional writer," then I was going to hack one myself.

The first time I felt that I might be on the right track was the summer before my senior year of high school, when I battled my way through the application process into an elite full-scholarship arts program called the Pennsylvania Governor's School for the Arts (PGSA). The five-week-long program, held on a college campus in Erie, featured arduous daily classes in your specific field of study, as well as in a chosen extracurricular art form.

In 1995, I was only one of nine fiction writers chosen, and needless to say, the experience was life-changing. Aside from the culture shock of leaving Somerton, I also experienced an absolutely idyllic summer for a writer. I did nothing but write, read, and write some more. I interacted with peers who shared the same passions and frustrations, and for the first time I met working writers—both my teachers and their invited guests—whose lives were not so dissimilar from the working-class existence I knew. They may have written books and published in *Poetry* magazine, but they also worked desk jobs to make ends meet and struggled every day to make time for their art. Suddenly, the writing existence seemed tangible. But every step forward I took in understanding what it took to be a writer brought up several more questions: *So to get a book deal, you need to get an agent. Okay. But wait . . . how do you do that? Oh, to get an agent you need to attract their attention by being published in magazines and journals first. Okay. But wait . . . how do you do that?* And so on and so on.

The more questions I asked these writers about their careers, the more they answered by asking me about my writing. Every time I would ask them if it was true that one needed connections "in the industry" to publish a book, they in turn would ask me if I had ever written a book, let alone one that I felt worthy of publication. If I asked a question about what made more strategic sense, pursuing a career in fiction or a career in nonfiction, they would respond with questions asking me about which genre I felt most passionate, to which genre I was more drawn, in which genre I was the most prolific.

As frustrated as I became with their responses, I began to realize the larger lesson they were teaching me: that there was something more important to creating a life as an artist than connections, more important than luck, and, heck, maybe even more important than talent. The most important aspect of making it as a writer was *work*.

You had to *work* to be a writer. You needed to write all the time. And you needed to read all the time. And you had to get comfortable with being uncomfortable: sending poems to places and being rejected, starting up a reading series and playing to near empty houses for weeks, buying every book a writer has to sell at his or her reading and then having him or her forget who you are ten minutes later. No matter what comes your way, the key is to stay focused and work, and work, and keep working.

This theory would be put to the test the following year, when I was accepted to NYU's Tisch School of the Arts as an undergrad and met Beau Sia. Beau Sia was known in our writing program for being the fast-talking, breakdancing Chinese American poet with an unshakeable confidence and a questionable work ethic. When we ended up in several classes together the next semester, Beau and I each started an unspoken campaign to be "the best writer in the class," with vastly different approaches.

I was the class workhorse, always first to arrive, always sitting in the front row, always prepared, my hand eager to pop into the air with the answer. Beau, on the other hand, was the brilliant slacker, always arriving late, sitting in the back, and asking for extensions on projects. But when he did show up with writing, it was envy-inducing genius. Fresh, free, and spontaneous, he approached the page with an absolute fearlessness. Needless to say, I hated him.

When I found out that he lived a double life—obnoxious college student by day and famous slam poet at night—my loathing for him only increased. *How was he already making a living as a writer?* I whined to myself. *How is that fair?*

As it turns out, he had just happened to be in the right place at the right time, joining the poetry slam scene just as it was preparing itself for a second cultural explosion. In a short matter of months, Beau was a subject for a documentary movie (*SlamNation*, 1998), had released a record (*Attack! Attack! Go!*, 1998), and had published a book (*A Night Without Armor II: The Revenge*, 1998).

When I was asked to interview Beau for our school's newspaper, I prepared all of my questions carefully. After peppering him with questions about his amazing recent run at success, I asked him point-blank: *But looking back at it now, don't you think your whole career is just based on luck?* And I remember his response to this day.

He said, *Of course, my whole career is based on luck. But that doesn't mean I wasn't prepared for that luck when it happened.*

And he was absolutely right. In my envy over his luck at stumbling into amazing opportunities, I had overlooked the fact that when those opportunities arose he had the work and talent to meet the challenge. In the decade or so since that fateful interview, Beau and I have competed with and against each other on numerous poetry slam teams, have cofounded a reading series (NYC-Urbana) that still exists today, and have grown to respect each other enormously as writers and as people. I still hold his philosophy of "preparing for luck" as one of my writing mantras and career tenets.

In the years since I graduated from NYU, I've been lucky enough to have a career in writing, with a few books under my belt and a community of writers I'm humbled to call my friends. My writing career by no means matches the "writing in your pajamas all day" fantasies I had when I was a teenager, but the fact that I can truthfully write the words "my writing career" makes me smile.

When I perform at high schools and colleges, I'm sometimes asked by a student what it takes to be a writer—*how do you do it?* Some of the kids will come from a background like mine and they'll have families or communities who are just as uncertain and skeptical as mine. And sometimes, I can see it in their eyes: They want to do it. They want to be writers. So I answer them honestly.

A writing career requires a lot of hard work, a lot of writing, and a lot of luck, I say. *The hard work helps you produce the writing, and trust me on this one, the hard work and the writing will produce that luck.*

Lit (Or to the Scientist Whom I'm Not Speaking to Anymore)

Don't say you didn't see this coming, Jason.

Don't say you didn't realize this would be my reaction
and that you never intended for me to get all worked
up,
because if that were true, then you are dumber
than Lenny from *Mice and Men*, blinder than Oedipus
and Tiresias put together and can feel less
than a Dalton Trumbo character.

You put the Dick in Dickens and the Boo in kowski
and are more Coward-ly then Noël.

But you don't understand any of these references,
do you, Jason? Because you "don't read."
You are a geology major and you once told me
that "scientists don't read popular literature,
Cristin, we have more important things to do."

Well, fuck you.

Be glad you don't read, Jason,
because maybe you won't understand this
as I scream it to you on your front lawn,
on Christmas Day, brandishing
three hypodermic needles, a ginsu knife
and a letter of permission
from Bret Easton Ellis.

Jason, you are more absurd than Ionesco.
You are more abstract than Joyce,
more inconsistent than Agatha Christie
and more Satanic than Rushdie's verses.

I can't believe I used to want to Sappho you, Jason.
I used to want to Pablo Neruda you,
to Anaïs Nin and Henry Miller you. I used to want
to be O for you, to blow for you in ways
that even Odysseus's sails couldn't handle.
But self-imposed illiteracy isn't a turn-on.

You used to make fun of me being a writer,
saying "Scientists cure diseases,
what do writers do?"

But of course, you wouldn't understand, Jason.
I mean, have you ever gotten an inner thirsting
for Zora Neale Hurston?
Or heard angels herald for you
to read F. Scott Fitzgerald?
Have you ever had a beat attack for Jack Kerouac?
The only Morrison you know is Jim, and you think
you're the noble one?

Go Plath yourself.

Your heart is so dark that even Joseph Conrad
couldn't see it, and it is so buried under bullshit
that even Poe's cops couldn't hear it.

Your mind is as empty as the libraries in *Fahrenheit 451.*

Your mind is as empty as Silas Marner's coffers.
Your mind is as empty as Huckleberry Finn's wallet.

And some people might say that this poem
is just a pretentious exercise
in seeing how many literary references
I can come up with.

And some people might complain that this poem is,
at its core, shallow, expressing the same emotion again,
and again, and again. I mean, how many times
can you articulate your contempt for Jason,
before the audience gets a little bored.

But you know what, Jason? Those people
would be wrong. Because this is not the poem
I am writing to express my hatred for you.

This poem is the poem I'm writing because
we aren't speaking, and it is making my heart hurt
so bad that sometimes I can't make it up off the floor.

And this is the poem I am writing instead of writing
the *I miss having breakfast with you* poem, instead
of the *Let's walk dogs in our old schoolyard
again* poem. Instead of the *How are you doing?* poem,
the *I miss you* poem, the *I wish I was making fun
of how much you like Garth Brooks while sitting
in front of your parents' house in your jeep* poem,
instead of the *Holidays are coming around and
you know what that means: SUICIDE!* poem.

I am writing this so that I can stop wanting to write
the *I could fall in love with you again so quickly*
if only you would say one more word to me poem.

But I am tired of loving you, Jason
'cause you don't love me right.

And if some pretentious-ass poem can stop me
from thinking about the way your laugh sounds,
about the way your skin feels in the rain,
about how I would rather be miserable with you
then happy with anyone else in the world.

If some pretentious-ass poem can do all that?

Then I am gone with the wind, I am on the road,
I have flown over the fucking cuckoo's nest,
I am gone, I am gone, I am gone.

I am.

All I'd Leave Behind

My mother has always been very laissez-faire about death.
When it's your time, it's your time, nothing you can do about it.
Sharing this philosophy has helped me through many mornings
in the city when everything seems too quiet. Like the morning

after the London bombings when the subways rattled empty
in what should have been the morning rush. My car held me
and five people all of whom were reading bibles. I thought,
if it's your time, it's your time and counted down my stops.

Living in New York City, it's too easy to imagine you'll die
in an act of violence just going to work. It's scary and a bit
egotistical, as if the site of me in business casual is enough to
press someone's small button. But you never know. And so

sometimes I think about what would be left behind, if I were
to evaporate into all that angry burning air: the letters left
unstamped, the half-finished poems, my wandering outlines.
The morning after the bombings I realized that my bag held

three books, all on the lives of serial killers, grim research
for a writing project, sure, but I admit I nearly laughed out loud
thinking about rescuers who would find me, how they'd look
in my bag and think, *Whoa, maybe this one was for the best!*

Gallows humor, I suppose, for a dark time. It's proof of what
I know to be true, this: My city still glitters despite it all.
All that hard-edged fearlessness, those worn bibles on laps,
the cups of coffee sipped from shaking hands. We still shine.

And if it's my time, it's my time, nothing I can do, but do
what I'm doing now, write what I write now, so that if
that dark day comes, the people at my office may smile
when they clean out my desk, its messy collection

of grant applications and dizzy comics, and maybe pause
to wonder at the post-it note still stuck in my drawer, a line
copied from a book of chinese love poems which reads:

Today at last a letter came,
and I've lit my lamp a hundred times
to read its words of love.

In Other Words

FOR AS LONG AS I CAN REMEMBER I HAVE STRUGGLED with finding a way to verbally express myself. As a kid, I panicked about communication. I was aware that my words and my thoughts didn't match up and that trying to explain anything was almost impossible. The worst possible question an adult could ask me was how I felt. I wanted to explode, as if someone were literally holding me down. I had little or no faith then that this would ever change. My lack of "socially sanctioned" interactions landed me in special education, which, believe me, was never very special. I remember wondering when I was going to learn "the other words," those that would help me to understand myself, the ones that no one I knew was using.

I grew up in Chicago, in a family where everyday life was filled with anxiety surrounding money, food, shelter, and emotional well-being. Often these elements were absent. The one important and consistent presence was that of my incredibly loving mother, an insanely strong woman, who worked her fingers and mind to the bone to provide for her kids. Alcoholism, depression, and poverty made her mission almost impossible. Our home was a gorgeous disaster, occasionally infused with the idea that anything was possible. Needless to say, education was very low on the priority list. I left school at fourteen, without basic reading or writing skills. In my home, *communication* meant anger, *feeling* meant getting wasted, and *art* only meant painting. It seemed clear to me that without an education, I would stay trapped in this cycle of frustrated expression, poverty, and abuse.

While roaming the streets of Chicago, usually high, I used to wander into galleries, coffeehouses, and clubs searching for meaning and art, and then I stumbled upon four women performers who would change my life forever: Kathleen Hanna at a Bikini Kill show, Lisa King at a poetry slam, Lynn Breedlove at a Tribe 8 homocore show, and Karen Finley performing at a benefit show for the Museum of Contemporary Art. I was in awe of these performers. Who were these women, and where the hell did they come from? They felt like a gift. This was my first introduction to feminism, my first sense that my own voice could be important, though I did not make that connection until much later.

I was twenty-one when I found those aforementioned "other words," language that existed outside of mainstream usage, the lexis for "outsiders." When I think about writing my first poem, I still can't tell if I was falling in love or if my heart was breaking. I only knew that the emotion was too much for my body to hold. That first poem dropped onto the paper from the back of my head; there was no editing, no structure, and no going back. The poem was completed and my life was different and, in a way, saved. Until that time, the only option for relief had come from drinking or shooting drugs.

Writing by no means rendered me clean—I have struggled with addiction for my entire life—but it did provide me one more outlet for relief. Two nights after writing that poem, I read at the Green Mill in Chicago. They asked me to come back the following week as a featured poet, and offered me a twenty-minute slot. Since I only had that one poem, I had some writing to do.

What followed was an extensive search for community, space, and education about art, culture, and emotional relief. Once I figured out that writing could be art, that other women shared some of my experiences and would thank me for writing what they couldn't say, that what I had been ashamed of all this time could be considered a strength, and that I had a voice that people responded to, I started to gain more faith in the idea that anything was possible.

For two years I performed in the male-dominated Chicago slam scene, where women were outnumbered and their work seemed like it could never be loud enough to make an impact. I wanted more, so I started a mixed-gendered gang of six poets in Chicago called Words to Swallow, poets with words to spit. It was my first attempt at creating community through art. Still, I was craving the company of queers. I needed to take the next step to find that home base.

In 1994, this search, along with yet another broken heart, led me to San Francisco, where I found the spoken word scene; unfortunately, it was just as male-dominated as in Chicago. I wanted to start an all-girl open mic and I already had a name for it: Sister Spit. A friend told me about this up-and-coming local writer named Michelle Tea who was funny, talented, and queer and was organizing readings in the city. We met over coffee at the Bearded Lady Café, and by the end of the conversation we had established a partnership as cohosts of this new open mic night. Sister Spit's first show was a week later. It felt like hope; it felt like a beginning.

Queer punk girls clearly were ready for this burgeoning art movement in San Francisco, and we were in the right place at the right time. Our first show was packed to capacity with girls leaning in from outside to hear the show. It was clear that this space was needed and desired. The idea took off. Girls who had never read their work out loud were hitting the stage, while those who were already writing found an amazing audience. It had a very righteous air to it. Righteousness was important at the time—we were demanding space.

Michelle and I were partners in crime for several years, bringing out countless incredible queer performers across the country, scraping together the money to tour by putting on local shows for months prior to our departure. I think that we inspired other queer communities to stand up and take personal and collective action. Those performances showed me that where there was pain there could be healing, where there was community there could be action, and where there was an idea there could be revolution. I needed to believe that I could confront personal and political injustice through my writing.

I often wonder where I would be without all the things that forced me to confront my life in different ways than my family did—art, this movement, my deep desire for creative justice. What if I fit in a little bit better with my family, if I weren't queer, if I weren't so angry about the injustices of women, and if I didn't struggle so loudly with addiction? I'm grateful that I discovered women, queers, and artists who have given me even more than a better life. They have given me faith—both in myself and in the power of community.

"God in You"

for kovick

There is something about living that nobody like god or
anybody ever showed me
My imagination whispers to me that this is our purpose in
life
To know why we live . . .
An understanding to be conquered then shared,
To save the minds of our friends and peers existing
desperately alone . . .
We spend our time in masses, praying to be removed from
painful moments, Together in drunk, in fuck, in noise, till
death do us fast enough.
Our sadness travels well in packs, without ever mentioning
it to each other.
Something bout life wont let me fear too much, a blessing,
a curse
Came at an early age, in a twisted-up package . . .
Wasn't anything too scary I came across that lived outside
my family
That is until true love came my way
There has always been something truly horrific and
romanticized about this great wish of humankind
A wish I've always thought for the naive and weak-minded
A protective few words I taught myself at a
young age . . .
I can be found telling myself mutable times on a daily basis,
That there is nothing worse than the letdown of love. . . .
Things change,
I've tripped over it, true and painful, a brutal accident,
A friend's embrace can sometimes feel like my last breath,

An unkind act, a murder of sorts.
I should tell you this feeling only comes in moments of pure
need . . .
And free of the act of sex, without the distractions of lust
and fluid . . .
The trueness of a friend,
I saw god in you.
I wanted to tell you that I got your message in the moment
of your passing.
Your eyes melted those packages I've spoken of for so long.
I can honestly say I've lived out your life's advice
to me . . .
Once or twice since you died . . .
A painful two moments.
A wish of love and being able to embrace it, to count on it,
and for me to exist in it . . . An enormous gift, that nobody
like god or anybody ever showed me.
And I believe that we all are god once or twice in our lives.
I heard god in a song today
She said keep your heart off your sleeve . . . and asked to be
cradled to sleep.
I found god in a friend of seven years on your afternoon of
relief and vodka,
Your painful departure.
She was right here all this time, along with so many
answers I claim to be searching for. A hand, a rest . . .
things that are underrated by my internal messages . . . my
broken record collection I've learned to like,
Worth the world to me and nothing to the world.
I'm speaking in code to you, poetry,
That nobody like god or any teacher could have showed me.
But you, looking back at you . . .

There were answers you were showing me all this time.
And a final lesson of true love, something you knew we
could both use.
A hand, a rest . . . your eyes,
And an embrace so full,
And not one ounce painful . . .

Say More

For me, for you

I want to run into the insane energy of love

I want to run into every wall the upper class puts up in our path

When you think you have nothing to say,

Stop and remember what you tell your friends

And when someone is trying to silence you,

Scream louder

I want to spit on sidewalks in front of men who take up way too
   much space

And when you're walking down the street, if you're a woman or
   a queer,

Take up more space

I think we should be making out more in front of people who are
   uncomfortable with it

And don't be afraid to be a punk-rock hippie

And don't be afraid to tell people how much you love them

If you are fortunate enough to have two working legs and a mind,

Run more

If you're not, demand that your people push you

Stop telling yourself you're dumb with nothing to say

And demand that your opinion be heard by your government

Remember that they work for us

If you're hurting, tell someone

If you can't afford your medication, demand that your state
   provide it for you

Remember that you're not the only one in the room right now
   who's panicking

And remember that health care in this country is a luxury, and
   that,

That is just simply wrong

Remember that you deserve clean needles if you need them

And remember that at some point in your life, you can live alive
and thrive without self-medicating

I want you to run into the idea that people think you're great,
and smart

And I want to be really cool to someone who's talking a bunch of
smack about me

Because that, that feels better

Remember it's not okay for anyone to physically, verbally or
mentally abuse you, anyone, not your friends, anyone, not
your girlfriend . . . anyone.

Listen to your family when they praise you

And tell them to fuck off when they are hurting you
intentionally

Remember that art is a very, very valid form of employment

Know that we couldn't survive without it

Remember right now you're thriving, you're thriving, you are
thriving.

Hey you know that sliding scale?

I don't always pay the bottom, and I'm poor.

Run to the stage when you're scared

Run to the kitchen when you're hungry

Stretch more, it feels good

When you hear someone say something fucked up to a young
girl on a bus,

stick up for her

And when you hear someone say something fucked up about
someone you care about,

stick up for them

Love can hurt, we'll live I swear

Know the power of positivity
And know that I really, really need you
And know that this,
This feels much, much better,
Than when I was writing it alone in my room

I want to run into the insane energy of love
I want to run into every wall
The upper class
Puts up in my path. . . .

I want you to run into the insane energy of love
I want you to run into every wall
The upper class
Puts up . . . in your path. . . .

Eileen Myles

In and Out of Spoken Word

WELL, LIKE ALL MOVEMENTS I'M THINKING SPOKEN word is something that many other things have flowed into. I would probably describe my own relationship to it starting in a poetry workshop in Harvard Yard in the '70s, where a woman in all black told us that she was influenced by the New York rock poet Patti Smith. I had never heard those two words, "rock" and "poet," put together like that before, and I went to New York a couple of years later anticipating something and I found it.

I did see Patti Smith perform in those early days, and I was mostly interested in her patter between songs and poems—a kind of vulnerability aimed at the audience, almost as if both were fans of *something else*, and she was inviting them to join in her enthusiasm about "it," and also the way she moved from poetry to song was part of it, and the poem just started to stutter and turn into rock 'n' roll. From then on it seemed to me that a poet couldn't be merely reading poetry— that the whole way she was up there counted. In my own poetry that meant something as simple as making a joke about the first poem always being a throwaway, and then bunching the poem up into a ball and throwing it away and hearing the audience laugh and knowing I had opened the room for myself through that act.

Around that same time and throughout the '80s, performance art reigned in New York. It seemed that poetry and punk rock ruled the '70s and merged into one another in many ways, but by the '80s you really couldn't utter the word *poetry* and be taken seriously, and instead everyone was into performance. I would watch Karen Finley or Spalding Gray perform and think, well, the delivery is radically different both in terms of pace and in terms of simply saying it or screaming rather than holding the poem and reading it. But calling it something else, not calling it poetry, seemed key because poetry seemed affiliated with a time that had now passed and along with it a whole style of living that asked for less than performance art. Performance art had ambition.

In terms of my own relationship to all this, I'd say I simply took it in. I spent about ten years memorizing my work, seeing how it felt to face the audience, emoting my poem, and for a poetry audience this was frequently uncomfortable-making because just like a poet wasn't used to looking at them, they weren't used to being looked at either.

From reciting the poem I got at a new sense of how alive a poem was in my body, that the language was in my muscles and everything and it came from there too—and that it was impossible to remember a bad or extra line, and that memorization is a great editor. And also that poems you memorize change constantly from the printed version. In tiny ways, but it indicates to me that any poem that you continue to spend time with will continue to fit to your body and change as you change. I think memorizing and performing poems gave me a sense of how songlike poems are, that they want to be sung, breathed.

I felt that I actually wanted something different from a poem than memorization, and that memorization actually caused me to write less, and I love writing new poems. Also I noticed that I stayed pretty still when I recited, and when I spoke I normally moved quite a lot. So the next phase of performing for me was to improvise talking in front of an audience. And I would generally tailor it to the group I knew I would face—for instance, once for a WOW (Women's One World) tenth anniversary performance at PS122, I told a story about getting raped. Again I saw the faces in front of me become somewhat tense and angry in some cases. But even then, improvising felt better to me, or more where I wanted to go, than reciting had. Talking to the people in front of me felt truly political, and I had been prepared for this by a lot of group work I had done around getting off of drugs and alcohol and realizing that if people are talking about anything important enough they forget themselves and are really interesting to watch and listen to when they forget to think about themselves.

During this time I started to find a multitude of uses of my new talking skills. Teaching poetry was one of them. I still teach, and it's supported me when writing didn't. I used to be afraid of teaching because I thought it meant you "weren't" something if you taught, but at later points in your career teaching allows you to go deeper with the things you are thinking about, and you generally don't have a scene by then and you are able to tell people younger than yourself what you are currently thinking about writing. It's a gift, and one you get paid for.

But the most prominent result of spoken word at this time (which is the early '90s in this telling) was running for president in 1992. I was doing the improvising thing and didn't know where it was going, but realized that political candidates pretty much fill the airwaves for one to two years and that I could colonize some of that space for my people, and so I did that all over the country, and the world to some extent, which I continued until 1992. Spoken word by now had morphed into fiction for me. I began writing novels, which seemed like a kind of long, ingrown telling. Maybe running for president was too far out for me and I needed to go way "in" for a long stretch, which is something you get from a novel. You can "talk" for, say, five years, then you publish it and tour it around for two. So, seven years from its inception. That's a long performance, a novel.

Now it's all mixed. I mean now in my writing, performing, speaking career. My feeling is that if you've performed your work consciously for any period of time, then you are always performing. Same with running for president. You'll never stop being a presidential candidate. I still think the patter between my poems is often the best part of the reading. But the poems feel very sung to me now, and I think if I'm on a panel, talking about this or that, I am actually still doing the improvising that liberated me from recitation in the '80s and early '90s. And I keep writing poems that I think might be nice recited, and I hope to do that on my next book tour (poetry), which is coming up. I'm probably also thinking I'd like to create some kind of show out of a reading, like an *evening with* kind of thing, kind of formal, but changing every night. I'm really interested in recording, too, which I've never put up front. Though I will.

Also—and I'm thinking here about the book in which this statement of mine will land—I mean in terms of *women* doing this kind of work, well, I'm increasingly less interested in having to discuss my work as being "female." I feel like having to talk about my work or my being in that way makes me feel like I'm still coming through the door, when in fact I'm way in, I mean into the middle (and past) of my life and performing, so perhaps I'd prefer to be a man at this moment and feel this question, the "woman" question, has already been answered, elsewhere.

An American Poem

I was born in Boston in
1949. I never wanted
this fact to be known, in
fact I've spent the better
half of my adult life
trying to sweep my early
years under the carpet
and have a life that
was clearly just mine
and independent of
the historic fate of
my family. Can you
imagine what it was
like to be one of them,
to be built like them,
to talk like them
to have the benefits
of being born into such
a wealthy and powerful
American family. I went
to the best schools,
had all kinds of tutors
and trainers, travelled
widely, met the famous,
the controversial, and
the not-so-admirable
and I knew from
a very early age that
if there were ever any
possibility of escaping

the collective fate of this famous
Boston family I would
take that route and
I have. I hopped
on an Amtrak to New
York in the early
'70s and I guess
you could say
my hidden years
began. I thought
Well I'll be a poet.
What could be more
foolish and obscure.
I became a lesbian.
Every woman in my
family looks like
a dyke but it's really
stepping off the flag
when you become one.
While holding this ignominious
pose I have seen and
I have learned and
I am beginning to think
there is no escaping
history. A woman I
am currently having
an affair with said
you know you look
like a Kennedy. I felt
the blood rising in my
cheeks. People have
always laughed at

my Boston accent
confusing "large" for
"lodge," "party"
for "potty." But
when this unsuspecting
woman invoked for
the first time my
family name
I knew the jig
was up. Yes, I am,
I am a Kennedy.
My attempts to remain
obscure have not served
me well. Starting as
a humble poet I
quickly climbed to the
top of my profession
assuming a position of
leadership and honor.
It is right that a
woman should call
me out now. Yes,
I am a Kennedy.
And I await
your orders.
You are the New Americans.
The homeless are wandering
the streets of our nation's
greatest city. Homeless
men with AIDS are among
them. Is that right?
That there are no homes

for the homeless, that
there is no free medical
help for these men. And women.
That they get the message
—as they are dying—
that this is not their home?
And how are your
teeth today? Can
you afford to fix them?
How high is your rent?
If art is the highest
and most honest form
of communication of
our times and the young
artist is no longer able
to move here and speak
to her time . . . Yes, I could,
but that was fifteen years ago
and remember—as I must
I am a Kennedy.
Shouldn't we all be Kennedys?
This nation's greatest city
is home of the business-
man and home of the
rich artist. People with
beautiful teeth who are not
on the streets. What shall
we do about this dilemma?
Listen, I have been educated.
I have learned about Western
Civilization. Do you know
what the message of Western
Civilization is? I am alone.

Am I alone tonight?
I don't think so. Am I
the only one with bleeding gums
tonight. Am I the only
homosexual in this room
tonight. Am I the only
homosexual in this room
tonight. Am I the only
one whose friends have
died, are dying now.
And my art can't
be supported until it is
gigantic, bigger than
everyone else's, confirming
the audience's feeling that they are
alone. That they alone
are good, deserved
to buy the tickets
to see this Art.
Are working,
are healthy, should
survive, and are
normal. Are you
normal tonight? Everyone
here, are we all normal.
It is not normal for
me to be a Kennedy.
But I am no longer
ashamed, no longer
alone. I am not
alone tonight because
we are all Kennedys.
And I am your President.

Merk

There's too much light in my life
there that's better
the street people recommend
don't let your brother fling his
leg & arm around you like
you're his girlfriend. Humpin your
kneecap, stuff like that
the vilest smell of all tonight
is human food
it's November when the moons switch
places. White is bad
black is good. Food stinks.
Carrying their buckets of soup
to their stupid abodes
furs around their necks, beasts.
What do humans eat? Dogs, more or less.
Ripping fruit from the vine
snipping the crop
maybe vegetables would like to
let their baby be too
and never never eat the human
that is a crime. Push my machine
to see what nazi called
me. Go out and kill her with my teeth
I'm a bored outsider
the season is cold
everywhere doors are slamming
and look who you're in the
room with now. Someone to eat
I hope. Think of Goethe

Werner Goethe with this leg
flung up on a rock in
Italy. Take a bite
of that fat calf.
He's like a big posing gondola
what's the idea
every poet I know is a partial artist
the lucky ones are dead
naturally incomplete
but look at everyone you think of
hanging on to some misapprehended
particle of modernism, all
plumped up with pillows
there's nothing
after a modern idea
for poets. All they do
is think & eat. If you call
that making something
& I don't, I don't call that art.
We must offer ourselves
up as food or eat
someone. If you can make there
be less of someone else
or someone could take
a bite out of you
then you could join in the incompletion
or excess of your age
I'm sick of seeing dunces celebrated
that's the job
someone that looks
good in ribbons
someone surrounded

by their editor's
arms. Love object
of a lesbian
but not being
one. Particle board
potential screen
play, plastic
hair, translates
well, millions will hold
you on the train
bite me now
bite me forever
in your two strong

o eat me read
me something

I am the daughter
of substitution
my father fell
instead of the dresser
it was the family
joke, his death
not a suicide
but a joke

how could I accidentally
get eaten
slipping into your
sandwich or refrigerator
sort of a dick
that crawls

up from the bottom of your
ice cream cone

it's too late for some
of us, but for others
it's never late
enough. Tonight
when they moved
the lights and everything
looked completely
horrible for
a change
I was looking
for sympathy
and you asked
me for the menu

I have escaped the unseemly
death of the alcoholic
yet I keep my ear so close
to the ground & I know
what they know
I begin to smell
funny, another fate

it was as if I was falling
last night
but I imagined
myself a bit
of food
& I was safe
in your mouth

& I would
never die

it is the legacy
of my family
to change in the air
& smash as
something
new

not a woman
but a chair
full of flowers

not a poet
but a donut
or a myth

go up there
& get me a cracker
darling
& proudly
I walked

Lynne Procope

Taco Shop
Tales

I FIRST READ MY POETRY OUT LOUD IN 1996, AT either a taco shop's open mic on West Nineteenth Street or a delicatessen on Fifth Avenue. What I remember most clearly is that the place was packed with people who cared a lot less about poetry than about eating all night long. My hands shook so badly that I could barely see the page, and my voice was soft, not just low in volume but mellifluous, with none of the concrete landing places of conviction.

When I reflect upon that time, I realize that I didn't believe anyone, including myself, wanted to hear what I was thinking or writing about—whether the topic was my fear of living in a new country, my concerns about other people's reaction to my body, my powerful anger about living in a racist society, or simply the brilliant miracle of coming into my own as a woman in a city that encouraged freedoms I hadn't imagined before. I also hadn't yet developed a sense of the written or spoken verse, not of its syntax and certainly not of its truth. I tended to end each line on the high, inquisitive note that so often demarcates the pattern of speech adopted by young women. I would continue to witness that insecure voice in the work of young, and even mature, women poets throughout my decade of performing.

Fortunately, by early 1997, I'd mastered "the shakes," primarily by closely observing my male poetry peers take to the stage with much more surety than I could imagine. Through them, I learned to perform my work with the idea that it deserved the space it was beginning to claim. My conclusion was that, because of whatever cultural constraints women had endured—social distress, trauma, harassment, abuse, denial of our inner voices or our rights to speak freely—we often carried a far greater challenge to the stage than just the poem. All of this often managed to supersede the pure pleasure of the art. Where our male counterparts could approach the mic as if it were the only noteworthy object in the room, we women would primp, adjust our clothing, lower our sight lines, attempt "cuteness" of one sort of another, or shut down and read through our hair. With each line, we would ask permission to speak; we'd assume with the high note at the end of each line that we were wrong to think as we did, or even to write at all.

At that time, I hadn't yet heard or read Daphne Gottlieb or Patricia Smith. I couldn't have imagined the up-and-coming Rachel McKibbens or Celena Glenn. The community of women poets that would come to me in the approaching years hadn't arrived. As a young woman, I spent a lot of time questioning my poems, indeed doubting whether I should write at all. I tossed out the first hundred poems I ever wrote without the slightest of hesitations. I know now that I imagined I was too young, black, immigrant, uneducated, and harmed—or unharmed—to write what I was writing, to question the status quo in verse. Furthermore, when I took the stage, I couldn't believe that the audience wouldn't hear my ignorance, my immense vulnerability. Also, I was never dressed like I imagined a poet would be, and didn't that expose me further? Didn't it stand to reason that the other poets in the room would see that I was a fraud, masquerading as a poet, when everyone knew that I didn't look the part? Wasn't everyone staring at my breasts, my legs, my mouth?

All of this took shape in my readings. I could craft a lovely line, full of a sense of its own power, then just as quickly dissipate that strength by racing through it in a soft, high voice begging permission for the line to exist.

After several months of taco shop readings and visiting open mics where I felt that I couldn't fit in because of either my style of poetry, my race, or my gender, I *was* finally sure that I wanted to push my boundaries. It was becoming evident to me that the self-satisfied readings from my journal, the disclaimer to the poem, and the work that I could easily discard weren't enough. I wanted to find a way to commit to the poems, to push into them more deeply and learn something new from them. At the Nuyorican Poets Café, Dot Antoniades was hosting the Wednesday night open slam, an exciting place for the poetic experiment. A good friend suggested that I try it out as an alternative to reading in taco shops. At the time, I believed that I went because I needed to read somewhere that didn't offer food as a draw. I know now that I went because I needed to be scared out of my mind and to see if I could navigate my fear in a challenging and unfamiliar space.

I was, and have always been, a working woman/poet. I have a full-time career—not a temp job I can opt out of in favor of art, but a career I've invested in building. I'd developed a habit of waking up to write before work several times each week. However, I'd come to the realization that after years of writing with no real expectation of calling myself an artist, I was at a point where if I didn't find something else in poetry I would easily walk away from it or treat it as simply a hobby. It was a fight-or-flight awakening that pushed me to do something more challenging with my writing.

I had a couple of new poems I wanted to read out loud, part of what I now realize was a small manuscript of poems I'd been building up. One was an erotic piece, which I then adapted and echoed in a second poem about rape, in response to an experience with an old lover who'd tried to muscle me into having sex with him a couple of years after an amicable split-up. I wanted to work on the two as companion pieces. The sex poem was a deliberate conjuring of time spent with a man who'd until that point been something special. The second poem, establishing a poetic discourse between the two, was about making a lover understand that someone who's always had your permission can become your rapist if they take that consent for granted. The second poem was, for my work back then, a delicate experiment, since I wanted to mirror the first sentiment closely, using as much of the original language as possible and keeping the structure, meter, and syllable count intact. I thought it would be good to hear them out loud, as an experiment in responding to my own work, and to try them in front of a new audience. I imagined that I might learn a couple of things about the twin poems. What ultimately happened changed my life.

The Nuyorican Poets Café at that time was an eclectic venue. A graduating cadre of poets, such as Crystal Williams, Cheryl Boyce Taylor, Beau Sia, and Willie Perdomo, had just taken their first full steps into the wider poetic landscape. It was still full of the freshest new voices and its slam scene was led by legendary slam master Keith Roach and by Dot, the nineteen-year-old ingenue goddess of all things strange and wonderful on the scene. Dot remains one of the freshest artistic voices that I've ever heard, and I miss hearing her poems; I'll be eternally grateful for the welcome that she offered at the Café.

On any given Wednesday night, up to thirty writers would sign up for the open slam, ranging from beat poets, actors, upcoming MCs, neo-academics, practiced performance artists, college students, and closet poets like me. The top ten poets would make it into the final round. When I performed in the first round and my hands shook, I thought, *Don't let them see you sweat. If they're listening to you they might not catch the tremors.* Despite imagining that an erotic poem should sound sweet and soft, I amped up the volume, intensity, and demand in my voice. I made eye contact with an audience of strangers and dared them to care about what I was saying. Ultimately I scored ten (out of ten) for each of my three poems and won the night. But more importantly—and this is a large part of why slam continues to be my favorite sport—I was suddenly doing something that I simultaneously loved and was terrified by.

That first moment at that slam performance allowed me to be exquisitely naked in a way that I hadn't been before. At the same time, a room full of strangers murmured back to me, *You go girl, bring it, damn, that's right!* For the first time I believed I might be in the right place at the right time. My next steps weren't yet clear, but something in the amazing democracy of the audience's response, in the diversity of the faces staring back at me, in the challenge of stepping up to respond to the dialogue that my fellow writers were throwing out on the Lower East Side, told me I'd found something I could commit to, a type of poetry that owned a conscience and a beauty that would continue to surprise me for years to come.

any closer to home and my heart will burst 2

the girl
with the patent leather shoes
knows the rain's gonna come. She raises
no tents, she's not warning the world of a need
for umbrellas, she's got *inevitable*
tattooed on her hip, she's got a mountain of bones
swelling her back pocket,
she calls them lineage. There are holes
in her underthings,   rot in her cupboards,
she watches the news
for walls of water.

and this city's a city for exiles, a city for refugees
from the spirit of sameness but they
all come bearing a disease, it's not hard to spot;
they're smoking the right
cigarettes, drinking the lite beer in the perfect
pants cut like an ad for the abyss. And the girl
with today's foxy dark blue patent leather shoes plans
for a change which she expects must come,
has begun to notice
signs for escape routes all along the paths of city buses

and whenever she crosses it, she counts the blocks
back to Atlantic Avenue, knows which way to turn
when she gets there, if she must run for the sea
or the sub urban sprawl, practices sprints from the good halal
    meat market past the cook shop
where a pot costs a hundred dollars just so you can fry up your

eggs, past the Afghan carpet store with its walls of mirrors
and frames and breakable things and the secret of brown paper
kites in the back. Even in her hard,
impractical shoes, she covers a mile/under a minute/she can break

a heart without even slipping to sweat, she practices what to do
if what comes/comes when she's wearing the wrong shoes/what
are the wrong shoes, if they come for the lesbians, militants or
poets and won't they know them by just those shoes? Like her
daddy says he knows lesbians by the way they cut their hair,
fags by their soft butter-cream hands and good-looking women
by their uncut soft locks, their slick legs, their simper?

and the girl is none of this. Just
shiny shoes and a plan for rain. She worries
that it's the way of iconoclasts to become the thing
you knew they'd always been, and that frightens her
cause maybe
all our hips *are* for babies, all our eyes for silence, all the bones
    in our feet
for breaking into dust and if we're silent, or at least apologetic
    for our wanting,
for our badass inclinations, if we moan with our mouths closed
    or a fist pushed
all the way in and then only when we're fucking, if nothing else
    truly cracks our hearts,
if we're careful never to break a rule even if it's our rule, even if
    the rules are crippling
our throats and searing our eyes, even if the rules make us want
    to bend until something
in our spinal fluid is too thinned out to hold, if we are careful to
    say the best things

as we've been trained
even when no one trusts us as our eyes betray our secrets, if we
      are sure
to arrive on time and be watching the watches as the hour
      hands click into place;
won't that make us right

or good or true if time is all
that tells us apart from savages—
she's not sure/she's dressed for this party but it's just—

ten blocks north to Atlantic and the dj is a white boy
rocking James Brown all night and the crowd gets funky
but they don't catch the beat and they're all scared
they done become their parents now, and ain't it too late
to worry about that when you're worrying about that/the girl
in her fuck me hot bright blue platform soled patent leather shoes,

she hopes that she *is* her momma cause what comes
is gonna get her and it better find her ready, so she turns

in these tight circles, she lets her body drop/hip and shoulder,
lets her body slide/head and shoulder, hip/and hip again
and it's all so good, she almost forgets the rain, almost
forgets that what wants you will follow you
from house to house/will wait beneath the stairs, will wait
till your holiday on some half-deserted beach, halfway round
the world or for the sound
of your other shoe—slipping so gentle
from your tired feet. So the girl's still dancing
when the music stops and the white boy dj is wiping the sweat
from the record, but oh she's dropping that hip into the void,
when the widows come knocking at the door and the good girls

are led away first, (good white girls
are often the first to go)
and the girl with the patent leather shoes that her momma gave
    her, plays
with her kinky-ass-overdried-cut-short-just-like-she-likes-it
    hair, and ain't she
a lesbian too in her Kevlar
and her lick-me lipstick/her close and tight contradictions
    ain't she
the thing her father fears most, and she remembers
that momma said, *black girls committin suicide*
are never sexy
or thin or tidy about that business.
Black girls who slit the wrist: cut it
thru to the bone,
the ones who take poison, swallow and
swallow that bitter stuff what cuts the bowels
and bubbles the throat and they gather in
their blue so purple it's black and they wail and some
don't even die that easy. So the girl considers

that she—won't go down
without a knuckle bare brawl, not without
bruising something down to the marrow
she will not be forgotten in the pain she leaves behind,
not without finally making a goddamn mess, the girl

rubs at a scuff in the toe of her shoe, she slides
her fingertips across *inevitable* as what comes
takes what it has come for with the wet hunger she expected,
sliding right by her spot where she's sunk into the couch, looking
for those more likely to want
when all is said and done.

Butterfly Nut House

in memory of Peter James Conti

We buried you, in a cold snap, during
a transit strike, nothing moving except
under the power of our own energies.

We whispered, *a cancer, what made it?*
and there grew a fear of our rash rough throats,
everything a threat. We shifted uneasy,

shoulder to shoulder, almost as in love
as we all were in the old days but for
this thrall of absolute ice, we owned

no explanations except perhaps sucrose,
and red wines too sweet for grownups. Peter.
How did we arrive here, without you?

Tonight I write at our old holy place.
The bartender does not know you're dead,
he gives me free beer; cold benediction.

He begins the list, asks after our circle.
This one still hungry, another married,
the youngest carries tumors; mistaken babies,

the loudest gone to where he can praise
an easier god and you; each time I'm asked,
I forget which words mean that you're dead;

underweight, 90 lbs when they cracked

the ice bound earth. I have not spoken aloud
since your first call to say, *Cancer.* Perhaps

your bare back exposed as a scandal and
all your lovely hungry boys. The last thing
I said was, *How do I apologize*

for letting in the monster that is eating you?
Was it your father's ministry, his holy,
the cracked closet door, your mother's deep cough,

or the voices that leached onto your ear?
When you stopped listening, did they migrate
south, inhabit your spine? You abdicated

madness. Was that it? You, younger, crazy
more naked, you louder, willing to sing
off key, off beat, all the wrong words. You said

you wanted babies and a lover with
a jaw like your father's, but a fistless,
godless man who'd look just like you. I said,

you were too young. I said, we had time for
all our vain mistakes but you murmured,
a baby. I want to be beautiful

for someone—want a body to love me
so that I'll be beautiful. I think
I promised that we'd love you, always.

I hope that I did and that it's enough now.

Still it seems the monster took a faster
path than love, arrived at always before us.
Perhaps laptops, black-pepper, pesticides.

Was it red meat or ten thousand bacon sandwiches,
the old days or our fashionable inhalations,
our mystic vegetation? We can't have been

so innocent. Perhaps naked to the moon,
something in the ether would not forgive us
and so had to have you.

Perhaps menthols, lead paint, asbestos or lye.
Something must be at fault. Perhaps religions
that swallow a gay black man whole in this

precious America where faith is what
we wear on our t-shirts. Dear Peter,
here is our religion; you are first generation

of this butterfly nut house, beekeeper
to us sons of immigrants, comic book inker
of scar wristed superheroines.

Peter, keep our brilliant-boisterous,
protect our cartoon alter egos, our truthless
selves. Know how I wish that I'd lied the day

you called to ask if, finally, we were growing up.
forgive us what we do in your memory.

Marty McConnell

You Say
You Want a
Revolution ...

ONE OF THE REASONS I HESITATE TO CALL myself an activist is that "causes" so often require a kind of blind faith I simply can't muster. I'm a middle-grounder by nature, more taken by the complex and muddy places than by the extremes. Despite defining myself clearly as a feminist—one of the few labels I will accept, and in fact self-apply—I can't hop on the bandwagon of lauding all female performance poets just because they have (or had) ovaries and choose to take the stage.

And I understand that it takes courage to write and perform a poem, particularly for women who have been systematically taught that we should sit still, cross our legs neatly at the ankle, and keep our mouths shut. I believe deeply in the potential of women. I despise the fact that girls are so often sold short, told that they shouldn't aim too high, or that there are specific, "appropriate" areas in which they can attempt to excel.

But as feminists and as artists presumably looking to grow and improve, we do ourselves a grave disservice by *cheerleading* rather than *leading*. Every artist goes through stages of development, and everyone deserves to be supported from word one through to the one-woman Broadway show. There is nothing wrong with wild applause in support of women as they take the stage, with seeking women out and encouraging them to continue writing and speaking.

What troubles me is the idea that in order to be supportive, we must be laudatory across the board. That those of us who curate venues should never turn down a fellow female poet for a feature, even if her work is not a good fit or ready for the audience. That we should expend our energies praising one another for our bravery as women performers rather than for our hard work at developing our craft. That the best thing we can do for each other is say, *You go girl.*

I believe that as members of a marginalized group—and many of us are members of more than one of those, being of color and/or queer in addition to being female—we must hold ourselves not just to the same standards to which we hold men, but to higher standards. Because for so long we were written off, we must make it impossible to ignore us, impossible to treat us as anything but artistic equals.

Hugs are nice, but hugs don't make great poets. And isn't that what we want to be?

A line commonly attributed to Emma Goldman says, "If I can't dance, I don't want to be part of your revolution." I say, if you don't want to work, you've got no place in *this* revolution. Performance poetry, spoken word, call it what you will, is about precise expression. About getting the words and their performance so close to the experience it's as if everyone in the room is having it with you, and simultaneously no one else could have expressed it as you have. That's hard work, and nobody gets there just by hearing how brave they are for taking the stage.

So what do we do? How do we embrace our sisters in a way that lifts all of us, that goes beyond cheerleading?

Women must insist on rigor. What I'm advocating is not the wholesale writing-off of poets who haven't reached some particular level of skill or craft, who are new or struggling or experimenting with something that's not quite working yet. What I'm advocating is a commitment by those of us who have the benefit of experience or education to connect and create community that both nurtures and challenges women who are new to poetry or performance.

Years ago, a group of women involved with the National Poetry Slam created a network within that scene and called it SlamSisters. We had a few meetings, created a listserv, and had preliminary discussions about what this group might have as its goals and purpose. In hindsight, I believe that there are two basic reasons the network never cohered, never found its driving force. In its forming it was reactionary, a response to what was perceived as men's dominance within the realm of competitive performance poetry. And, more importantly, there was no structure created for the group to do anything but cheerlead—all nurture and no challenge. All kumbaya and no ass-kicking.

Of course it's not only women new to poetry and performance who need communities that insist on rigor—those of us who've achieved some level of success or count ourselves experienced still need people around us whom we can trust to tell us the truth, to hail us when we soar and to haul us back when we've gone off course. We must challenge each other toward constant improvement, new levels of risk and growth.

Workshops, whether formal or casual, structured or loose, are a great way to create systems through which constructive criticism becomes the norm. The all-female writing circle in Chicago in 1998 where a common critique was, "This line sucks. Fix it!" was as valuable to my development as a poet as my first MFA workshop at Sarah Lawrence. More than anything, we must engage each other on a level that creates not only the space for but also the expectation of critical feedback, as opposed to mutual backslapping.

Women must work together. We must not allow ourselves to succumb to the fragmenting nature of competition, or patriarchal capitalism's insistence on the lack mentality, the notion that "there is only so much room at the top." The power of women taking the stage together, traveling together, writing and speaking and moving together, does more to destroy the stereotype of cattiness, and to demonstrate the possibility of cooperative, synergistic female relationship, than a thousand feminist essays.

When I was traveling with the Morrigan, an all-female performance poetry troupe I cofounded in 1999, what we heard most consistently from women and girls was their astonishment at our belief in our ability and right to speak our truth onstage. We heard time and time again how empowering it was to see a group of fierce women working together. Men, on the other hand, were more inclined to ask us if we fought or fucked; apparently, for them, three strong women in one vehicle for two months was a recipe for a continual string of catfights or orgies.

What we knew, from watching and talking to the women of Sister Spit, from observing the circles of aunts and female friends who informed our mothers' lives, from reading June Jordan and Audre Lorde and Adrienne Rich and bell hooks, was that not only was what we had to say important, it was important that we said it.

Women must create spaces that value and honor the present and the past. Who came before us? We must make ourselves the keepers of the institutional memory: Who made it possible for us to exist? Who paved the roads we travel? How are we passing this knowledge on to new generations of women who write and perform?

Creating community means creating space, be it exclusive space or a safe circle within an open space. When I was fairly new to the performance poetry world and living in Chicago, a group of about seven women met weekly for critique and practice. We'd venture to open mics throughout the city, armed with the poems we'd worked on and with the confidence of numbers. It was remarkable to see the shift we could make in a room as it became clear that we planned to be vocal about misogyny and about supporting women on the mic. People changed their minds about what poems they'd read that night based on how we might react. One man even asked us to look at his poem before taking the stage. We created our own space, our own safety zone, within a community that, while not overtly hostile to women, had no structures in place for supporting or encouraging them. And our safety zone extended to other women in the room, in the audience, in the community; we weren't just protecting ourselves, we were actively insisting on respect for voices outside of the male-centric mainstream.

In recognizing that women's voices are marginalized and often dismissed or ignored, it's crucial that we create spaces where the work of female poets is celebrated and taught. These spaces might be open mics that include readings of women's work, workshops, tribute nights, or discussion groups; the format is less important than that these events occur and engage women across the spectrum of experience, acknowledging the variety that exists within the construct of "female."

None of what lies ahead for us is easy, but none of it is impossible either. If we value the movement, however we define it, and if we value the women who are unquestionably a crucial part of it, we will do what it takes to create space within that movement for rigor, risk, and growth. We will become our own brand of feminist/poet/performer activists, not crusading against all that opposes us, but working to bring to fruit the great seed residing in each of us.

instructions for a body

praise the miracle body: the odd
and undeniable mechanics of hand,
hundred-boned foot, perfect stretch
of tendon
tell me there are no gods then,
no master plans for this anatomy
with its mobile and evident spark
someone says "children of light"
and another, "goddessfragment" and
another, "chosen" / a dozen makers,
myriad paths, one goal:
some scalpel, some chisel, some crazed
sentimental engineer giving rib, giving
eyelash, giving gut and thumb—
all mattering. all set down
in a going world, vulnerable
and divine
in the beginning was the word.
or before time there was a void
until a voice said "I" and was
or there was star and dust,
explosion and animal, mineral, us:
praise the veins that river these wrists
praise the prolapsed valve in a heart
praise the scars marking a gallbladder absent
praise the rasp and rattle of functioning lungs
praise the prearthritic ache of elbows
and ankles
praise the lifeline sectioning a palm
praise the photographic pads of fingertips

praise the vulnerable dip at the base of a throat
praise the muscles surfacing on an abdomen
praise these arms that carry babies
and anthologies
praise the leg hairs that sprout
and are shaved
praise the ass that refuses to shrink
or be hidden
praise the cunt that bleeds
and accepts, bleeds
and accepts
praise the prominent ridge of nose
praise the strange convexity of ribcage
praise the single hair that insists on growing
from a right areola
praise the dent where the mole was clipped from the back
of a neck
praise these inner thighs brushing
praise these eyelashes that sometimes turn inward
praise these hips preparing to spread
into a grandmother's skirt
praise the beauty of the freckle
on the first knuckle of a left little finger
we're gone / in a blizzard of seconds
love the body human
while we're here, a gift of minutes
on an evolving planet, a country
in flux / give thanks
what we take for granted, bone and dirt
and the million things that will kill us
someday, motion and the pursuit
of happiness / no guarantees / give thanks

for chaos theory, ecology, common sense that says
we are web. a planet in balance or out, the butterfly
in tokyo setting off thunderstorms in iowa,
tell me you don't matter to a universe that conspired
to give you such a tongue, such rhythm
or rhythmless hips, such opposable thumbs—
give thanks or go home a waste of spark
speak or let the maker take back your throat
march or let the creator rescind your feet
dream or let your god destroy your good and fertile mind
this is your warning / this
your birthright / do not let
this universe regret you.

Joan of Arc to the $2,000-an-hour woman

Jason would be saying, "Natalia is the greatest escort in the history of the world, as good as Cleopatra or Joan of Arc," and I'd be like, "Jason! Joan of Arc was not an escort, she was a religious martyr."
—New York Magazine, *July 18, 2005*

at least your pimp has a name, a neck
you could put your two good hands around.
he loves you like all men love
what they sell, what comes back
in gold. make no mistake, my God
was a man. men with their mouths
at the entrance to the cave, whispering,
men dripping hallucinogens into the milk,
men insisting *lead us, lead us, have this horse*
this sword this sentence this pyre. men naked
under their robes, their armor, their teeth
bartering my skin for their country, a cause
I would have sworn was mine.

Cleo and I place bets on women like you.
from this distance, your dance looks like ours.
and Vashti's, and Salome's, and Helen's,
and you're acquainted with the Magdalene.
our mythical knees locked or spread,
bringing men to theirs and us to the gallows
the tower the stake / trade your corset for a habit
and they'll hate you all the same: whatever cannot
be possessed is poison. the body is never bought
but rented which is why he wants your heart, bound
like feet, dancing only for him.

let me tell you something about possession. never
let a man dictate your wingspan or your footwear.
there's a god on every corner and not one
would have you mortgage your given body
for this man and his fur-lined tongue. don't think
I don't know about love; more goes unreported
in history than in myth. sell your story, Natalia,
before they scrape it from under your fingernails
as evidence / cut your hair. buy a building
in Brooklyn. lay down on a bed of teeth, alone.
peel back their fingerprints one by one, each incision
the hot face of a god, unfolding.

Bitch

Spilling Ink

IF I HAD A NICKEL FOR EVERY TIME A WOMAN SAID "sorry" to me, simply for standing there, for *existing*, as I squeezed past her in the subway, I would be nearing the same tax bracket as Oprah. Women are constantly sent both subtle and blatant messages reprimanding us to hush up. Rarely are stalwart, outspoken women reflected back to us in mainstream media. As a result, we have become skilled at deflecting our opinions, shriveling up, not filling either physical or emotional space.

Confronting this societal lack of entitlement just may be women's singular battle as we begin to explore writing. I have seen far too many women apologizing for their work, and this leads me to contemplate how many great female writers have gone to their graves without ever sharing their poetry, much less creating it in the first place.

So many women's stories get lost, and we must be dedicated to preserving our experiences. I see this happen over and over again. My girlfriend's great-grandmother passed away a few years ago, and during the painful process of clearing out her house, my girl discovered that her great-grandmother was a poet. She watched, increasingly agitated, as her uncles poured through trunkloads of documents, meticulously safekeeping their grandfather's business plans while readily tossing their grandmother's writing into recycling containers. Ever methodical, my girlfriend dove headfirst into the tubs to rescue the so-called "ramblings of an old woman."

As women writers, it is vital that we identify both our externally imposed and self-imposed limitations, then access, embrace, and pursue our most primitive emotional signposts, and not let our inner critic get in the way. I link my own beginnings as a poet to my first heartbreak. When I was eleven, my family moved from Pittsburgh to Detroit, forcing me to leave my very best friend, Nancy. Devastated, I would repeatedly play my older sister's Depeche Mode cassette as I walked to and from my new middle school. I dub this time my "suicide poetry years," not because I was actually suicidal, but because this suddenly huge loss propelled me to write rhyming, singsong poems about the death of me and my love, Nancy.

Perhaps these singsongs were the beginning of my current career as a poet and musician, and my stint as half of the former duo Bitch and Animal. As a young kid, though, I don't recall second-guessing those poems that came from my gut. Years of living as a girl and then as a woman changed that. I first recognized how easily my inner critic could plug my creative outlet during a session with Animal, my former musical partner. Writing a song called "Boy Girl Wonder," we were struggling to find the last rhyme of the phrase:

> But you're so caught up in your boyfriend jock
> And he fits right in and he hits the spot
> But the spot you missed was the one of me—

When Animal busted out with the line "The Boy Girl Wonder from Queens!" I felt a rush of embarrassment, a visceral aversion to her claiming this "superhero" status. I resisted. I felt awkward. My immigrant parents' voices crowded my head, dying for assimilation, longing to quiet any sense of "sticking out." But there was Animal shining, letting herself dream big, and I was trying to quell that? Resistance was futile. The line proved golden—the true key to the song. Now, when I am writing, I know that I have hit creative pay dirt when I sense that embarrassment. Any opposition most likely transpires from a fear of revealing myself, deafening me to my true divine voice.

My poetry is most authentic when I force my internal editor toward the back row, thus freeing my imagination to run wild. It is also important for me to find out who that editor is. Is it a critic? Is it some voice from the outside telling me that my creativity has no value? What makes me doubt what I make or say? I ask myself, "What's going to happen if I just let these words flow, if I just let myself be?" I try to allow some inner voice to guide my pen. Why not? Dioxin-free paper, after all, is cheap!

As Virginia Woolf said, "The cheapness of writing paper is, of course, the reason why women have succeeded as writers before they have succeeded in the other professions." I strongly believe that the economic structure that has created women's poverty has attempted to silence us.

In order to share our remarkable stories with the world, to stand up for life and what we believe to be true for the good of all sentient beings everywhere, we must not be limited in who we think we are. We must not be limited in who we tell people we are. Most importantly, we must not limit ourselves based on people's reactions to who they think we are.

Each of us contains a voice out of which a writer could be born; we simply need to harness our courage, playfulness, and power. Our words matter. Not only because they serve as mirrors of, and messages to, the world, but most significantly because they are our messages to one another.

After a recent performance a woman approached me, joyously exhibiting her Sharpie-scribbled palm, and exclaiming that, until tonight, she had not written poetry in fifteen years. Her joy was clearly linked to her inspiration to write, and by joy, I don't mean cheap happiness. I mean feeling the weight of yourself in the world. Daring to spill ink onto a page. Exposing your most raw self, regardless of how it will be interpreted.

I strive to be a reminder that there is a necessary function in all societies for artistic souls. When I dress up in many colors, wear my hair green, and adorn my neck or arms with bold costume jewelry, I almost always get comments akin to: "That's very—*colorful.*" My general response is: "That's one of my jobs!" Artists have worked to combat conformity throughout herstory. Capitalism, and its "come be a cog in my wheel" mentality, does everything in its power to convince us that this is some sort of absurd or selfish way to live.

We must acknowledge the sexism, racism, and homophobia that controls whose stories get told, and then whose stories are preserved and retold. We must eke out whatever shred of truth is left in us, as survivors of an imperialist world, to carry on for generations to come. Whether the ink-stained woman dies with her palms to the sky, or if I blush through my own creative dreaming, we must acknowledge that human beings are creators. It is in our cellular makeup to make. We must follow the truest voice inside us. We must discover who we are by mining through layers of societal voices in order to find the jewels of wisdom that await us in our internal landscapes. Capitalism may be hell-bent on keeping us from these gems, but be not the cogs, be the wheels! Reinvent the wheels! Let's kick up so much dust that everything shifts! Then we will be more like nature: changing, raging, bursting, settling, circling and humming and taking up space. Paper may be cheap but words, my dear coconspirators, are not.

Pussy Manifesto

Manifest this motha fucka #1:
Every living thing comes from and returns to (get it?)

Manifest this Muddafucka #2:
Let Pussy speak to me through every living thing.
As all creatures move and grow,
let them bring forth the open ness and warm ness
that flows in the energy of Pussy . . .
the life force on which we all depend.

Manifest this Muthafucka #3:
I'm sick of my genitalia being used as an insult. Are you?
It's time to let my labia rip and rearrange this.
Here we go:
"That was so Pussy of you to help me move to my new place!
Especially since I'm living on the thirteenth floor.
You've really made this a Pussy move!"

Manifest this Motherfuckrr #4:
The power of Pussy could be blinding.
Do not misinterpret its strength and fear it.
Do not try to control it. It is light, rich and full of warmth.
Use it wisely and with jeweled intentions.

Manifest this Muthefucka #5:
The Egg says, "Don't forget me, Muddafucka!"
The Egg must not be understated.
Let the Egg be the symbol of all courage!
Here we go:
"Honey, that took Eggs for you to tell your customer off

for not tipping you 20 percent!"
The Egg, like courage, is a delicate intricate shell surrounding
ever-changing nutritious life!
Let the Egg be the teacher and the Pussy be its nest.

Manifest this Motherfuckrr #6:
Employ the Pussy!
*teacher
*whore
*philosopher
*president
Pay her well!

Manifest this Motherfuckrr #7:
The Pussy is a traveler!
No matter where your Pussy energy leads you,
let the Pussy be your clock.
Allow the "ticking" to be measured by
gathered and dispersed
gathered and dispersed
gathered and dispersed
one should not outweigh the other . . .

Manifest this Mothafucker #8:
Let Pussy manifest and let freedom sing!

Red Roof In

Every time I focus my view
Every time my camera zooms
I get this commercial by you
Ubiquitous you

Everywhere wears the badge of ads of you
You oh country sold out to capital
Shit, you dress my friends in it
The lens I view it with
The invisible space in the air
The soundwaves cast
Your insipid glare

I'm under your "red roof inn"
Your murder marketing system
Calling it Christian
Christ was a freak like me
You think he'd be down
With all the forests being paved with his name
Or some war being waged with his fame
Or he wasn't getting it on with Mary or Jane

Just cuz they killed him don't kill me
Don't go kill a bunch of people back in Iraq
Then put that fish up next to your support-our-troops flag
Follow this asshole dictator
Daddy's little imitator
Give him your money your love and your veins

If Christ died for my sins
He died in revolution
The one we're trying to make
So stop trying to take
My view
My true
My ocean blue

Anyway, I was trying to say
That somehow you just can't stop our joy
You just can't stop our basic need for people-ness
It springs up in the craziest cracks
And we are finding our roots now
We have to fight just to keep our space
We are finding our roots now
We will fight to keep our space
In the race and the pace
Of the land over take
In the race and the pace
Of the land over take

Turiya Autry and Walidah Imarisha

Good Sista/
Bad Sista

"I HEARD THAT!"

"Oh she didn't say that! Say it again girl!"

"Amen!!!"

Smiles split our faces as we met one another's eyes, hearts beating, blood surging, after finishing our first ever duo-poem together: "No You Don't Know Me," our diatribe-manifesto-mantra-rant-poem about being black women living in what was (and is) one of the whitest major cities in amerika.

Born out of our collective frustration and our demand to be heard, the piece included direct and unapologetic lines like, "Do you get confused when more than one black person enters the room?" "Do you have problems keeping your Turiyas and Walidahs straight?" and "We may be only 3 percent of Oregon's population, but goddamnit, we're taking over!" The Black History Month crowd, mostly black and brown faces packing the Portland State University Multicultural Center and for once rendering it truly multicultural, applauded and cheered, beaming back at us. Raw and unrefined, poetic and pissed off, we had never written poetry like that on our own, or received such an overwhelming response.

This 1999 event, Tribute to the Black Woman, helped to incubate and birth the fire-spitting, bicoastal poetry duo Good Sista/Bad Sista. Walidah was nineteen years old, Turiya was on the verge of turning twenty-seven, and we were both students at Portland State University. As part of the less than 1 percent black student population, and as two spoken word sistas, it was inevitable that we would run into each other, around campus and out in the community. However, though we were definitely friendly, we had never really spent a lot of time together. That was, until a brother named Dramaine, from the Black Cultural Affairs Board at PSU, began calling and hounding us both until we relented and agreed to do a collective fifteen-minute set at the Tribute to the Black Woman event. He knew of our work individually and thought it would be powerful to have us do a joint piece. Of course, he gave us only two weeks to make it happen.

When we started preparing, we had no intention of becoming a poetry "duo." We had both come to performance poetry through the very male, white-centric, individualistic, and competitive Portland, Oregon, slam scene, not a loving scene nor one fostering collaboration. Neither of us had positive experiences writing with other folks to reference as a model, and as fiercely independent women we were used to tackling the world on our own. So, we had simply planned on weaving two separate pieces we had already written together and calling it a day. But then, on the phone trying to figure out what the hell we were going to do, and in our initial meetings and rehearsals, we discovered something that would change the whole course of our lives as organizers, artists, cultural workers, and people: We were, in fact, better *together*. Turiya's romantic, poetic heart naturally expressed itself in beautiful metaphors and visions, which Walidah found incredibly inspiring. Walidah's up-front, in-your-face, cut-the-bullshit attitude inspired Turiya to say things that she had always wanted to voice but had held back.

We also had similar backgrounds. Raised in mostly white areas, we both experienced periods of isolation and distance from our black heritage. Initially inspired by literary figures like Sylvia Plath, Walidah began writing poetry in high school, work that was intended to be shared only with her muse. Her artistry had no connection to the political work she was engaged in: working against racism in the small town of Springfield, Oregon, supporting political prisoners like Mumia Abu-Jamal, and learning about the Zapatistas. She did not even, in fact, call herself a poet, because she did not see herself reflected in the title, and she had no idea then she could stretch poetry's skin to become hers. Turiya, likewise, grew up black and outnumbered, surrounded by and raised in predominantly white neighborhoods and attending white schools. Her first years of college at San Francisco State University further fueled her interest in politics and activism. She spoke out at rallies, protesting Desert Storm, became active in students of color organizations, and marched through the city after police officers were acquitted for the Rodney King beating. Marrying young and starting a family shifted her priorities to the home front and education. She focused her revolutionary efforts toward community building and raising her children. After several years of distance from her inner writer, Turiya rediscovered her love and need for poetry as a necessary release valve for the frustrations of divorce and difficulties of single parenthood.

In the process of writing with one another, we realized that not only did we share similar global perspectives, but also that poetry was in fact relevant to all the facets of our lives. Our different writing styles pushed each other to be better, badder, and bolder than on our own accord. There was a freedom in being as crazy as you wanted to be, indeed as you had to be, knowing that at least one person had your back.

The birth of Good Sista/Bad Sista was inevitable—not just because of our individual connection and histories, but because of the new relationship we were able to establish with our audiences as a duo. During that Black History Month performance, which was our first time performing before an almost all black crowd, we transcended being "coauthors of a poem," and became cocreators in collective expression, a collective history. Our collaboration represented a pact between us and the audience. By taking up space as black women, we added to the communal voice of the oppressed. We could be loud enough to clear out some space for ourselves and for others, and we could be poetic enough to envision something to fill that space. Standing side by side on the makeshift stage, we witnessed audience members rolling out of their folding chairs in laughter and tears. We could see then that this poetry thang had the potential to be more than either internal personal therapy or expressive political articulation. Our work was a collective scream in the car, with all of the windows finally rolled down, a way to connect folks with a big "Hell yeah, I been thinking the same damn thang!"

We became close friends over the next year and continued to grow as co-artists. A stranger actually christened us with our name unintentionally in 2000, when we were joining the bill at a Black Anger's show in Seattle. After attempting unsuccessfully to pick up on both of us, the young man declared, "Oh, you must be the bad sister, and she must be the good sister!" While it initially seemed trivial, even irritating, most people did assume we were actual siblings, and the name grew on us and stuck. We saw the irony in the title; after all, what is considered "good" and "bad" is oftentimes a matter of perspective, environment, and circumstance. As women of color, we are often expected to shield our anger and be "well-behaved" even though most times society needs a smack. We joke that the duality represents the ability to make sure our verbal ass-whoopin' leaves folks wanting more, and however a situation demands we come, we know we have the arsenal to supply it.

When we attended the 2000 National Poetry Slam competition in Rhode Island, we met dozens of professionally touring spoken word artists, two of whom were the Twin Poets, who were the first other poetry duo we had ever met. They were actual brothers, and their style of intertwining lines and bodies while performing was captivating. We performed during the group performance showcase at the Nationals, and saw that while collaborative pieces flourished, established duos were rare. That was also the time that we decided that we should organize a serious tour for ourselves.

Walidah relocated to Philadelphia soon after and began getting familiar with the East Coast. We decided we would focus our tour in that region, since major cities were relatively near each other. The following summer, leading up to the 2001 National Poetry Slam competitions in Seattle, we embarked on the Sho-Nuff Show tour, performing at over thirty venues in a month and a half. We toured venues throughout the Northeast Corridor, Texas, and the Northwest; we performed at nightclubs, slams, coffee shops, and concerts. We spent every waking and sleeping moment together for six weeks. A less solid relationship would have cracked under the pressures of sharing space on couches and floors, eternal Greyhound rides, and the humidity of Texas in the summer. We thought that the road would be an opportunity to write a book of new verses, but we soon realized, in between the exhaustion of performing every day (we only scheduled two free days not on a bus) and the horrible movie selection on Peter Pan bus services in the Northeast (*The Legend of Bagger Vance, Crimson Tide, What Dreams May Come* . . . we felt there was a conspiracy to only play films with subservient, "safe" black folks), it was not going to be possible. What we did manage, though, included perfecting delivery and timing and getting to a place of comfort with our pieces where we could improvise on the spot and ad-lib lines that we would later continue to incorporate. Some days we opted to sit at opposite ends of the bus, when we were truly exhausted by each other's company, but we found we preferred the known irritant over the unknown passengers, and found ourselves side by side again before the end of the ride.

Touring as a pair could be trying, but we learned we could push ourselves to the limit, and come back better and stronger. Together, we shared the responsibilities of keeping records, printing and assembling new chapbooks, and overall coordination. Traveling together also provided a sense of security and the safety of not being alone. Certainly, it was no perfect utopia. We worked on each other's last nerves; we didn't always want to practice at the same time, eat at the same places, or indulge in the same activities during our limited free time; and our schedule was extremely tight and fast-paced. But Turiya's "goodness" helped smooth over difficulties with organizers and individuals, and Walidah's "badness" helped us survive subways, too-friendly strangers, and assholes. Neither of us could imagine doing an endeavor of that length and geographical span alone. At the end of the day, we were each other's shoulders and mirrors.

Our subsequent tours have been much shorter in duration. Oftentimes now we travel to a city for a weekend to do a show or two, or incorporate performances into our schedules when we visit each other across coasts. Family members who helped watch Turiya's children during her travels have gone on to have their own children and responsibilities, which makes it harder to be gone for long periods. We are both still traumatized by buses and PB and J, so those two factors are definitely eliminated from our trips now. While we still perform at different kinds of venues and are very committed to performing in community spaces for free, we attempt to anchor shows with university gigs or other performances that can better cover expenses. During the Sho-Nuff Show tour we broke even and made some profit due to merchandise sales, but there was no ecstatic skipping to the bank for large payloads. The motivation was never wealth, but exposure: We wanted the audiences to hear our work, and we wanted to experience multiple audiences. Being on the road and performing for various crowds sharpens what a performer delivers and leads to immeasurable growth and inspiration.

We both maintained, and continue to maintain, hectic daily home lives that have, for the last few years, lessened the amount of performances we are able to do together. Turiya is a parent of two teenagers and an instructor at Portland State University, and works with several arts education organizations to provide workshops and performances to youth throughout Oregon. Walidah currently works full-time as an administrator with a Philadelphia foundation that provides grants to artists creating social change, as well as giving nearly full-time energy toward organizing political projects that pay only in love. Meanwhile, we are our own publicists, web developers, booking and travel agents, editors, publishers, and marketers. Initially, one can enter the realm as a dedicated artist with heart and ambition, but eventually, to be truly successful, the business aspect is crucial. Two sets of eyes and ears are an asset when it comes to promotion and detail work. Taking on that responsibility also keeps the power in our hands. We decide how we market ourselves and for what ends. As women of color, we understand the importance of controlling how we are represented along with the content of our material (we saw how they did Queen Latifah in *Bringing Down the House* and Halle Berry in . . . well, everything). We are each other's counsel and point of reference. While we both do more shows as individuals due to the current geographical distance between us, people are constantly contacting us about Good Sista/Bad Sista. Undeniably, when the two of us are together, the impact is exponential. Our bicoastalness allows us to utilize the many contacts we've each made and merge that wealth of resources.

Over the past eight years, we have now toured cross-country several times, and performed at hundreds of venues. We've shared many memorable moments onstage. Some that stand out were performing after Nikki Giovanni at a conference in Washington state and having one of our personal heroes give us a perfect "ten." Our first time featured together for a packed house at the historic Nuyorican Poets

Café in New York was literally a dream come true; as Walidah remembers, on her first visit to the Rotten Apple, she stood outside the Nuyo and said, "One day, one day." We've performed to our largest audience ever at Michael Franti's 2002 Power to the Peaceful event in San Francisco's Golden Gate Park; thirty thousand people rolled through. Some cities stand out because the audiences are so live; Houston gave us so much love we couldn't help but grow fond of our visit to Texas, even though it was initially a place we were nervous about visiting. We still run into and meet people who have seen us randomly in some venue around the country, and it makes us realize the level of impact all of us have on the people around us, and feel the heaviness of that responsibility, as well as the beauty of that honor.

We have taught and facilitated, we have acted and sang, we have rioted and rebelled. We have tried to write a new world with our tongues. We have carried with us the understanding that it is important for us to walk through this world together, as sistas, as best friends, as compas and comrades. As angry and fragile, strong and bruised, funny and intelligent black women, we remind one another of our beauty in a world that reflects back ugliness. Good Sista/Bad Sista are tied together as part of a greater good and the larger whole. We have a responsibility to each other, to our community, to our ancestors, to our children, and most importantly, to ourselves.

Ultimately, we have realized that the truths of two big-haired, bad-assed revolutionary sistas, unafraid to speak their piece, resonate with black folks everywhere, since we all negotiate and navigate the systems of white supremacy on the daily. We create together because, as dead prez said, "one dreadlock is stronger than one strand." We speak and scream and yell because, as Frantz Fanon said, "I want my voice to be harsh, I don't want it to be beautiful . . . I want it to be torn through and through." Every individual is endowed with unique gifts; finding and utilizing them for the sake of bettering the world is the true calling of the artist. Through our voices and our ability to take up space we create pathways for others because we know the pain and impact of feeling unrepresented, unheard, and underappreciated. We do all that we do because, as June Jordan said, "We are the ones we've been waiting for." It took us time to find each other and grow our art, but we were definitely worth the wait.

Supa Soul Sistas

i always wanted to be a superhero marvel comic book character
action packed thrill a minute type of girl
just hug my curves and hold your breath

but i'd do it with a twist,
cause i didn't want to be no wonder woman or bionic woman
and i definitely didn't want to be invisible woman
(shit, I did that every day)

no, i wanted to be a black female superhero
kicking ass and looking damn good
i wanted to be storm from the x-men
command the elements with a single thought
shake entire continents with my wrath
and quiet the fiercest monsoons

i used to wish to be storm
so when some stupid muthafucka
asked me why i was so angry
my eyes would widen
with the awesome power of nature

i would raise my hands above my head
power pulsating in between my fingertips
i would make the sky darken and rumble my answer
and then from the bowels of the clouds
a lightning bolt would flash
and shoot him in the ass

aah . . . yeh! that was a badass sista!

then the movie came out
and my idol was . . .
Halle Berry?
Oh hell no!
come on now!
storm was a goddess, worshipped by entire villages
but she's going to get her ass whipped by a toad with a sticky
    tongue?
and Halle Berry does *not* have the thighs to be storm!
look at the comics
sista has some sho-nuff black girl thighs
thighs for days!
but of course for the movie they put her on some
jazzercise thin and trim routine

i knew then that no known image of black women,
created by white men
(of course)
could satisfy my longing to be a superhero
i would have to figure it out for myself
i would have to make myself over into . . .

a supa sooooooulllllll sista!

that's right
the white man will not be saving the universe this time
not Willis, not Schwarzenegger, not Ash Ketchum, and not
that bratty whiny Skywalker
    ("But Uncle Owen I wanted to go to Tosche and get some
    power converters")

instead the next superhero is a sister

and not the generic, ratings are going down
we need something to perk up the show
safeway select of superheroes
generic brand of freedom fighter

no, this will be a sister
who can fly above the chains of ignorance
and whip out the tongue lashing of a lifetime

"you think you know me?
i call upon the forces of Isis and Harriet Tubman
Sojourner Truth and Nefertiti
Assata Shakur and Cleopatra
to reign down the fury of centuries of oppression
degradation and silence on your head
because we will not be silent anymore
and with the voice of a hundred million
sistas moaning across the bloody pages of history
you will feel our rage!
because I have the power to resurrect the past
train it like a pit bull
and sic it on your ass!"

Ahhh Yeah!

or maybe my power would be held captive
trapped like an angry storm cloud whipping out of my head
my hair would rise up around me like a cobra's hood
spitting venom and years of pent up frustration
of not good enough, not light enough, not white enough
and you can touch it if you want to
but I can't be responsible for the consequences!

instead,

i'll be responsible for conquering corporate dominance with a
    smackdown

ending racial profiling with a swift crackdown

coming soon to a theater

(and streets) in your town!

then I can tap into my special super empathy powered third
    eye . . .

and I . . .

sense . . .

racism nearby . . .

damn, girl, that ain't a super power

that's just simple common sense!

you're right! every black woman

action figure or not

comes equipped with that option

KAPOW

this shit won't be televised

cause the networks can't handle

this much angry black woman juice

but it will be in your face

and we don't need syndication

to open a can of whupass five times a week

and twice on Sundays

take that for slavery

    and that's for segregation

and that's for integration
    that's for the glass ceiling
and that's for that futuristic movie bullshit
where i am still Aunt Jemima
talking bout "have a cookie and you'll feel better"
and this is for my not ever being able to find
flesh colored pantyhose
or my hair care products at the corner store

DOUBLE SMACK
forget the wonder twins!
we're the thunder twins!

KABLAM!
knocked that smirk right off the face of patriarchy
rewrote history and started my own galaxy
beyond the silver surfer's reach
cause you know he be trying to gentrify that shit
and no we ain't letting them in to fuck up the new solar system
    too!
and hell no the chief of police can't page us with a strobe light
shaped like an afro pick shining on the night's sky
Charlie won't be on the intercom
and if he tries to page us tell him
we've decided to stop moonlighting as angels
cause we've come down to earth
and pawned our wings for weaponry

you'll be captivated by our graceful motions
as we kick the asses of Judge Sabo, Pete Wilson,
George Bush (first and second)
Giuliani, Charlton Heston

(Chuck, let my people go!)
and every great white hope that ever arose
we will whoop them like we was Muhammad Ali

"i wrestled with an alligator
tussled with a whale
handcuffed lightning
and threw thunder in jail"

hold up!
instant replay that shit
so I can watch it again!

aah sookie sookie now

but don't even think about trying to get some
cause we ain't clark kent
and you ain't no lois lane
(and definitely not the other way around)
and we will unfurl a fury of afro swipes
Black Belt Jones *Enter the Dragon* style

cause we are Supa Soooooooullll Sistas
and you just found your way
onto the bad side of our hair

No You Don't Know Me

	Black folks
Woman	
	Colored
Women	
	African American
I am	
	Black
We are	
	Mulatto
Names	
	Darkie
Titles	
	Mammy
Assigned	
	High Yella
But who are we	
	Jezebel
Really?	
	Nigga

People are always trying to categorize us, demystify us.
Flatten us and straighten us and define us our parameters.
But they really don't have a clue.

Don't I know you? You look so familiar!

No you don't know me!
I didn't used to sit next to you in second period math class
I wasn't friends with your second cousin's best friend

I didn't live in Philly in '92
And no you didn't see me on *Soul Train*
But thanks for asking

>Black
>I am the universe before the stars
>Fertile chamber of things to come
>Buried secrets
>Deep beneath the ground
>Deep beneath the deck of slave ships named jesus
>We multiply and reproduce
>A mass movement coming from the underground
>Grassroots taking over the landscape
>We clone ourselves in preparation for the slave insurrection

Do you get confused when
More than one black person enters the room?
Do you have problems
Keeping your Walidahs and Turiyas straight?

>Colored
>I am muted brown
>Child of Ham
>Searching for a sign
>To point me in
>The right direction
>But that path is labeled whites only.
>How can you know me when you're afraid to get close to
>me?

Is it a genetic drift
That pushes you

To the other side of the elevator every time I get on?
If you think you're scared now, you should hear what we say
    when you're not around . . .

You know, Portland is the whitest major city in amerika
We used to be number two but now Omaha has that honor!
Moving on up! (Moving on down!)

    Surrounded
                Don't get me wrong . . .
    Trapped behind every lines
                I'm not a racist . . .
    Closing in from all sides
                I mean some of my best friends are . . .
    May day! May day! This is not a drill!
    I repeat this is not a drill
    This is reality!

It's just that every once in a while
We would like to get away!
I mean, they even show up at reggae shows!   *Bomba Clot!*

We may be only 3 percent of Oregon's population
But goddamnit, we're taking over!!!

We don't have any smiles for you today
We're throwing in our masks
We're not going to steppin fetchit for you anymore
The minstrel show is over!

Sometimes we are tired . . .
Of you . . .

It happens.

And for as much as we remain silent with our thoughts,
Seems like white folks don't have problems expressing what
  they think:

> *It's not like you're black; it's more like you're white . . .*
> *Oh you speak so well!*
> *You're so lucky. It's like you have a year round tan!*
> *You're so angry. Why are you so gosh darn angry?*
> *Can I touch your hair?!*

HELL NO!!!!!!!!!!!!!!!!!!!!

Tonight on the six o'clock news
An epidemic of jungle fever is running rampant
Spreading throughout the nation
Causing white boys to get pretty fucking bold!

> *You know, white girls just don't do it for me.*
> *I don't know why.*
> *I don't date anything lighter than a cinnamon.*
> *Baby, can I get some of your brown suga?*
> *Would you like a little cream in your coffee?*

Interracial relationships
From the slave quarters to the big screen
Sexin' us up wasn't part of Martin's "I Have a Dream"
Look, Black isn't some two-hour movie
Starring Oscar award winning performances
Or some thirty-minute laugh track sitcom
Where widened grins mask our suffering.

People need to turn that shit off!

We are more than MTV personifications
twenty-first-century reinterpretations of slave plantations

Shit!
Forget everything *Good Times* ever taught you
About black folks:
    DYNOMITE!
And just listen . . . really listen
So when you say that you *"know me"*
You can say it with honesty.

Lynn Breedlove

A Boy Among
Weemoon

YESTERDAY I WAS IN THE PAJAMA STORE IN
San Francisco, where people, especially The Gays, should know
something about gender variants like myself. My girlfriend was
buying me PJs from some old daggers who insisted upon calling
me "she" even though my girlfriend kept referring to me as "he."
I assumed the old dykes would figure it out, but hardly anybody
ever seems to, except an occasional transfeminist femme like my
girlfriend. Not even my mom gets it. The girlfriend says, "If you
want people to know, you have to correct them." But I say, you
gotta choose your battles. Every time I correct somebody, I have
to explain, teach, lecture, and defend. I have to watch as old-school
and often even new-school feminists, feeling abandoned, abandon
me. As straight people cock their heads to the side like confused
dogs. As my parents stare little smiles that try not to betray: "Our
kid is crazy."

   This pronoun confusion is part of the life of a no-op tranny. If you
do not do hormones or surgery, how can you expect people to know
you are a dude? I passed as a teenage boy for decades, but now it's

no longer "Yes, sir" but "Hey, lady." I have become Peter Pan, an eternally small boy always played by a middle-aged woman.

The change happened slowly. At first, watching my pals transition in the early '90s, I was by turn jealous of, fascinated by, and pissed off at these "fence jumpers." As time passed, however, I came to understand that their trans existence gave me permission to be the boy I had always been since I was old enough to say my real name: Johnny. The combination of feminist theory, heteronormative pressure, and my fag hag–faux queen mom had convinced me for forty years that I should leave my tiny boy behind and celebrate, if not my woman-ness or lesbianism, then at least my dykehood.

Over the last few years, I may have evolved from boy to teenager to mature Uncle Lynnee, but I still get my ass grabbed for being a chick and punched for saying fuck off. I still get dirty glares for looking like an old bull dyke with a hot young babe twenty years my junior. So I get homophobia for coming across as a woman who is not giving it up to boys, for not being sad about not embodying anything a straight bio boy would want, and for stealing hot young babes that should rightfully be in their dating pool.

It doesn't matter to the haters that I am a dude. They don't know I am a dude, because I'm not on hormones, have had no lower surgery and no operations. I could wear a big sandwich board that says:

IF YOU'RE GONNA HATE ME, HATE ME FOR BEING A TRANSSEXUAL, NOT FOR BEING A DYKE. IT'S NOT MY SEXUALITY YOU HATE. I'M A STRAIGHT GUY. IT'S THE FACT THAT I DON'T HAVE A DICK, OR THAT I DO AND IT STAYS UP LONGER THAN THREE MINUTES AND I ACTUALLY KNOW HOW TO OPERATE IT BETTER THAN YOU WHO WERE BORN WITH THE MOTHER-FUCKER ATTACHED. GET THE HATE MOTIVE RIGHT, PAL.

But then I would look like those really crazy people who walk around downtown San Francisco with the personal billboards that tell you how you're going to hell because you're a fornicator and on what page you can find it in the bible, or all about how the aliens are coming to get you.

I'm still not quite ready to bang Vitamin T (testosterone). First off, I'm a broke-ass artist. Not to mention that I have, just recently, gotten used to my "seventeen-year-new" clean and sober self. That chemical transition was hard enough—going from doing speed, ecstasy, pot, and 'shrooms, and drinking beer every day for ten years, to imbibing only coffee and cigarettes. Now you want me to get accustomed to a brand-new hormonal situation? I don't know if I have another chemical evolution in me. All that partying likely left me with liver damage that I'd be loathe to exacerbate with testosterone.

Plus, I don't like change. Hate it. If my girlfriend dyes her hair, without giving me six months' advance notice, I freak out and leave her. How is a guy who hates change that much going to approach a gender transition? Very slowly. I started out by straddling the barbed wire fence between dykes and trannies. Gradually, I acclimated to answering the preferred pronoun question with "shim, herm, zie, hir, they, it."

In the end, since I'm a Cali boy with years of therapy, it all came back to the inner child. I began to remember that in all of my made-up childhood stories I had referred to myself, the boy antihero, as "he," and in order to get back to that little boy, I had to climb over a lot of bad experiences with men. After all, a lot of women I loved had been terribly wronged by this identity I hated. One day, I answered, "I prefer he," and that just felt right even though I was still obsessive over hair removal. What can I say, I'm a metrosexual.

One of the main reasons I hesitated so long in admitting I was a guy was my fifteen-year stint as lead singer in my band Tribe 8. I was a vengeful motherfucker, yelling anthems by, for, and about dykes. "Frat Pig," one of our biggest hits, was a little ditty about gang rape; our answer was to gang castrate. I wrote and sang it before I was a dirty old bastard, and I used to get in trouble with feminists for being pissed off, perverted, and violent. But it's not that great of a poem. It just felt good to yell, "Frat pig, it's called gang rape. We're gonna play a game called gang castrate."

For years I wrote a semiautobiographical novel about a transgendered bike messenger. I read it aloud everywhere I went with Sister Spit and in San Francisco cafés. In the first edition, Jim has girl junk. In the second version, he has boy junk. Since it's in the first person, I was able to skirt the pronoun issue. At first, I didn't really stand up for Jim, and allowed publishers and press to describe Jim as a "she," because they wanted to be "clear." But then I shot a short film based on my book, and I had to write and talk about Jim in promoting the film. I was finally brave enough to let my real-life pronoun choice self-reflect.

Why did I take so long to come out? My parents had just gotten used to me being a dyke; but mostly it was because my dyed-in-the-wool dyke fans expected me never to change, and relied upon me to give voice to their struggles and keep fighting asshole males forever. Well, no worries, kids, I am still a righteously indignant feminist. Even though I am ostracized by some feminists for being a guy, I am proud to say my early work has allowed some of said Weemoon, Birkenstock babes to get in touch with their pissed-off, perverted, and violent sides. Their anthem?

> Women's love it's so friendly, women's love like herbal tea, women's love it empowers me . . . I just want to manipulate my girlfriend I just want to play games with her head I want her to do some mental pushups I want her to apologize and beg.

And then there's a recent rap I wrote about being a boy with boyboobs. Yep; I am a boy, but nobody knows. Nor will anyone believe me now that I am in an anthology of women's writing, begging to be ostracized by other trannies for being a poseur, opportunist, fence sitter, or unclear on the concept of what's woman and what ain't.

I am in this anthology because this is about a body of work, most
of which was written when I identified strongly as a dyke. A castrating, man-hating, kill-'em-all-let-god-sort-'em-out bulldagger. A mofo
who ran all over the stage, all tits and dick, brandishing a knife, soliciting BJs from straight boys with the promise that this would prove
they were punk.

Do I speak, rap, or sing words to get love? Nah. I do it to get an
answer back. All the answers and questions from everyone who's ever
heard me make me question who I am. All the transmen, all the dykes,
all the queers who want to be represented, demand realness from me.
Without them, I wouldn't know myself.

Knuckle Sandwich

What's uncle sam tellin you to do?
he's tellin you
to worry about predators with guns
so you scurry about limiting your fun in the dark
when in fact the attack
like a stab in the back
where you gotta watch your mouth
is in your own house.
love shack jackee.
ain't no out-the-bush-jumpin stranger
in the park ya gotta watch out for.
just when ya think it's cush it's Mr Danger
bite like his bark kickin it on yer couch.
You think a 12-year-old ho thought o that on her own?
why she ran away from home sweet home?
in the arms of a pimp it's better than it once was.
all her kiddie porn pals are dead in a dumpster.
if in the end she's alive she'll a been traumatized
like 9/11 survivors.
moms what you gonna do when your boyfriend eyes her?

if he's a jerk call a high alert
i gotcher war on terrorists
fix yer man a sandwich
knuckle sandwich

yeah them democrats they got your back.
DOMA? defense of whose marriage act? no love for the homos.
    where's my princess bride? I got FOMO.
you must be in a coma if you think gay marriage

is a carriage to hell.
we need the courage to heal from uncle dad's treachery
raising bambinis for twenty-first-century slavery machinery
penitentiaries cheaper than a factory
like what's fucked up by broken trust can be corrected at
   correctional facilities.
all my homos in the big house
came up in a hell house
of rapes beatins shameful secrets.
generations keep repeating
how we gonna beat this?

if he's a jerk call a high alert
i gotcher war on terrorists
fix yer man a sandwich
knuckle sandwich

it's so nice to have a man at least around the house.
feels right until his sanity goes down south.
at midnight you gotta jam to your feet and roust the kids out
beat it from the beater and the heat
run away on an underground railway.
wanted in fifty states they say you snapped
kidnapped your own babies when bailing
was all you could do to save them from the raving
madman sworn to protect them.
what's that about?

if he's a jerk call a high alert
i gotcher war on terrorists
fix yer man a sandwich
knuckle sandwich

dads diddlin their children
killin their women every day
don't get half the space in the press
of the one crazed babe who drowns the kids
she don't know how to save
while the front page raves how it can't explain
Why Maternal Instinct Turned to Rage!
cuz babes are just plain unstable

if they're so stable why do guys strangle
chix with their bare hands? cuz they can.
judge is willin to let em serve two to six
women rebellin with a gun or an ice pick
will soon be chillin on death row.
you gotta know kung fu to take a life.
you'll do less time than for a bullet or a knife
still pay more than a man
who offs his wife
cuz what? your life ain't worth as much?
damn make a stand
like j lo: had enough? rough him up.
9-10 he's out for the count.
why you gotta be the one to leave your own house?
he ain't down

if he's a jerk
call a high alert
i gotcher war on terrorists
fix your man a sandwich
knuckle sandwich
knuckle sandwich

Breasticles

i'm a boy
i got boyboobs
breasticles like testicles but higher
in the hierarchy of male identity
i feel dead
they be
sendin me to the periphery cuz i eschew surgery and vitamin T
i got no money
already had my body modified
traumatized needles and knives
i'm no-ho no-lo
no op-at-all
i spell M-A-N
balls—balls to the wall—that's all
gonna start a support group cuz
i need hugs
called the Big Titty He-Man Woman Hater's Club for big lugs
    bugged by manboobs—jugs
we'll exchange tips on over-the-counter strapper-downers
flatteners wrappers so yer flappers
dont impede ya get between ya
when yer tryina pound her into the ground
missionary style but yer mounds are drownin her
cuz i'm no-ho no-lo no op-at-all
i spell M-A-N
balls—balls to the wall—that's all
i apologized
for havin tits
cuz i'm scared o knives
but you got pissed

i'm more attached to em than i was at first yunno—don't take it
    personal
me talkin bout me
don't amount to cursin ya
I'm my own personal art project
self-obsessed? that's manly yes
but a real man ain't so sensitive
he's confident
my choice don't make me best
yer chest don't make you less
we just want a squishy place for our____
so live and let live and don't trip
(every song about you should be a love song
every song about me should be a love song
every song about us should be a love song)
she don't even make naked feel fake
skin all raw from yanked duct tape
her gaze makes pecs outta cupcakes
some guys get pushed outta shape
by pretty boys feelin shitty bout titties
but cut or not cut ain't cut-rate
outside changed or unchanged
inside self-same top shelf maing
cuz i'm no-ho no-lo no-op
you're not
we spell M-A-N
balls—balls to the wall—that's all

Stacyann Chin

Poet for
the People

I HAVE ALWAYS BEEN A STUDENT OF LITERATURE,
particularly enjoying the cadence of poetry. In Jamaica, I grew up
learning the words of classic poems and reciting them along with the
other students in my class. The cultural regard for poets in Jamaica is
similar to that in the U.S. The page poet is regarded as a creature to
be revered. He or she is thought to have sharpened sensibilities. The
performance poet is, for the most part, entertainment: held in high
regard by the outcast communities, privately ridiculed and scorned by
the greater number of academics. Mutabaruka, Louise Bennett, and
Mikey Smith were not taught as individual poets; rather, their poems
were occasional additions to the general poetry courses. The same
is true in this country; the Derek Walcotts and Joseph Brodskys are
almost never in the same room with Sonia Sanchez or Amiri Baraka.

Moving to America was pivotal in my trajectory from literature
student to writer. Though I'd penned a tragic confessional verse or
two in college, it wasn't until I came to America that I made a con-
certed effort to write. And I have to say, I *happened upon* writing
poetry for the page. Alone in New York, poor and confronted with

the terror of being other—I was accented, looked Black, and was half-Chinese—I was forced to chronicle the emotional effects of the transition in a journal. One Friday night, in 1997, a woman invited me to the Nuyorican Poets Café. There were poets of all ages and colors and cultural backgrounds. The room was teeming with a sort of underworld intensity. I have no other way to say it except that I caught the fever of the room and signed up for the open mic. Somewhere after midnight I dared to share an entry from my journal. The crowd stood up and cheered and shouted my name. I had no way to make sense of the experience. I only knew that I wanted to feel that way again. On that stage, I felt powerful, and heard, and *seen*.

I walked into the Nuyorican Poets Café because I wanted to get into the aforementioned woman's pants, so I would say I was motivated by lust at first. I told her I wrote poetry in the hopes that it would impress her. I spent my first year as a poet performing at the Nuyorican Poets Café. The next year, the Louder Arts Collective wooed me away with their emphasis on craft rather than performance. I actually qualified for the Nuyorican national slam team, but chose to go to Chicago with the Louder Arts Project instead.

I eventually decided to stop "slamming" and to start touring as a spoken word poet. The competitive process was very seductive. Being in the spoken word scene gave me access to a wide and varied demographic. As a young writer, I was electrified with the buzz of winning. But as the number of slams I won increased, I became uncomfortable with the desire to use cheap tricks to get a rise out of the audience and the judges in order to win. Finally, I decided that my pen needed room to create outside of the slam. Allan Buchman of the Culture Project had been "pestering" me to write a one-person theater show. In the absence of the competition, I wrote my first play in poetic vignettes, *Hands Afire*.

Since that time, I have toured as a professional performer nonstop and have been blessed with countless and diverse venues both

here and abroad. One of the most recent and breathtaking perfor-
mances, one that reminded me why I embarked upon this journey, was
at the 2006 Gay Games on Chicago's Soldier Field stadium, for tens of
thousands of diverse queers. It was big and open and loud, and it was
gay. I offered up an intense critique of our increasingly "white, rich,
media-friendly" queer cultural face, not knowing if I was going to be
well-received. And apart from one or two dissenting voices—the ones
who complained that my negative portrayal of the present LGBT com-
munity tarnished what was supposed to be a celebration—the stadium
was a roar of voices. I heard this response as an admission that we had
strayed from the intent of Stonewall, and Audre Lorde and all those
people who fought so hard to create a political gay identity. It restored
my faith in the power of saying your truth out loud. I now know that
if you shout and shout and shout a truth, eventually, someone hears
it, and sometimes if you are really lucky, and if the words are just the
right pitch, the crowd will shout along with you.

When I address lesbian college students in the U.S., one of the
first concerns I address is the political apathy in our communities,
followed swiftly by the disappearance of women's spaces, of lesbian
spaces, of spaces where real, sharp, radical politics can be debated:
health care, AIDS, and violence against women. I also challenge the
growing generational divide within feminist culture, wondering if
these young college students know the work of Barbara Smith and
bell hooks and Andrea Dworkin. In this mad rush to find themselves,
young women are missing each other. If we continue like this, the
daughters of the next generation will not even recognize each other
as people who share a history of gender and sexual oppression.

Performing outside of the United States can also be a challenge.
The names, the topics, and, most especially, the genre are almost
always *new* to the audience, and they are less impressed by flashy
metaphors and stomping feet. I was really at home in South Africa.
The women there still have a recent memory of apartheid. They still

remember why radical activism is important and necessary for our
survival as women, as lesbians, as creatures who will be held account-
able by the next generation for what is happening now. It was hard
to see the poverty, to hear the stories of rape and disfigurement of
women. But it was good to be among people who seemed bonded by
a common struggle for equality. I always feel my double conscious-
ness in most white countries. In Scandinavia, I am never quite sure
if they like my poetry, or are seduced by my accent. In Jamaica I am
always at odds with myself. Some performances are received with
open palms; others, I am booed and almost thrown from the stage.
And it is complicated, because it is home.

I first went home to Jamaica, as a professional poet, to read for
the Calabash writers' festival in St. Elizabeth. I had no idea what
my family's response would be. The trip home was wrought with all
sorts of anxieties. I was already on HBO's *Def Poetry Jam*, and had
appeared in many on-air performances. The island had already seen
what I do. I was afraid I was going to be stoned off the stage for my
overtly lesbian politics. The gathering was mostly people from the
upper and middle class. But there were also a few Rastafarians and
local prophets who considered work like mine dangerous to the spiri-
tual safety of the island. Much to my surprise, the audience applauded
and was deeply moved. The newspapers did stories on my perfor-
mance, and Mutabaruka invited me to do an interview on his popular
radio talk show. No one was surprised. There were people who were
upset, but the consensus was that I'd always been a controversial
individual and no less was expected when I "became" a lesbian and
promptly went on to become a public poet.

Taking on the responsibility of the work I put out, as a political
public figure, has been a slow, cautious process. I know I want to make
the world safer for marginalized groups, and I am particularly moved
by the suffering of people who share my cultural or political genesis.
I care about Black people, and lesbians, girls, and children—and I

know I will spend what remains of my life agitating the powers that could make the lives of those people better. Every day I get better at knowing that it is not a choice to be an activist; rather, it is the only way to hold on to the better parts of my human self. It is the only way I can live and laugh without guilt.

Before being a writer, or a poet, or a theater performer, I am a "poet for the people." It is how I came to the art of writing. I want to fuck up the political power structure in the world. I know I cannot do that by myself. So I want to belong to a group of badass, radical, feminist thinkers who I can run with, ride with, and maybe have sex with, all while we change the world. I am always grateful when anything is canonized in this era of "Drink now, piss it out later." I like being recognized for the work that I have done. But it is also important to note that there are women who have done far more than I who will not be "canonized." This only says that I was here, that I ran, in a sea of women who were moved by the word. It is the documenting of a history. And when I am not even memory, not even dust, the word will remain to count me as present, to mark that I was here.

Cross-Fire

Am I a feminist
or a womanist
the student needs to know
if I do men occasionally
and primarily am I a lesbian

Tongue tied up to my cheek
I attempt to respond with some honesty—

This business of dykes and dykery I tell her
is often messy
with social tensions as they are
you never quite know what you're getting
—girls who are only straight at night
—hardcore butches who sport dresses
between nine and six during the day
    sometimes she is an endangered chameleon
trapped by the limitations of our imagination

primarily I tell her
I am concerned about young women
who are raped on college campuses
    in cars
after poetry readings like this one
    in bars
    bruised lip and broken heart
you will forgive her if she does not come
forward with the truth immediately
for when she does it is she who will stand trial
as damaged goods

Everyone will say she asked for it
dressed as she was she must have wanted it

The words will knock about in her head
horny bitch
slut
harlot
loose woman
some people cannot handle a woman on the loose

you know those women in silk ties and pinstriped shirts
those women in blood-red stilettos and short pink skirts
these women make New York City the most interesting place
   and while we're on the subject of diversity
   Asia is not one big race
   and there is no such country called the *Islands*
   and no—I am not from there

There are a hundred ways to slip between the cracks
of our not-so-credible cultural assumptions of race and religion

Most people are surprised my father is Chinese—like
there's some kind of preconditioned
look for the half-Chinese lesbian poet
who used to be Catholic but now believes in dreams

Let's keep it real
says the boy in the double-X hooded sweatshirt
that blond haired blue eyed Jesus in the Vatican ain't right
   that motherfucker was Jewish, not white

Christ was a Middle Eastern Rastaman
who ate grapes in the company of prostitutes
and drank wine more than he drank water
born of the spirit the disciples also loved him in the flesh
but the discourse is on people who clearly identify as gay
or lesbian or straight
the State needs us to be left or right
    those in the middle get caught
in the cross—fire away at the other side

If you are not for us you must be against us
People get scared enough they pick a team

Be it for Buddha or for Krishna or for Christ
God is that place between belief and what you name it
I believe holy is what you do when there is nothing between
    your actions and a truth

never one thing or the other—
I am everything I fear
    tears and sorrows
    black windows and muffled screams
in the morning I am all I ever wanted to be
    rain and laughter
    bare footprints and invisible seams
always without breath or definition—I claim every single dawn
for yesterday is simply what I was
and tomorrow
even that will be gone

Poem for the Gay Games

Being queer has no bearing on race
or class or creed
   my white publicist said
true love is never affected by color
or country or the carnal need for cash

I curb the flashes of me crashing across the table
to knock his blond skin
from Manhattan to Montego Bay
to bear witness to the bloody beatings
of beautiful brown boys
accused of the homosexual crime of buggery

amidst the newfangled fads and fallacies
the new-age claims that sexual and racial freedom
has finally come for all
these underinformed, self-congratulating
pseudointellectual utterances
reflect how apolitical the left has become

I can't explain why
but the term lesbian just comes across
as confrontational to me
why can't you people just say you date people?

Tongue and courage tied with fear
I am at once livid, ashamed and paralyzed
by the neoconservatism breeding malicious amongst us

Gay
Lesbian
Bisexual
Transgender
Ally
Questioning
Two spirit
Non-gender-conforming—every year we add a new letter
our community is happily expanding beyond the scope
of the dream Stonewall sparked within us

yet every day
I become more and more afraid to say
black
or lesbian
or woman—every day
under the pretense of unity
I swallow something I should have said
about the epidemic of AIDS in Africa
or the violence against teenage girls in East New York
or the mortality rate of young boys on the south side of Chicago

even in friendly conversation
I have to rein in the bell hooks–ian urge
to kill motherfuckers who say stupid shit to me
all day, bitter branches of things I cannot say out loud
sprout deviant from my neck

fuck you-you-fucking-racist-sexist-turd
fuck you for crying about homophobia
while you exploit the desperation of undocumented immigrants
to clean your hallways

bathe your children and cook your dinner
for less than you and I spend on our tax deductible lunch!

I want to scream out loud
all oppression is connected you dick

at the heart of every radical action in history
stood the dykes who were feminists
the antiracists who were gay rights activists
the straight men who believed being vulnerable
could only make our community stronger

as the violence against us increases
where are the LGBT centers in those neighborhoods
where assaults occur most frequently?
as the tide of the Supreme Court changes
where are the LGBT marches
to support a woman's right to an abortion?
what are we doing about health insurance
for those who can least afford it?

HIV/AIDS was once a reason for gay white men to act up
now your indifference spells the death
of straight black women
and imprisoned Latino boys
apparently
if the tragedy does not immediately impact you
you don't give a fuck

a revolution once pregnant with expectation
flounders
without direction the privileged and the plundered

grow listless
apathetic and individualistic no one knows
where to vote
or what to vote for anymore

the faces that now represent us
have begun to look like the ones who used to burn crosses
and beat bulldaggers and fuck faggots up the ass
with loaded guns
the companies that sponsor our events
do not honor the way we live or love
or dance or pray
progressive politicians still dance around
the issue of gay parenting
and the term marriage is reserved
for those unions sanctioned by a church-controlled state

for all the landmarks we celebrate
we are still niggers
and faggots
and minstrel references
for jokes created on the funny pages of a heterosexual world

the current LGBT manifesto
is a corporate agenda/and outside that agenda
a woman is beaten every twelve seconds
every two minutes
a girl is raped somewhere in America

and while we stand here well-dressed and rejoicing
in India
in China

in South America—a small child cuts the cloth
to construct you a new shirt/a new shoe
a new imperialism held upright
by the old hunger and misuse of impoverished lives

gather round ye fags, dykes, trannies
and all those in between
we are not simply at a political crossroad
we are buried knee deep in the quagmire
of a battle for our humanity

the powers that have always been have already come
for the Jew, the communist and the trade unionist

the time to act is now!
Now! while there are still ways that we can fight
Now! because those rights we still have are so very few
Now! because it is the right thing to do
Now! before you open the door to find
they have finally come for you

Exceeding
Expectations

I FIRST BEGAN PERFORMING SPOKEN WORD IN
2002, just a year after my transition from male to female.
Transitioning had been a tumultuous experience for me. It was a
period full of intense highs—for the first time feeling comfortable
in my own skin and being honest and open about seeing myself as
female. There were also lows—in particular, having to constantly
manage other people's reactions toward my transsexuality. My
coming-out process dredged up all sorts of memories from my child-
hood and young adulthood that had remained dormant for decades.
And the surreal experience of having other people perceive and
treat me as female after having lived for thirty-some-odd years
as male resulted in numerous anecdotes and observations about
gender that I was anxious to share with the rest of the world.
Almost unconsciously, these perspectives and experiences began
to come together in my mind in the form of spoken word poems
(most likely as a result of me having been a regular attendee at Bay
Area poetry slams for a number of years). Before I knew it, I was up
onstage myself, sharing my story and opinions with audiences.

As writers, we may be able to choose the words we use and the manner in which we speak them, but we are not always in control of the ways in which other people will interpret or react to what we have to say. This reality really hit home for me during that first year of performing at poetry slams. Highly personal poems about discovering my female identity as a young child would garner responses like, "I really enjoyed that poem by that man . . . woman . . . transvestite?" And after performing a righteous, kick-ass feminist rant, I'd have someone come up to me afterward and the only thing on their mind would be, "Is it really true that you used to be a guy?" It became apparent to me that, for many in the audience, I was the first real-life transsexual they had ever knowingly encountered. And for many of them, my words were of secondary interest compared to their fascination regarding my transsexuality.

This divide continues to be one of the most challenging aspects of performing spoken word. When we read a poem or an essay off the page, we tend to make very few assumptions about the author—we only know those aspects of their life that they explicitly share with us. But as soon as a spoken word performer steps onto the stage, we immediately begin to make all sorts of presumptions about them, even before they utter a single word. We judge them, consciously or subconsciously, based on their race, size, age, appearance, and countless other factors—including, of course, the gender we perceive them to be. Over time, I began to realize that any time I performed a piece that touched on my experiences as a trans person, I had to grapple with two very different audience expectations. Initially, people would tend to read me as a somewhat tomboyish, freckly-faced "girl next door" type. Then, as soon as I'd mention that I was trans, I'd have to deal with an entirely different set of assumptions: all of the stereotypes and misconceptions that people have about transsexual women.

As I became increasingly cognizant of these audience expectations, I began to explore ways in which I could exploit them in order to challenge the audience. I know that it's really trendy for people in feminist and queer activist circles to talk about gender as a "doing" or a "performance," but during my transition I found that that wasn't always the case. Even though my personality, mannerisms, and actions did not change with my transition, other people began reacting to those same behaviors in very different ways now that they perceived me to be a woman rather than a man. I took advantage of this understanding to craft pieces that illuminated the fact that all of us view the world through gendered lenses. In many of these performances, the "coming out as trans" moment was highly choreographed—perfectly timed to ensure the biggest impact on the audience, to allow them to reflect upon all of the assumptions that they had initially made about me. I learned how to weave moments where I exceeded the audience's expectations into my poetry and performance—they became a part of the language of the piece itself.

Performing spoken word not only offered me a way to challenge many commonplace presumptions people have about femaleness and maleness, but also provided me with an opportunity to debunk many of the myths and prejudices that people harbor toward transsexual women. Many people—even those who are highly attuned to the ways in which women and other marginalized groups are regularly misrepresented by the media—often accept media stereotypes of trans women at face value. TV and movie producers may try to pigeonhole transsexual women as either drag queens, sex workers, or middle-aged men donning dresses, but in reality we (like women in general) happen to fall all over the map with regard to our gender expressions, presentations, and politics. The fact that I did not dress in a high-femme manner, and that most of my poems were unapologetically feminist, offered audiences the chance to appreciate the fact that there are many different types of trans women.

While I have found challenging audience expectations to be extremely empowering and rewarding, I've also had to accept the fact that there are limits to what I can do within the context of a three- to five-minute spoken word piece. Most people, having absorbed a lifetime of gender socialization, are not going to immediately embrace everything that I have to say. In many ways, being out as a transgender poet can be a double-edged sword. By speaking publicly as a trans person, I am able to bring much-needed visibility and attention to transgender issues and perspectives. At the same time, however, as soon as I come out to people, they immediately begin to see me differently. They actively scan my body and behaviors for any real or imagined signs of my former maleness. They start slipping up my pronouns. They begin using words like "imitate" or "impersonate" when referring to my female identity. In other words, they begin to view my femaleness as artificial and illegitimate. People often describe transsexuals as "passing" as one sex or the other, but I take issue with that description. I do not "pass" as a woman—I *am* a woman. If I "pass" for anything these days, it is as a cissexual (i.e., someone who is not transsexual). While I am not in any way ashamed of my transsexuality, it does sadden me that I cannot be open about that aspect of my person without having some people demean or dismiss my identity and lived experiences as a woman.

Despite the fact that audiences do not always view me the way that I view myself, I still find myself constantly gravitating toward spoken word performance. I think part of the reason for this is that spoken word can be so much more than just words—it incorporates sights, sounds, motion, and the energy of the space. Spoken word performance is undoubtedly the most intimate and immediate artistic medium that I have experienced. It allows my words and experiences to emotionally resonate with the audience. It offers audiences the chance to identify with me, with my perspective, if only for a brief moment. As a poet and as a trans activist, I realize how vital these small moments can be. Perhaps that's why spoken word performance has been such fertile ground for artists of all persuasions to explore the subject of identity. It provides a rare moment where we can transcend borders and bring the audience into our world. It allows us the rare chance to exceed other people's expectations.

sleeping sickness

in the name of the father
the son
and the holy spirit
amen

that's how it begins
my nights are spent
composing insomniac open letters to you
two-hour-long monologues
that end in exhaustion
and sometimes in the middle of my day
i'll remember that i fell asleep
before ending my previous night's prayer
with a proper amen
and i'll wonder whether my channel to you is still open
my every word an invocation
the sounds of my atari games
little league practice
and eighth grade history class
becoming the annoying background noise of heaven

and maybe forgetting to say amen
makes my life one long continuous prayer
and if so, then you were there that afternoon
when i tucked my penis tightly behind my legs
just to see what i'd look like without it
when i wrapped bedroom curtains around my body
like a prom dress
turned tattered shoelaces
into necklaces and bracelets

and you were there later that same night
when i began another prayer within a prayer
to once again beg for your forgiveness

wanting to be a girl
never came up in CCD or sunday mass
and it's not covered in the ten commandments
but from everything the nuns and priests taught me about you
i know that you do not approve
and when i turn to your holy words
to look for anything that might shed some light
onto whatever this is that i'm going through
i keep returning to the same story
the one about abraham
and how you commanded him to sacrifice his son to you
stopping the blade only seconds before
he actually went through with it
and forgive me father
for i can't help but think
that that was a fucked up thing to do

and maybe i'm like abraham
and this is just another one of your tests
maybe you put girl thoughts
into the heads of twelve-year-old boys
just to see how they'll react
maybe i'm an experiment
and you're up in heaven looking down on me
taking notes as i tear myself apart in self-hatred
tossing and turning in bed
as if acting out my inevitable burning in hell

and at first
my sins made me even more devout
i'd lie awake each night
clutching the glow-in-the-dark rosary beads
that my grandmother gave me
repeating the words that i once heard her say
"blessed are those who have not seen yet believe"
and i want to believe
but more and more it just feels
like you're torturing me
and i'm doing the best that i can
to plug up all the holes
in this disintegrating dam
as my brain bleeds rivers of bad thoughts
that pour out of my mouth and hands
like wounds that won't clot
and i can't understand
why you won't help
when i've asked you over and over again
to please either turn me into a girl
or else make these thoughts stop

the nuns say that you answer all prayers
it's just that sometimes the answer is no
well, i'm tired of praying to a god
who only offers me
thou shalt not's
i'm tired from lack of sleep
from keeping secrets
that burn so much that they hollow me out
i am tired of hurting so much
that sometimes i pray

that i don't wake up
so forgive me father for i have sinned
i have dared to share
all of myself with you
forcing you to watch
one long sacrilegious prayer
within a prayer
within a prayer
within a prayer
like a serpent swallowing its own soul
like a serpent swallowing itself whole
and maybe tonight
i'll finally be cured of this sleeping sickness
because the last few years
of living in absolute shame
and unbelievable pain
has made me fearless enough to finally say
amen.

vice versa

i almost forgot about her
buried alive in the back of my mind
at the time
i was a twenty-six-year-old closet case
self-described occasional crossdresser
and she was just like me
only vice versa

i met her in kansas city
at my first transgender support group meeting
the chairs were set up in a circle
and most of the seats were filled
with transvestites in their forties and fifties
painstakingly dressed
wearing sunday's best
floral prints
and muted pinks
with just a hint of five o'clock shadow
looking strangely sweet
almost equal parts aunt and uncle

and she seemed so out of place there
the only one in t-shirt and jeans
and genetically speaking
she was the only girl in the room
and chronologically
we were the only two in our twenties

after the meetings minutes
and a guest speaker from mary kay
offering makeup tips

she introduced herself to me
she told me her name was joan
i told her mine was tom
and after a bit of random chitchat
she asked if i wanted to hang out some time
and i said sure
and a week later we did

i drove to topeka where she lived
and i remember
the two of us sitting on her bed
listening to tom lehrer
on her portable cassette player
when i asked her what her deal was
she said she wasn't sure what to call herself exactly
she was attracted to men
but when she masturbated
she imagined herself with a penis topping them
and i could tell she was embarrassed
until i told her
that i knew exactly what she meant
because i was just like her
only lesbian

so i told her
the first time i told anyone
about when i was in the seventh grade
and had the biggest crush on kathy patterson
and every preteen fantasy i had about her
began with me being turned into a girl somehow
and only afterwards
would we run away together

then joan told me
about her high school boyfriend
who told her he was gay
and she replied
that she wasn't surprised
and that she liked him that way

and we told our gender histories
like we were swapping war stories
experiences we couldn't share
with our families or friends
because they were never there
and they would never understand
but that night
sitting on joan's bed
for the first time in my life
i didn't feel
quite so much like an alien

and the last time i saw her
was a saturday evening we spent
watching a star trek next generation rerun
(the episode where beverly crusher
falls in love with a trill)
and we both sat still on her couch
next to one another
and when our bodies touched
we knew that it was the first human contact
that either of us had in a while
and at one point
i put my arm around her
and she leaned into me

and it felt like we were pretending
that i was the he
and she was the she

and for a moment
i thought one thing might lead to another
maybe we'd make out on her sofa
and wake up naked next to one another
and somehow it almost made sense
like we were each other's long-lost complement
the way two odd numbers add up
to make an even
but the problem was
we weren't really a perfect match
we were more like exact replicas
the same only vice versa
and while there was definitely some mutual attraction
nothing ever happened
because after all
i wasn't a gay man
and she wasn't a lesbian

now it's eight years later
and i'm not in kansas anymore
i'm a woman living in oakland
and that bedroom in topeka
literally feels like a lifetime ago
and every now and again
when i find myself feeling alone
i think about joan
and i wonder how he's doing

Patricia Smith

Name-Calling

SLAM POETRY LEGEND PATRICIA SMITH IS A FOUR-
time individual champion of the National Poetry Slam. She spoke with
anthology editor Alix Olson about artistic and political self-identifica-
tion, avoiding cookie-cutter poetry, and performing for twenty-five
thousand Japanese businessmen.

**As a four-time individual champion of the National Poetry Slam, what
advice would you provide to up-and-coming spoken word artists and/
or slam poets, either in terms of actual study and/or life experience?**
First, listen to everyone. Everyone with a voice has a lesson for
you—the Baptist preacher, the pump jockey, that bitch on the train
bellowing into her cell phone. All their sounds have an effect on the air
around them, and you need to study that effect. Listen to little kids
mispronounce words in rap songs, listen to drivers cursing traffic, lis-
ten to your lover sing absentmindedly while dicing veggies. Then, once
you've learned to revel in sound, listen to the stories. That's where
your substance will come from, that's where the pulse of your poems
are. In your stories, and in theirs. . . . Secondly, don't listen to anyone.

Nowadays, so much of slam is cookie-cutter. Poet sees poem about joy of doughnuts, poet writes poem about joy of doughnuts. One mad poet equals several thousand mad poets—they're mad about being black, mad about being female, mad about being black and female, mad about racial profiling, mad about Amadou Diallo, mad about George Bush, et cetera . . . and that's all they are is mad. Ask them why, and they'll tell you they saw it on television. Or heard it from that cat at the open mic. . . . While I wouldn't trade a millisecond of my life in slam, it's now having an unexpected effect, one I couldn't have predicted. Because the slam is so public, such a lightning rod, I can't shake it. No matter where I go, no matter what I do, I'm slapped with the label "slam poet," and I'm expected to perform. I haven't slammed, officially, in more than ten years, but I can't tell you how many times I've been introduced or touted as "that slammer." It doesn't matter how many books I write, how many awards I win, that's my designation. I've been fighting against it lately, calling folks on it whenever it occurs, but I'm beginning to think that it's something I'll never completely shake. But hey, there are worse things to be called. After all, I can walk on any stage in the world and conquer it. How many folks can say that?

What have you learned most about poetry and about yourself as a poet through teaching?

I often say that if I had had a poet come into my classroom when I was eight or nine years old, a poet who said, loud and clear, "This is what I do, and it is an option available for you," my life would have been changed that much sooner. I try to do that.

Do you identify as a "political," "feminist," and/or "Black" poet? And what is your view of these types of self- and/or externally imposed identifications upon artists?

I hate those cheap little categorizations we let just about anybody slap on our world and work. What's worse is when we slap the labels on ourselves. If you've got enough courage to stand up tall in this dipsy world and say, unequivocally, "I am a writer," then you should also be committed to writing in as many ways as possible, with any voice or from any perspective that hits you. I'm a woman, so I don't have to be a "feminist" anything; hell, anybody with ovaries who lives in this country has to be a feminist—a brass-balled woman—just to slice through the muck that's thrown at us every day. Every syllable we conjure is political. And of course, being black influences every breath I've ever taken, every word I'll ever write. The only people who need to name it are those who need to keep its meaning, its importance, small and pliable. If I'm a "black poet" or a "feminist poet," then I can't effectively be anything else. Well, I'm every damned thing. I was raised watching Ed Sullivan and John Wayne and Richard Nixon and seeing the Beatles punch the world in its gut, so you can't tell me I can't write from a white, male, mainstream perspective. I've been surrounded by "white as right" ever since I can remember. But if I don't stay in my box, what will you do with me? For Chrissakes, what will you call me? We spend entirely too much time with names. It's as if we can't do what we do until we know what we're called. Then that's all anybody ever expects us to do. Nonsense.

What has been your experience touring internationally? How have you been received, for example, as a U.S. poet?

Once, I won a citywide poetry contest in Chicago, which remains one of the best places in the world to be a poet. There was this far-flung competition—the organizers worked hard to pull poets from the whole of the city—and the winner was rewarded with a trip to one of Chicago's sister cities. This was a big, big, deal—a teeny and tasteful parade, party at city hall, and then this all-expense-paid jaunt to, in this case, Osaka, Japan. All you had to do was write a poem that would eventually wow a panel of Chi-town bigwigs. But, of course, it couldn't be just any poem. The poem had to be about a tree, or spoken about a tree, or carved into the skin of a tree. The winning trip was to some sort of agricultural/environment fair, and somebody who'd had way too much beer figured it would be a great idea to have the winning poem tie in somehow. That's right, I said the poem had to be about a tree.

So I wrote a poem about a tree on Chicago's lakefront. I write a lot of persona pieces, and while this wasn't exactly in the voice of the tree, it might as well have been. I had lines about how the chilly water felt on the tree's "thick ankle," and how it felt when "hopeful lovers scratched their names into her skin." And, I'll admit it, the end of the poem was totally manipulative. Here it is (remember, we're talkin' about a tree here):

> She has a name for the moan that worries gently in her hair
> It is called Chicago.

Yeah, yeah, shameless, I know. You can't put a competition in front of a slammer. But I won, and I was going to Japan.

Before I got there, there was the matter of my poem. It had to be translated, because it was going to be projected on a huge screen beside me when I read. (Oh, did I tell you the reading was in front of approximately twenty-five thousand Japanese businessmen?) So I had this translator calling me, completely frustrated because trees *can't talk*. He'd try to talk me through a line before collapsing completely and hissing, "You know that trees cannot think? You know this!" I apologized, but I couldn't help him out. The poem was what the poem was. Pretty soon he stopped calling.

I'm convinced that when I took the stage and that screen clicked into light behind me, my poem didn't appear. Instead, I imagine, the lines said over and over, in Japanese, "This silly woman thinks that trees can talk. Please applaud politely when she is done with this silliness."

My second favorite touring story is doing "Skinhead" in a dank East German bar with skinheads in the audience—it's an experience I treasure, but do not recommend. In the middle of the poem, a framed picture fell off the wall and hit me in the head, knocking me unconscious. The poets I was traveling with thought I'd been taken out by a neo-Nazi.

My third story also takes place in Germany, years later. There was this wonderful event where a train full of poets took off across the countryside, stopping in town squares and giving readings. I was on hand in Berlin when their train returned, and it was the most amazing thing. There were so many people waiting to welcome them that they had to close the station down—this was Berlin's main train station, and closing it was a huge deal. As the poets got off the train—one by one, like stepping out of a limo at the Oscars—there were deafening cheers, flags waving, tears, music. Some of them were hefted and carried about on the crowd's shoulders. I had never, ever seen poets treated with such giddy reverence. It was then I realized that—in the rest of the world, at least—we're national treasures.

Your poetry volumes have been adapted for the theater. What was your favorite experience with this?

My favorite experience was being "discovered" by Derek Walcott, who just happened to be exploring the juncture of poetry and theater when he happened upon a reading I was doing. He produced my show—which was really just a number of poems I was already doing, linked with dialogue, backdrop, and music. It played for weeks at the Boston Playwrights' Theatre, sold out shows, and was reviewed like an honest-to-goodness theatrical production. After seeing how successful it was, Derek packed up the whole shebang and took us to Trinidad, where we set up shop in the Trinidad Theatre Workshop, had way too much fun, and drank way too much beer. I felt like a real celebrity, and I got rid of another silly line separating the genres.

Since then, theater has seemed very accessible to me. I've done a couple of other shows, and felt very comfortable and competent onstage. I was a writer-in-residence at the Eugene O'Neill Theater Center, where I hobnobbed with actual working, big-time playwrights like Adam Rapp and Regina Taylor. They thought I was one of them! My time there opened up a world of possible collaboration. Poetry has no boundaries. I've played Carnegie Hall with Bill Cole's Untempered Ensemble, an avant-garde jazz band, and right now I'm working on a huge, kinda hush-hush project with Urban Bush Women.

What was your biggest compliment within this work, and what did it mean for you?

One [compliment] was something written by Emily Van Hazinga, a reporter for the Fitchburg, Massachusetts, *Sentinel and Enterprise*. She called me "a testament to the power of words to change lives," and I've never forgotten that. I'm always preaching about that power, to students and other poets, and I'm thrilled to be considered an example of what that power can do.

And in October of last year, during a ceremony at the Gwendolyn Brooks Center of Chicago State University, I was inducted into the Literary Hall of Fame for Writers of African Descent. After the ceremony, we were shown the place where our photos would hang, alongside the other honorees. There was Zora Neale Hurston, Langston Hughes, Toni Morrison, Robert Hayden, and Gwen Brooks. And me. Damn.

What is your wish for the future of the spoken word movement?

I'd like it to stop being a movement. It's here, it's always been here, and it's a victim of our inexplicable need to "name" everything. I hope poets can stop counting on other poets to forge their own voices. I hope the "spoken word movement" gets so big that you can't see it at all. Then we can stop talking about where it's been and where it's going. Then we can just write, and work. Then we can just be.

Asking for a Heart Attack

for Aretha Franklin

Aretha. Deep butter dipped, scorched pot liquor,
swift lick off the sugar cane. Vaselined knees
clack gospel, hinder the waddling south. 'retha.
Greased, she glows in limelit circle,
defending her presence with sanctified moan,
that ass rumbling toward midnight's neighborhood.

Goddess of Hoppin John and bumped buttermilk,
girl know Jesus by His *first* name.
She was the one sang His drooping down
from that ragged wooden T,
dressed Him in blood red and shine,
conked that holy head,
rustled up bus fare
and took the Deity downtown.
They found a neon backslap, coaxed the DJ
and slid electric till the lights slammed on.
Don't know where you goin', but you can't stay here.

Aretha taught the Almighty slow, dirty words
for His daddy's handiwork,
laughed as he first sniffed whiskey's surface,
hissed him away when he sought to touch His hand
to what was blue in her.
She was young then, spindly and ribs paining,
her heartbox suspicious of its key.
So Jesus blessed her, opened her throat
and taught her to wail that way she do,
she do wail that way don't she do that wail the way

she do wail that way, don't she?
Now when 'retha's fleeing screech jump from juke
and reach been-done-wrong bone,
all the Lord can do is stand at a respectable distance
and applaud. And maybe shield His heart a little.

So you question her several shoulders,
the soft stairs of flesh leading to her chins,
the steel bones of an impossible dress
gnawing into bubbling obliques?
Ain't your mama never told you
how black women collect the world,
build other bodies onto their own?
No earthly man knows the solution to our hips,
asses urgent as sirens,
titties bursting with traveled roads.
Ask her to tell you what Jesus whispered to her that night
about black girls who grow fat away from everyone
and toward each other.

Building Nicole's Mama

For the sixth grade class of Lillie C. Evans School, Liberty City, Miami

I am astonished at their mouthful names—
Lakinishia, Fumilayo, Chevellanie, Delayo—
their ragged rebellions and lip-glossed pouts,
and all those pants drooped as drapery.
I rejoice when they kiss my face, whisper wet
and urgent in my ear, make me their obsession
because I have brought them poetry.

They shout me raw, bruise my wrists with pulling,
and brashly claim me as mama as they
cradle my head in their little laps,
waiting for new words to grow in my mouth.

You.
You.
You.
Angry, jubilant, weeping poets—we are all
saviors, reluctant Hosannas in the limelight,
but you knew that, didn't you? Then let us
bless this sixth grade class—forty nappy heads,
forty cracking voices, and all of them
raise their hands when I ask. They have all seen
the Reaper, grim in his heavy robe,
pushing the button for the dead project elevator,
begging for a break at the corner pawn shop,
cackling wildly in the back pew of the Baptist church.

I ask the death question and forty fists
punch the air, *me!*, *me!* And O'Neal,
matchstick crack child, watched his mother's

body become a claw and nine-year-old Tiko Jefferson,
barely big enough to lift the gun, fired a bullet
into his own throat after Mama bended his back
with a lead pipe. Tamika cried into a sofa pillow
when Daddy blasted Mama into the north wall
of their cluttered one-room apartment,
Donya's cousin gone in a drive-by. Dark window,
click, click, gone, says Donya, her tiny finger
a barrel, the thumb a hammer. I am shocked
by their losses—and yet when I read a poem
about my own hard-eyed teenager, Jeffery asks

He is dead yet?

It cannot be comprehended,
my eighteen-year-old still pushing and pulling
his own breath. And those forty faces pity me,
knowing that I will soon be as they are,
numb to our bloodied histories,
favoring the Reaper with a thumbs-up and a wink,
hearing the question and shouting *me, me,
Miss Smith, I know somebody dead!*

Can poetry hurt us? they ask me before
snuggling inside my words to sleep.
I love you, Nicole says, Nicole wearing my face,
pimples peppering her nose, and she is as black
as angels are. Nicole's braids clipped, their ends
kissed with match flame to seal them,
and *can you teach me to write a poem about my mother?*
*I mean, you write about your daddy and he dead,
can you teach me to remember my mama?*

A teacher tells me this is the first time Nicole
has admitted that her mother is gone,
murdered by slim silver needles and a stranger
rifling through her blood, the virus pushing
her skeleton through for Nicole to see.
And now this child with rusty knees
and mismatched shoes sees poetry as her scream
and asks me for the words to build her mother again.
Replacing the voice.
Stitching on the lost flesh.

So poets,
as we pick up our pens,
as we flirt and sin and rejoice behind microphones—
remember Nicole.
She knows that we are here now,
and she is an empty vessel waiting to be filled.

And she is waiting.
And she
is
waiting.
And she waits.

Acknowledgments

First, I am indebted to Erin Raber, my lead editor, for initiating this much overdue project, for her soft but firm handle on the process, and for her intelligent and patient guidance. Thanks also to the rest of the Seal Press team, including Tabitha Lahr, Hannah Cox, Laura Mazer, and Darcy Cohan, for steering this anthology toward fruition.

Eve Ensler, the Great Vagina Warrior, who packs her political theater with an eloquent punch and a Cheshire grin, thank you for blessing this project.

I am honored to have been a member of the slam poetry family for the past decade—thanks to each of you. I gratefully acknowledge all of the venues, nationally and worldwide, that sustain the spoken word revolution, particularly the Nuyorican Poets Café, my special breeding ground. Keith Roach, thanks for changing the direction of my life.

Many thanks to all of the festivals that have incorporated spoken word and the college student organizations that work diligently to bring us to your campuses.

I have immense gratitude for my past public school teachers, especially Naomi Era, Judy Smullen, Len Perrett, and Roger Hudak, who each had a delicate hand in sculpting my love affair with words. To my Wesleyan University professors, especially Kate Rushin, Jessica Shubow, and Christina Crosby, thanks for stretching my brain like it was putty in your hands (it was).

I am fortunate for my feisty family, especially Laura Katz Olson, Kathleen Kelly, Liz Devlin, and Gary Olson, my consistent landmark of a dad. I am equally nurtured by Sarah Kowal, David Vine, Lyndell Montgomery, Chris Pureka, Samantha Farinella, Jill Dunn, Natalia Kay, Elizabeth Still, and Pamela Means, who good-naturedly endured my whiny relationship with deadlines.

I have so much appreciation for the *Word Warriors* contributors, many of whom I am lucky to count as friends, and all as allies in the fight for social justice.

In loving memory of Lisa King, your words still reach us.

Finally, thank you to the warrior poets before us, who have made this anthology possible, and a welcome to those on the brink of arrival.

SINI ANDERSON is a performance artist, producer, and director who lives in San Francisco and New York City. She has been performing and touring her work for fifteen years. Anderson was a chief curator and co–artistic director for the National Queer Arts Festival and a coproducer for the Nectar Stage at San Francisco's Pride; she has also served as the president of the board of directors for the Harvey Milk Institute and co-chair of the board of directors for the Queer Cultural Center. When Anderson is not making shows, she works in independent film as an assistant director. She was the cofounder and co–artistic director of Sister Spit and Sister Spit's Ramblin' Road Show from 1994 to 2000.

TURIYA AUTRY AND WALIDAH IMARISHA (GOOD SISTA/ BAD SISTA) write and reincite powerful, provocative, and political performance poetry with attitude. They have dropped their verbal hand grenades in slams, slums, schools, and streets throughout the United States, and unleashed their lethal word weapons on television, radio, and records.

MELIZA BAÑALES originally hails from Los Angeles and is the youngest of four kids from working-poor parents. The first Latina ever to ever win a Bay Area slam championship, Meliza has been a fixture in the poetry slam community for the past six years. She has performed in parks, bars, street corners, universities, restaurants, and also internationally, with everyone from schoolchildren to Alice Walker, June Jordan, and Ana Castillo. Meliza's work has been published in numerous anthologies and magazines, including

Revolutionary Voices, Lodestar Quarterly, and *Laundry Pen,* and in her own books (Chula Press and Monkey Press).

BITCH is an entertainer and songwriter who has pulled audiences to their feet worldwide with her politically charged and personally wrenched lyrics, atypical instrumentation, minimalist sound, and wildly dramatic stage persona. Her former band, Bitch and Animal, released three albums: *What's that Smell?*, *Eternally Hard* (voted one of the *Los Angeles Times*'s top ten albums of 2001), and *Sour Juice and Rhyme* (nominated for the GLAAD Media Awards' Album of the Year). Bitch has toured all over the world and been featured in *Spin*, the *Advocate*, the *Village Voice*, *Playboy*, *Girlfriends*, and many other publications. Her new CD is titled *Make This/Break This.*

LYNN BREEDLOVE, lead singer and songwriter for infamous dyke-punk band Tribe 8, has been performing throughout the United States, Canada, and Europe for more than a decade. Breedlove has published one novel, *Godspeed* (St. Martin's Press), and is at work on a screenplay of the same name. Breedlove currently teaches at the Harvey Milk Institute in San Francisco.

CHERYL BURKE is an award-winning poet and creative nonfiction writer from Brooklyn who has performed, published, and produced literary events under the name Cheryl B. since 1993. Her work appears in over two dozen anthologies and literary journals, most notably *The Guardian; BLOOM; Reactions 5; Pills, Thrills, Chills and Heartache; The Milk of Almonds;* and *The World in Us.* Cheryl has toured extensively throughout the United States and Great Britain and performed at the Edinburgh Festival Fringe. Cheryl is also the creator and producer of *PVC: The Poetry vs. Comedy Variety Show.* She is online at www.cherylb.com.

C. C. CARTER is the author of the recent release *Body Language* and the chapbook *Letters to My Love*. She has appeared in the film documentary *Living with Pride: Ruth Ellis at 100*, in *Kevin's Room*, and on *Chic-A-Go-Go*. A member of the performance ensemble A Real Read, Carter has won the Gwendolyn Brooks Open Mic competition and the Lambda Literary Foundation's National Poetry Slam. She has been nominated for a Lambda Literary Award. Currently, she is an adjunct professor at Columbia College, where she teaches performance poetry workshops.

STACEYANN CHIN was the winner of the 1999 Women of Color Conference's Poetry Slam and the 1998 Lambda Literary Foundation's National Poetry Slam, and the winner of *WORD: The First Slam for Television*. Since then, she has toured extensively and internationally. Staceyann has appeared on HBO's *Def Poetry Jam* on more than one occasion. Her one-woman spoken word shows, *Hands Afire* and *Unspeakable Things*, have enjoyed off-Broadway runs at the Bleecker Theater. Staceyann's work has been featured on NBC, CNN, CBS, and BET, and in the *New York Times*. She is the recipient of a Tony Award for her contributions to *Def Poetry Jam* on Broadway.

Writer/performer AYA DE LEÓN lives in the Oakland Bay Area. Her critically acclaimed work has been featured on *Def Poetry Jam* and in *Essence*. She was named best discovery in theater for 2004 by the *San Francisco Chronicle* for her solo show *Thieves in the Temple: The Reclaiming of Hip-Hop* (now available on video). She has received a Goldie award from the *San Francisco Bay Guardian* in spoken word, and in 2005 was voted "Slamminest Poet" in the *East Bay Express*. Aya has released three spoken word CDs and is currently working on two novels, a collection of essays about self-love, and a project on spirituality and hip-hop. She is a slam poetry champion and the director of June Jordan's Poetry for the People program, teaching poetry and spoken word at UC Berkeley.

EVE ENSLER is a playwright, performer, and activist. She is the award-winning author of *The Vagina Monologues*, which has been translated into 45 languages and performed in over 112 countries. Ensler's other plays include *Necessary Targets, Conviction, Lemonade, The Depot, Floating Rhoda and the Glue Man*, and *Extraordinary Measures*. Her play, *The Good Body*, which debuted at ACT in San Francisco followed by a run on Broadway and a national tour, was recently premiered in a three-person version at Pittsburgh's City Theatre. Ensler's newest play, *The Treatment*, premiered in September 2006 at the Culture Project in New York City. In October 2006, Ensler released her first book, *Insecure At Last: Losing It in Our Security Obsessed World*, published by Random House. Ensler is the founder/artistic director of V-Day, a global movement to end violence against women and girls, which has raised over forty million dollars in eight years. She is the recipient of many awards including the Guggenheim Fellowship Award in Playwriting, and has received numerous honorary degrees.

KAREN GARRABRANT is the cofounder of Cliterati, the twice-monthly, Atlanta-based open mic and touring collective for redeemable/trans/punk/queer spoken word. Karen curates and organizes spoken word events for Ladyfest South and Estrofest's Seen + Heard festival, and is currently a performer and co–slam ma'am for the Art Amok/Slam Amok! series at Atlanta's 7 Stages theater. Karen has performed in venues ranging from ForWord Girls in San Francisco to the National Women's Studies Association, and has been a two-time host for the women's mic at the Individual World Poetry Slam.

ANDREA GIBSON is a queer poet and activist who took third place at the National Poetry Slam Individual Championships in 2006 and 2007.

Andrea is also a member of Vox Feminista, a multipassionate performance tribe of radical, political women bent on social change. Her work has been showcased on Free Speech TV, *Dyke TV,* the documentary *Slam Planet,* and independent radio stations nationwide, she is currently a member of the prestigious Bullhorn Collective, comprising thirty of the world's highest-ranking slam poets and most accomplished performance poets. Andrea has two self-released CDs, *Bullets and Windchimes* and *Swarm,* as well as one book, *Trees That Grow in Cemeteries.*

DAPHNE GOTTLIEB stitches together the ivory tower and the gutter just using her tongue. She is the author of four books of poetry, most recently *Kissing Dead Girls.* Additionally, she is the author of the graphic novel *Jokes and the Unconscious* (with Diane DiMassa), and the editor of *Homewrecker: An Adultery Anthology,* as well as a forthcoming anthology tentatively entitled *Fucking Daphne,* expected in 2008. She is the winner of the 2003 Audre Lorde Award for Lesbian Poetry and the 2001 Firecracker Alternative Book Award. She lives in San Francisco and teaches at New College of California.

SUHEIR HAMMAD was born in Amman, Jordan, to Palestinian refugee parents in 1974, immigrating with her family to Brooklyn when she was five years old. Suheir has been able to travel throughout the world via her poetry. She has read her poems in Ivy League universities and on Brooklyn street corners. Her work has appeared in award-winning anthologies, and in zines stapled together by queer youth collectives. Suheir was the first Palestinian to star in a Broadway show (the Tony Award–winning *Def Poetry Jam*), and she continues to be the first Palestinian in many artistic spaces throughout the United States.

LEAH HARRIS is the mother of sixteen-month-old Sami, and lives in Washington, D.C. Her prose and poetry have been published in *Off Our Backs, D.C. Poets Against the War, Mizna, Literary Mama,* and

Beltway Poetry Quarterly. Leah has performed and organized with the D.C. Guerrilla Poetry Insurgency and D.C. Poets Against the War. She is active in the psychiatric survivor movement and works with such organizations as the National Association for Rights Protection and Advocacy, the National Empowerment Center, and MindFreedom. She currently works in mental health policy reform and is writing a memoir about her experiences as a psychiatric survivor.

THEA HILLMAN is the author of two books, *Depending on the Light* and *For Lack of a Better Word*. She has performed and given presentations at festivals, conferences, and colleges throughout the United States. Thea has produced groundbreaking intersex and queer performance events such as ForWord Girls, Intercourse, Shameless, Rated XXXY, Fixed/Broken, and *Class Action Suit*, which won *Curve* magazine's Lesbian Theater award in 2004. For more information, visit theahillman.com.

NATALIE E. ILLUM is an activist, writer, and federal employee. Natalie is a founding board member of mothertongue, a spoken word and creative writing organization in D.C. for women and girls. She has an MFA in creative writing from American University and teaches poetry through a variety of local community venues. She also promotes independent writers, musicians, and artists through her production company, 3Word Productions. Currently, Natalie is touring nationally with her most recent chapbook, *Ground lover*, and is almost ready to work on a disability-related memoir titled *Spastic*.

SARAH JONES is a Tony Award–winning playwright, actor, and poet. Her multi-character solo shows include the critically acclaimed, long-running smash Broadway hit *Bridge and Tunnel*, as well as *Surface Transit*, *Women Can't Wait*, and *Waking the American Dream*. Most recently, Jones has been commissioned by the W. K.

Kellogg Foundation for a piece entitled *A Right to Care*. Her theater honors include an Obie, a Helen Hayes Award, two Drama Desk nominations, HBO's U.S. Comedy Arts Festival's Best One Person Show Award, and an NYCLU Joseph Callaway Prize. She has made numerous TV appearances on HBO, NBC, ABC, CBS, PBS, CNN, and in her own special, *The Sarah Jones Show*, on Bravo.

RACHEL KANN, an *LA Weekly* award-winner, works within the confines of page poetry, spoken word, and hip-hop, and then breaks down these boundaries to do something genuinely different. Rachel has three self-produced CDs, has been on three national slam teams, and has performed her poetry for HBO's *Def Poetry Jam*, BET's *The Way We Do It*, and ABC's *Eye on L.A.* She leads poetry workshops in public schools, youth detention facilities, and rehabilitation centers, and was recently commissioned to create poetry curricula for kindergarten through fifth graders throughout the Los Angeles Unified School District.

KATZ, hailing from Atlanta, Georgia, with his Jewish roots dressed in cowboy boots, has toured nationally since 2003. He has shared the stage with the Indigo Girls, Ani DiFranco, the Butchies, and Michelle Malone. From a sports bar in San Diego to a sold-out crowd at the Bowery Ballroom in New York City, Katz has struck a chord in the most diverse of audiences. Katz has one self-released CD and another CD, *Rose Cuts the Cake*, released on Daemon Records.

NOMY LAMM is a writer, musician, and activist who first became known for her writing at age seventeen, with her zine *i'm so fucking beautiful*. Now thirty, Nomy is a regular columnist for *Punk Planet*, a publisher of *Clamor*, and the founder and creative director of More Than Just Phat, a body empowerment project for youth. She also sings and plays accordion in the genre-blending ensemble Tricrotic.

BETH LISICK has published poems, essays, and a short fiction collection. Her stage and screen collaborations with writer/performer Tara Jepsen resulted in a short film, *Diving for Pearls*, which continues to tour the international film festival circuit. Beth co-organizes the Porchlight Storytelling Series, a monthly show for amateur storytellers in San Francisco. She has performed at Lollapalooza and the National Poetry Slam, toured with Sister Spit, and performed at Berlin's Deustche Guggenheim and Paris's Shakespeare and Company. Beth's band the Beth Lisick Ordeal played at Lilith Fair. Her most recent book, *Everybody Into the Pool*, was a *New York Times* extended list bestseller and made *Entertainment Weekly*'s top ten nonfiction books of 2005 list.

ELLYN MAYBE is the author of *The Cowardice of Amnesia*, *The Ellyn Maybe Coloring Book*, *Putting My 2 Cents In*, *Walking Barefoot in the Glassblowers Museum*, and *Praha and the Poet*. She has read at the Poetry Project, Taos Poetry Circus, South by Southwest, Lollapalooza, and Bristol Poetry Festival, on the BBC, and throughout Germany. *Writer's Digest* named her one of ten poets to watch in the new millennium. Her work appears in anthologies including *Another City: Writing from Los Angeles*, *Poetry Nation*, *The Outlaw Bible of American Poetry*, and *American Poetry: The Next Generation*. She was on the 1998 and 1999 Venice Beach slam teams. Her Web site is www.ellenmaybe.com.

MARTY MCCONNELL cofounded the Morrigan, a nationally touring all-female performance poetry troupe. She cocurates the flagship reading series of the louderARTS Project, a New York City literary nonprofit, and she has appeared on two seasons of HBO's *Def Poetry Jam*. Her work has been published in anthologies including *Will Work for Peace*, *In Our Own Words*, and *Women of the Bowery*, as well as literary magazines including *Rattapallax*, *Fourteen Hills*, *Thirteenth Moon*, the *2River View*, *Lodestar Quarterly*, and the *Blue*

Fifth Review. She competed in the 2000, 2001, 2002, and 2003 National
Poetry Slams, and has performed and facilitated workshops at schools
and festivals around the country.

LENELLE MOÏSE is a self-identified "culturally hyphenated pomo-
sexual poet." In 2005, Planned Parenthood hired her to facilitate I AM
. . . Renaming the Sexual Revolution, a series of "slam poetry meets
sex ed" workshops and a nationally distributed spoken word CD. Her
prose is featured in the anthologies *We Don't Need Another Wave*, the
Lambda Literary Award–nominated *Red Light*, and *Homewrecker.* Her
essays and interviews have been featured in *Altar* magazine, *Queer
Ramblings*, *The F-Word*, and *Velvetpark*. A working theater artist,
Lenelle earned her MFA in playwriting from Smith College in 2004. She
is currently touring *Womb-Words, Thirsting*, her autobiographical one-
woman show. Lenelle recently produced her debut CD, *Madivinez*.

TRACIE MORRIS is an award-winning interdisciplinary poet who
has worked extensively as a sound poet and multimedia performer.
Her poetry has most recently appeared in *Callaloo, Social Text*, and
Chain magazines, as well as in her own collections, *Intermission*
and *Chap-T-her Won*. Ms. Morris has contributed to, and been writ-
ten about in, several anthologies of literary criticism, including *An
Exaltation of Forms, The Outlaw Bible of American Poetry, The
Stamp of Class*, and *Aloud: Voices from the Nuyorican Poets Café.*
Ms. Morris holds an MFA from Hunter College and a PhD from New
York University.

EILEEN MYLES has written thousands of poems since she gave
her first reading at CBGB in 1974. *Bust* calls her "the rock star of
modern poetry" and the *New York Times* says she's "a cult figure to
a generation of post-punk females forming their own literary avant
garde." Her books include *Skies* (2001), *On My Way* (2001), *Cool for
You* (a novel, 2000), *School of Fish* (1997), *Maxfield Parrish* (1995),

Not Me (1991), and *Chelsea Girls* (stories, 1994). She's a frequent contributor to *Bookforum, Art in America*, the *Village Voice*, the *Nation*, the *Stranger, Index*, and *Nest*.

CRISTIN O'KEEFE APTOWICZ is the author of four books of poetry and the nonfiction book *Words in Your Face: A Guided Tour Through Twenty Years of the New York City Poetry Slam* (Soft Skull Press). Founder of the three-time National Poetry Slam championship venue NYC-Urbana, Cristin has performed her work on such diverse stages as Australia's Sydney Opera House, Joe's Pub in NYC, and the Paramount Theatre in Seattle, as well as at universities and festivals around the world. She lives in New York City.

LYNNE PROCOPE is a poet from Trinidad and Tobago. She is a founder and executive director of the louderARTS Project. She is a poet-in-residence with the experimental new music ensemble VisionIntoArt, and a member of the Piper Jane Project. She was a member of the 1998 National Poetry Slam Championship team from NYC. She is a coauthor of *Burning Down the House*. Her work appears in *Drums Voices Revue, Poetry Slam, Bowery Women: Poems, The Spoken Word Revolution Redux*, and *Washington Square Review*.

JULIA SERANO is a poetry slam champion and the host and curator of GenderEnders, a trans/intersex/genderqueer-focused performance series and open mic. In addition to self-publishing several chapbooks, Julia has contributed essays to the anthologies *BITCHFest* and *TransForming Community;* excerpts from her work have appeared on NPR and in the *Believer* and the *San Francisco Chronicle*. Julia is the author of *Whipping Girl: A Transsexual Woman on Sexism and the Scapegoating of Femininity*. She will soon be releasing *Six Small Words*, a DVD of her performance poetry.

PATRICIA SMITH's voice originates from the true ground zero of the slam poetry movement: Chicago in the late 1980s. Smith has read her work at the Poets Stage in Stockholm, Rotterdam's Poetry International Festival, the Aran Islands International Poetry and Prose Festival, Expo '90 in Osaka, the Bahia Festival, and the Sorbonne in Paris. She has also performed at Bumbershoot, the Writer's Voice, South by Southwest, the Bisbee Poetry Festival, the Poetry Project at St. Mark's Church, the Black Roots Festival, the Painted Bride in Philadelphia, and Lollapalooza. Smith was featured in the nationally released film *SlamNation*, recently appeared on the HBO series *Def Poetry Jam*, and performed the poem "Awakening" at the 1991 inauguration of Mayor Richard M. Daley in Chicago.

MICHELLE TEA is a writer, performer, and literary event wrangler. She cofounded Sister Spit, which began as an all-girl open mic in the early '90s and morphed into a national tour. She is the author of four memoirs, including *The Chelsea Whistle*, the award-winning *Valencia*, the illustrated *Rent Girl*, and the novel *Rose of No Man's Land*. She has also edited several anthologies, most recently *Baby Remember My Name: An Anthology of New Queer Girl Writing*. In 2007, she organized a Sister Spit performance revival tour called Sister Spit: The Next Generation.

GENEVIEVE VAN CLEVE lives and works in Austin, Texas, and has been a part of the national poetry slam community for ten years. She is a spoken word artist, activist, workshop leader, and member of the Xenogia Spoken Word Collective. She just wrapped her first one-woman show, *Chick on the Team*. She was a member of the 1995, 1997, 1998, 2002, 2003, and 2006 Austin Poetry Slam teams. Genevieve teaches for the Boys and Girls Clubs of America and runs a regular poetry workshop for NARAL Pro-Choice Texas volunteers.

About the Editor

ALIX OLSON is an internationally touring folk poet and progressive queer artist-activist. She has performed at poetry and music venues, festivals, colleges, and political events throughout the United States, Canada, Europe, Australia, and South Africa, and has headlined HBO's *Def Poetry Jam*, graced the covers of *Ms.*, *Curve*, *Lambda Book Report*, and *Velvetpark*, and been featured in numerous publications, including *The New York Times*, the *Washington Post*, *Utne*, *Time Out*, the *Progressive*, *Girlfriends*, the *Advocate*, *Out*, *Poets and Writers*, *Venus*, *Lesbian News*, and *Salon*. Olson and her work have also appeared on WXPN's World Café, Air America, Oxygen, CNN, *In the Life*, LOGO, *Dyke TV*, Holland National Radio, and Australia National Radio. Since winning the 1998 National Poetry Slam with her New York City team and the OutWrite LGBT slam in 1999, Olson has coauthored *Burning Down the House* (Soft Skull Press), published two books of poetry, produced two award-winning spoken word CDs, starred in the award-winning documentary *Left Lane: On the Road with Alix Olson*, and has contributed to many anthologies and CD compilations. She is a monthly columnist for *Inside Out*, a regular contributing writer for *Velvetpark*, and a national slam poetry camp instructor. Olson is also the recipient of a New York Foundation for the Arts grant, a Hedgebrook Foundation fellowship, and the OutMusic's 2004 OutArtist/Activist of the Year and *Venus* magazine's Activist of the Year awards. Alix lives in Brooklyn, NY.

Credits

POETRY

"Subtle Sister" by Alix Olson was originally printed in *Burning Down the House* (Soft Skull Press, 2000).

"montana de oro" by Rachel Kann first appeared in the anthology *Literary Angles* (Sybaritic Press).

"titular" by Rachel Kann first appeared in http://getunderground.com.

"Pigeon Manifesto" and "The Beautiful" by Michelle Tea were originally published in *The Beautiful* (Manic D Press, 2003).

"sleeping sickness" by Julia Serrano was originally published in *Clamor* magazine vol. 23 (November/December 2003).

"vice versa" by Julia Serrano originally appeared in *The Big Ugly Review* (Issue #1, 2004).

"Ball and Chain Record Store" by Ellyn Maybe was originally published in *The Cowardice of Amnesia* (2.13.61 Publications, 1998) and *The Outlaw Bible of American Poetry* (Thunder's Mouth Press, 1999).

"Ellyn Maybe's Dream" by Ellyn Maybe was published in *Praha and the Poet* (2006) and *poeticdiversity* (2006).

"your revolution" © Sarah Jones 1997. All Rights Reserved.

"wax poetic" © Sarah Jones 2006. All Rights Reserved.

"Monkey Girl" and "Empress of Sighs" by Beth Lisick are reprinted with permission from *Monkey Girl* (Manic D Press, 1997).

"Lit" by Cristin O'Keefe Aptowicz was originally published in *Dear Future Boyfriend* (The Wordsmith Press, 2007).

"All That I'd Leave Behind" by Cristin O'Keefe Aptowicz was originally published in *Working Class Represent* (The Wordsmith Press, 2007)

"An American Poem" by Eileen Myles was originally published in *Not Me* (Semiotext(e), 1991).

"Merk" by Eileen Myles was originally published in *School of Fish* (Black Sparrow, 1997).

"Death Drive" © 2001 by Daphne Gottlieb. Reproduced by permission of Soft Skull Press, Inc.

PHOTOGRAPHY

Eve Ensler © Joan Marcus

Alix Olson © Desdemona Burgin

Sarah Jones © Deb Marcano

Michelle Tea © Lydia Daniller

Lenelle Moïse © Vanessa Vargas

Daphne Gottlieb © Reverend Michel St. Germain

Natalie E. Illum © Kendra Kuliga

Aya de León © Aya De León

Leah Harris © Hani Akil

Meliza Bañales © J. Waite

Karen Garrabrant © Nadj Goodvin

Beth Lisick © Winni Wintermeyer

Genevieve Van Cleve © Peter Ravella

Cheryl Burke © Matthew David Powell

Katz Athens Boys Choir © Harvey Katz

C.C. Carter © Anthony Dowdell

Suheir Hammad © Tarek Aylouch

Rachel Kann © Greg Frederick

Nomy Lamm © Caldwell Linker

Andrea Gibson © Emily Clay

Thea Hillman © Luna Maia

Ellyn Maybe © Cindy Beal

Tracie Morris © Tracie Morris

Cristin O'Keefe Aptowicz – courtesy of Cristin O'Keefe Aptowicz

Sini Anderson © Jenny Shealy

Eileen Myles © Angela Carone

Lynn Procope © Peter Dressel

Marty McConnell © Peter Dressel

Bitch © Roberto Portillo

Turiya Autry and Walidah Imarisha © Vagabond

Lynn Breedlove © Kerstin Buchwald

Staceyann Chin © Desdemona Burgin

Julia Serano © David Huang

Patricia Smith © Peter Dressel

Selected Titles

For more than thirty years, Seal Press has published groundbreaking books. By women. For women. Visit our website at www.sealpress.com.

LISTEN UP: VOICES FROM THE NEXT FEMINIST GENERATION edited by Barbara Findlen. $16.95, 1-58005-054-9. A collection of essays featuring the voices of today's young feminists on racism, sexuality, identity, AIDS, revolution, abortion, and much more.

COLONIZE THIS: YOUNG WOMEN OF COLOR ON TODAY'S FEMINISM edited by Daisy Hernandez and Bushra Rehman. $16.95, 1-58005-067-0. An insight into new generation of brilliant, outspoken women of color how they are speaking to the concerns of new feminism, and their place in it.

IT'S SO YOU: 35 WOMEN WRITE ABOUT PERSONAL EXPRESSION THROUGH FASHION AND STYLE edited by Michelle Tea. $15.95, 1-58005-215-0. From the haute couture houses of the ruling class to DIY girls who make restorative clothing and create their own hodgepodge style, this is the first book to explore women's ambivalence toward, suspicion of, indulgence in, and love of fashion on every level.

VOICES OF RESISTANCE: MUSLIM WOMEN ON WAR, FAITH, AND SEXUALITY edited by Sarah Husain. $16.95, 1-58005-181-2. A collection of essays and poetry on war, faith, suicide bombing, and sexuality, this book reveals the anger, pride, and pain of Muslim women.

WE DON'T NEED ANOTHER WAVE: DISPATCHES FROM THE NEXT GENERATION OF FEMINISTS edited by Melody Berger. $15.95, 1-58005-182-0. In the tradition of *Listen Up*, the under-thirty generation of young feminists speaks out.

WHIPPING GIRL: A TRANSSEXUAL WOMAN ON SEXISM AND THE SCAPEGOATING OF FEMININITY by Julia Serano. $15.95, 1-58005-154-5. Biologist and trans woman Julie Serrano reveals a unique perspective on femininity, masculinity, and gender identity.